.NET Core in Action

DUSTIN METZGAR

MANNING
SHELTER ISLAND

For online information and ordering of this and other Manning books, please visit
www.manning.com. The publisher offers discounts on this book when ordered in quantity.
For more information, please contact

    Special Sales Department
    Manning Publications Co.
    20 Baldwin Road
    PO Box 761
    Shelter Island, NY 11964
    Email: orders@manning.com

 Recognizing the importance of preserving what has been written, it is Manning's policy to have
the books we publish printed on acid-free paper, and we exert our best efforts to that end.
Recognizing also our responsibility to conserve the resources of our planet, Manning books
are printed on paper that is at least 15 percent recycled and processed without the use of
elemental chlorine.

Manning Publications Co.
20 Baldwin Road
PO Box 761
Shelter Island, NY 11964

Development editors:	Cynthia Kane, Kristen Watterson
Review editor:	Aleksandar Dragosavljević
Technical development editor:	Mike Shepard
Project manager:	Kevin Sullivan
Copyeditor:	Andy Carroll
Proofreader:	Melody Dolab
Technical proofreader:	Ricardo Peres
Typesetter and cover designer:	Marija Tudor
Illustrator:	Chuck Larson

ISBN 9781617294273
Printed in the United States of America
1 2 3 4 5 6 7 8 9 10 – DP – 23 22 21 20 19 18

contents

foreword

.NET Core is what we've always asked for as .NET developers: an open source, fast, and portable runtime for C#, VB, F#, and more. The book you're holding is a great on-ramp to the world of .NET and .NET Core. You'll learn the why, what, and how of building systems on this new platform. You'll utilize a host of open source libraries to test your code, access databases, build microservices, and ultimately go live! You'll also learn how to debug and profile real code in the real world with practical tips and a pragmatic perspective.

.NET Core brings the Common Language Runtime not just to Windows, but also to Mac, Linux, and beyond. You can run .NET Core in a Docker container on an ARM-based Raspberry Pi if it makes you happy! You can code against the .NET Standard and create libraries that can be shared among all these platforms as well as iOS, Android, and even an Apple Watch.

.NET Core is yours and mine, and I'm thrilled you're joining us on this adventure. The .NET community has rallied alongside .NET Core like nothing we've seen before in the Microsoft development community. Over half the pull requests for the .NET Core framework come from outside Microsoft! You can run .NET Core apps in Azure, Amazon, Google, and more. Large-scale open source container orchestrators such as Kubernetes can build sophisticated hybrid systems that include all the languages that make you productive—all running side by side on the OS of your choice.

SCOTT HANSELMAN
PRINCIPAL PROGRAM MANAGER, .NET, MICROSOFT

preface

Software developers keep learning throughout their careers. It's part of the appeal of the field. The more I learn, the more I discover how much I don't know (the "known unknown"). The times when I learned the most were the times when an "unknown unknown" became a "known unknown"—when a whole category of development was revealed to me that I hadn't heard of before. Subjects such as performance profiling and localization never even occurred to me when I started out. Yet they have an important role in professional software development.

With so much information available through blogs, tweets, Stack Overflow, conferences, and online documentation, some may wonder if physical books can still be relevant, especially with a subject like .NET Core, where the book may be outdated by the time it reaches print. I believe the true value of a book, what gives it lasting impact, is the revelation of the unknown unknown to the reader. The book should cause you to ask questions you haven't asked before and provide new context and ways to process the avalanche of information out there on a particular topic.

While this book is about .NET Core, a lot of the concepts have been part of the .NET Framework for years. By opening .NET Core to other platforms, Microsoft hopes to reach a new audience of developers. I'm fortunate enough to be in the right place at the right time to write a book that introduces not only .NET Core but also some important aspects of software engineering and how they're accomplished in the .NET ecosystem. It's my goal with this book to make you a better developer and pique your curiosity about aspects of software engineering you may not have thought about before.

A significant portion of my career has been spent on .NET. My introduction to .NET happened while I was working as a consultant for enterprise resource planning (ERP) systems. A salesman for the consulting company didn't know (or care) that our web ERP portal product was written in Java. The customer liked the portal but wanted to customize it and to use .NET. We worked to rebuild the portal in .NET in a few months and collaborated with the customer's development team on their customizations. That turned out to be my favorite consulting job. Years later, I was fortunate enough to be hired by Microsoft and work on the .NET Framework itself. I got to work with many talented developers and wrote code now used by countless applications.

When .NET Core started, I was excited about its potential and got involved early. An editor at Manning saw some of my early work and gave me the opportunity to submit a proposal and table of contents. I'd always wanted to write a book, so I jumped at the chance. It takes a special kind of naïveté to think you have time to write a book after the birth of a child and after taking a larger lead role at work. Not only that, but .NET Core was a moving target in the beginning, which resulted in my having to throw out or rewrite finished chapters and parts of the table of contents.

This book took way longer to write than I expected. But I learned a lot along the way, and I'm pleased with the result. I'm also proud that I was able to deliver most of the ambitious table of contents I originally planned. I hope you finish this book not only with the ability to write and publish libraries and applications in .NET Core, but also with a desire to learn more.

acknowledgments

This book wouldn't have been possible without the support of my wife, Sherry. Our son is a handful sometimes, so I really appreciate you giving me time to write. I doubt I would have finished without your encouragement.

Thanks also to the editors at Manning who kept the bar high and helped me write the book I wanted to write: Kristen Watterson, for guiding me to production; Cynthia Kane, for helping me through writing most of the manuscript; Mark Renfrow, for getting me to my first MEAP release; and Greg Wild, for giving me the chance to write this book and some useful advice along the way.

My thanks also go to Mike Shepard, my technical editor, for telling me when my writing was crap.

I'd also like to thank Samer Alameer for his help with the localization chapter. He not only helped me with the Arabic, but also taught me some important points about localization.

Finally, thank you to all who bought the early access version of this book, to Ricardo Peres, for his technical proofread, and to the team of reviewers who provided invaluable feedback along the way, including Andrew Eleneski, Angelo Simone Scotto, Bruno Figueiredo, Daniel Vásquez, Daut Morina, Eddy Vluggen, Eric Potter, Eric Sweigart, George Marinos, Hari Khalsa, Igor Kokorin, Jeff Smith, Jürgen Hötzel, Mikkel Arentoft, Oscar Vargas, Renil Abdulkader, Rudi Steinbach, Srihari Sridharan, Tiklu Ganguly, and Viorel Moisei.

about this book

.NET Core in Action was written to help you build libraries and applications in .NET Core. It takes you through many important aspects of developing high-quality software for release. Concepts are introduced "in action" with examples to show their practical application.

Who should read this book

Whether you're new to .NET and C# or a seasoned .NET Framework developer, this book has plenty of useful information for you. While all this information may be available online through documentation, blogs, and so on, this book compiles and organizes everything into a format that's clear and easy to follow. The book assumes that you have a working knowledge of imperative, object-oriented programming languages, such as C++ or Java. Although this isn't an instruction guide on C#, key concepts are explained to aid you. The book also assumes some proficiency with terminals or command lines and text editors.

How this book is organized: a roadmap

This book has 12 chapters:

- Chapter 1 introduces .NET Core and .NET Standard—what they're for and why you should learn them.
- Chapter 2 gets you started creating .NET Core applications.
- Chapter 3 explores the MSBuild build system and how to edit project files.
- Chapter 4 covers unit testing with xUnit. xUnit documentation online tends to be scattered, so this chapter will be useful as a reference later on.

- Chapter 5 introduces working with relational databases, a common thing for developers to do. .NET Framework developers familiar with relational databases may want to move on to chapter 6.
- Chapter 6 covers object-relational mappers (ORMs). It introduces two different types of ORMs: Dapper, a micro-ORM, and Entity Framework Core, a full-featured ORM.
- Chapter 7 explores building a REST endpoint with ASP.NET Core, as well as how to make HTTP calls to other services.
- Chapter 8 explores different options for debugging, from IDEs to command line.
- Chapter 9 introduces performance testing with xUnit.Performance and profiling with PerfView.
- Chapter 10 covers the internationalization process and how to make applications world-ready.
- Chapter 11 looks at how to build .NET Core libraries and applications that rely on framework- or operating system–specific constructs.
- Chapter 12 covers how to prepare your .NET Core library for release and distribution.
- The appendixes contain specific details useful for writing .NET Core applications, such as target framework monikers and what's in each version of the .NET Standard.

About the code

This book contains many examples of source code, both in numbered listings and in-line with normal text. In both cases, source code is formatted in a `fixed-width font like this` to separate it from ordinary text. Sometimes code is also **in bold** to highlight changes from previous steps in the chapter, such as when a new feature adds to an existing line of code.

In many cases, the original source code has been reformatted; we've added line breaks and reworked indentation to accommodate the available page space in the book. In rare cases, even this was not enough, and listings include line-continuation markers (➥). Additionally, comments in the source code have often been removed from the listings when the code is described in the text. Code annotations accompany many of the listings, highlighting important concepts.

The source code for the book is located at https://github.com/dmetzgar/dotnetcoreinaction. This GitHub repository contains source for examples in all chapters except chapters 1, 8, and 12, which aren't focused on particular examples.

The source code is also available from the publisher's website at www.manning.com/books/dotnet-core-in-action.

Book forum

Purchase of *.NET Core in Action* includes free access to a private web forum run by Manning Publications where you can make comments about the book, ask technical questions, and receive help from the author and from other users. To access the forum, go to https://forums.manning.com/forums/dotnet-core-in-action. You can also learn more about Manning's forums and the rules of conduct at https://forums .manning.com/forums/about.

Manning's commitment to our readers is to provide a venue where a meaningful dialogue between individual readers and between readers and the author can take place. It is not a commitment to any specific amount of participation on the part of the author, whose contribution to the forum remains voluntary (and unpaid). We suggest you try asking the author challenging questions lest his interest stray! The forum and the archives of previous discussions will be accessible from the publisher's website as long as the book is in print.

Online resources

At the end of each chapter, you'll find a section called "Additional Resources" with references to books and online resources related to the contents of that chapter.

about the author

DUSTIN METZGAR has been developing software professionally since 2003. His industry experience includes building software in areas such as enterprise resource planning, supply chain management, insurance, and loan origination. He joined the .NET team at Microsoft around the time of the .NET 4.0 release and later worked on Azure services. Currently, Dustin and his team own a few libraries in the .NET Framework and .NET Core, an Azure service, and some parts of Visual Studio.

Dustin lives near Redmond, Washington. When not spending time with his son, he's either bicycling or trying to weld sheet metal. You can find Dustin online through Twitter (@DustinMetzgar) or his blog at http://mode19.net.

about the cover illustration

The figure on the cover of *.NET Core in Action* bears the caption "A Turk in a pelise." The members of the Turkish court would wear certain outer robes linked to the season; of course, it was the sultan who decided when the season had changed and so the robes should too. The illustration is taken from a collection of costumes of the Ottoman Empire published on January 1, 1802, by William Miller of Old Bond Street, London. The title page is missing from the collection, and we've so far been unable to track it down. The book's table of contents identifies the figures in both English and French, and each illustration also bears the names of two artists who worked on it, both of whom would no doubt be surprised to find their art gracing the front cover of a computer programming book 200 years later.

The collection was purchased by a Manning editor at an antiquarian flea market in the "Garage" on West 26th Street in Manhattan. The seller was an American based in Ankara, Turkey, and the transaction took place just as he was packing up his stand for the day. The Manning editor didn't have on his person the substantial amount of cash that was required for the purchase, and a credit card and check were both politely turned down. With the seller flying back to Ankara that evening, the situation seemed hopeless. What was the solution? It turned out to be nothing more than an old-fashioned verbal agreement sealed with a handshake. The seller proposed that the money be transferred to him by wire, and the editor walked out with the bank information on a piece of paper and the portfolio of images under his arm. Needless to say, we transferred the funds the next day, and we remain grateful and impressed by this unknown person's trust in one of us. It recalls something that might have happened a long time ago.

The pictures from the Ottoman collection, like the other illustrations that appear on Manning's covers, bring to life the richness and variety of dress customs of two centuries ago. They recall the sense of isolation and distance of that period—and of every other historic period except our own hyperkinetic present. Dress codes have changed since then, and the diversity by region, so rich at the time, has faded away. It's now often hard to tell the inhabitant of one continent from that of another. Perhaps, viewed optimistically, we've traded a cultural and visual diversity for a more varied personal life. Or a more varied and interesting intellectual and technical life.

We at Manning celebrate the inventiveness, the initiative, and, yes, the *fun* of the computer business with book covers based on the rich diversity of regional life as it was two centuries ago, brought back to life by the pictures from this collection.

Why .NET Core?

This chapter covers

- What is .NET Core?
- The advantages of .NET Core
- Differences from the .NET Framework

Learning a new development framework is a big investment. You need to learn how to write, build, test, deploy, and maintain applications in the new framework. For developers, there are many frameworks to choose from, and it's difficult to know which is the best for the job. What makes .NET Core worth the investment?

To answer this question, it helps to know where you're starting from. If you're completely new to .NET, welcome! If you're already a .NET developer, I'll provide some guidance as to whether .NET Core is right for you at this time. .NET Core is still evolving to meet customer demands, so if there's a critical piece of the .NET Framework that you need, it may be good to wait a few releases. Whether you're already familiar with .NET or are just learning about it, this book will get you writing professional applications with .NET Core in no time.

1.1   *Architecting enterprise applications before .NET Core*

Early in my career, I worked for a car insurance company. Its developers were attempting to improve the efficiency of claims adjusters. When you get into a car accident, a representative of the insurance company—a claims adjuster—will sometimes go directly to the scene of the accident and assess the damage. Adjustors would collect information, usually on paper, and then head back to the office where they could enter the data into an application on a desktop or laptop computer. The process was slow and required a lot of manual work.

The insurance company wanted to enable claims adjusters to enter the data directly into the claims system from the scene. They would then be able to get cost estimates and access the car owner's insurance policy on the spot. For the insurance company, this meant quicker claim resolution and less cost. One of the secrets I learned about the car insurance industry is that they want to get a disbursement to the claimant quickly. The less time the claimant has to reflect on the estimate, the less likely they are to negotiate for a higher payout.

Accessing the claims system from the scene meant changing the architecture to incorporate mobile devices. Figure 1.1 shows the high-level design.

In the past, implementing this kind of architecture equated to substantial costs. Creating cell phone and tablet applications required either hiring developers for both iOS and Android ports or standardizing on hardware to limit the number of platforms. An adjuster might travel to a remote location with poor or nonexistent cellular

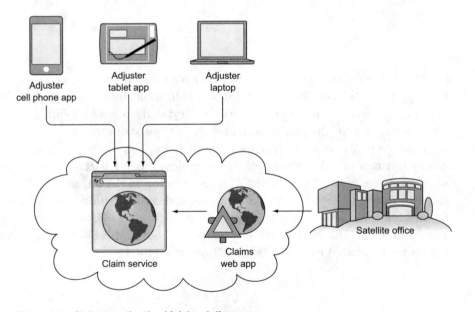

Figure 1.1   Claims application high-level diagram

service, so the application needed to operate offline. The different languages and platforms used in each piece of the architecture made integration and maintenance difficult. Changes in business logic meant rewriting the logic in several languages. At the time, scaling was too slow to adjust for demand during the workday, so the hardware requirements were based on peak load. The expenses kept piling up.

What if you could use not just the same code but the same libraries across the applications, website, and services? What if you built one app and it worked on iOS, Android, and Windows? What if your website and services could fit into small containers and elastically scale in response to demand? If all that were possible, it would dramatically reduce the cost of building and maintaining systems like the claims architecture.

These questions are no longer hypothetical. .NET Core is a software framework that makes all of this possible. Developers aren't confined to a particular language, operating system, or form factor. .NET Core is engineered to be small and modular, making it perfect for containers. It's built and supported by Microsoft but is also open source, with an active community. Having participated in software projects like the claims application, I'm excited about the possibilities introduced by .NET Core.

1.2 If you're a .NET Framework developer

For some .NET Framework components, .NET Core is a reboot, and for others, it's a chance to work cross-platform. Because the .NET Framework was built mostly in managed (C#) code, those portions didn't need code changes to move to .NET Core. But there are libraries that depend on Windows-specific components, and they had to either be removed or refactored to use cross-platform alternatives. The same will apply to your applications.

1.2.1 Your .NET apps can be cross-platform

Once they're ported to .NET Core, your existing .NET Framework applications can now work on other operating systems. This is great for library authors who want to expand their audience or developers who want to use the same code in different parts of a distributed application. It's also great if you'd just like to develop in .NET on your shiny new MacBook without having to dual-boot to Windows.

Although not all of the Framework has been ported to .NET Core, major portions have. There are also some API differences. For example, if you use a lot of reflection, you may need to refactor your code to work with .NET Core. Section 1.7 provides more information on the differences, which can help you determine if it's feasible to port to .NET Core.

1.2.2 ASP.NET Core outperforms ASP.NET in the .NET Framework

The ASP.NET team built a new version of ASP.NET for .NET Core called ASP.NET Core. The difference in performance between ASP.NET Core and Framework ASP.NET is many orders of magnitude. Much of ASP.NET was built on the legacy System.Web library, and the .NET Framework supports older versions of ASP.NET projects.

That constraint has restricted ASP.NET's evolution. With .NET Core, Microsoft decided to rewrite the whole stack. Although this does mean breaking changes, the gains are worth the effort of migrating.

1.2.3   *.NET Core is the focus for innovation*

One of the critical principles of the .NET Framework is that new releases shouldn't break existing applications. But this backwards compatibility is a double-edged sword. A lot of effort goes into making sure that changes made in new releases of the .NET Framework usually won't break existing applications. But this goal of avoiding breaking changes restricts innovation. Changes to the .NET Framework need thorough justification (usually from customers), exhaustive testing, and approval from many levels of product groups. I've been in meetings where people argued over one- or two-line code fixes, which caused me to reconsider my life choices.

With .NET Core, it's much easier for internal Microsoft teams to work on their library independent of the core libraries. Changes to core libraries, like System.Collections, still require the same rigor as with .NET Framework, but it's easier to make substantial changes to ASP.NET Core or Entity Framework Core without being constrained by backwards compatibility. This allows for greater innovation.

.NET Framework ships as one product, whereas Core is broken up into pieces. Developers can now choose which version of a library they want to use, as long as it's outside the .NET Standard Library, and .NET Core teams can innovate with less difficulty. This is why, in the future, you'll see only bug fixes for the Framework. Core will get all the new features.

1.2.4   *Release cycles are faster*

If you've ever encountered a bug in the .NET Framework and reported it to Microsoft, you're aware of how long it takes for a fix to be released. The Framework has long release cycles, usually measuring at least a year, and there are tiny windows during these cycles for feature work. Each code change can cause issues in unexpected places elsewhere in the Framework. To give each team enough time to test, there are many times when code changes are restricted or heavily scrutinized. If you find a bug in .NET, you're better off finding a workaround than waiting for an update.

.NET Core follows a faster release cadence. Developers can use nightly builds to test early. Libraries that aren't part of the .NET Standard Library can release at their own pace. Because everything is open source, any developer can propose a fix if Microsoft doesn't respond quickly enough. If the fix isn't accepted, the discussion is held in public so everyone can see why that decision was made.

1.3   *If you are new to .NET*

On Windows platforms, the .NET Framework hasn't had much competition. Microsoft could make changes to everything from the OS kernel layers up through the high-level .NET libraries. By taking .NET to other platforms, the playing field has changed.

.NET must now compete with all the other development frameworks out there. Here are some things that set .NET apart.

1.3.1 C# is an amazing language

The flagship language of .NET, C#, has many distinguishing features, such as Language Integrated Query (LINQ) and asynchronous constructs, which make it powerful and easy to use. It's not my intention to teach C#, but I will be using it throughout this book. You'll get to experiment with some of the many cool features of C#.

C# also continues to innovate. The C# team designs the language openly so that anyone can make suggestions or participate in the discussion. The compiler (Roslyn) is entirely modular and extensible. I recommend picking up another Manning book, *C# in Depth, Fourth Edition* (2018) by Jon Skeet, to learn more.

1.3.2 .NET Core is not starting from scratch

.NET has been around since before 2000. The Framework code has been hardened over the years, and its developers have benefited from the experience. Much of the Framework code that has been ported to Core is untouched. This gives .NET Core a head start in terms of having a reliable framework for building applications. .NET Core is also completely supported by Microsoft. A lack of support can keep some organizations from adopting open source software. Microsoft's support decreases the risk of using Core for your applications.

1.3.3 Focus on performance

The Common Language Runtime (CLR) team at Microsoft has been optimizing garbage collection and just-in-time (JIT) compilation since the beginning of .NET, and they're bringing this highly tuned engine to .NET Core. They also have projects underway to perform native compilation of .NET Core applications, which will significantly reduce startup times and the size on disk—two important characteristics for fast scaling in container environments.

1.4 What is .NET Core?

To understand .NET Core, it helps to understand the .NET Framework. Microsoft released the .NET Framework in the early 2000s. The .NET Framework is a Windows-only development framework that, at its lowest level, provides memory management, security, exception handling, and many other features. It comes with an extensive set of libraries that perform all kinds of functions, from XML parsing to HTTP requests. It also supports several languages and compiles them into the same common intermediate language, so any language can use a library built in any other language. These key concepts are also present in .NET Core.

In 2016, Microsoft acquired Xamarin and released .NET Core 1.0. Xamarin was responsible for porting large parts of the .NET Framework to run on Linux/Unix-based operating systems in the past. Although some of the code could be shared between the .NET Framework, Xamarin, and the new .NET Core, the compiled

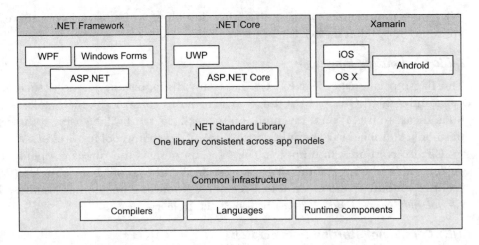

Figure 1.2   .NET Framework, .NET Core, and Xamarin all implement the same standard called the .NET Standard Library.

binaries could not. Part of the effort of building .NET Core was to standardize so that all .NET implementations could share the same libraries. Figure 1.2 shows what this standardization looks like.

Xamarin and the .NET Framework were previously silos, where binaries couldn't be shared between them. With the introduction of the .NET Standard Library and the common infrastructure, these two frameworks are now part of a unified .NET ecosystem.

What is .NET Core, then? In figure 1.2 it appears that .NET Core is just another framework that includes UWP (Universal Windows Platform) and ASP.NET Core. In order to make .NET Core a reality, however, the authors also created the .NET Standard Library and the common infrastructure. .NET Core is really all three of these things.

1.5   Key .NET Core features

.NET Core borrows the best from the .NET Framework and incorporates the latest advancements in software engineering. The following sections identify a few of the distinguishing features of .NET Core.

1.5.1   Expanding the reach of your libraries

With .NET Core you can write your application or library using the .NET Standard Library. Then it can be shared across many platforms. In figure 1.3, MyLibrary is deployed across cloud services, web servers, and many client platforms.

The same library can work in your backend service on your premises or in the cloud and also in your client application running on a cell phone, tablet, or desktop. Instead of building separate apps for iOS, Android, and Windows, you can build one app that works on all platforms. .NET Core is small and perfect for use in containers, which scale easily and reduce development time.

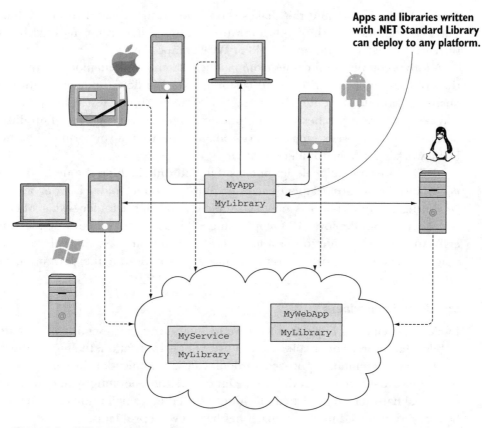

Apps and libraries written with .NET Standard Library can deploy to any platform.

Figure 1.3 .NET Core development

.NET Core and the .NET Standard Library establish a common standard. In the past when a new version of an operating system or a new device came along, it was the responsibility of the developer to rebuild their application or library for that new run-time or framework and distribute the update. With .NET Core there's no need to rebuild and redistribute. As long as the new runtime or framework supports all of your dependent libraries, it will support your application.

1.5.2 Simple deployment on any platform

Microsoft products tend to have complex installation processes. COM components, registry entries, special folders, GAC—all are designed to take advantage of Windows-only features. The .NET Framework relies on these constructs, which makes it unsuit-able for other operating systems.

When shipping an application that relies on the .NET Framework, the installer has to be smart enough to detect whether the right .NET Framework version is installed, and if not, provide a way for the user to get it. Most modern Windows versions include the .NET Framework, and this makes certain applications easier to install, but it can cause complications if the application uses features that aren't installed by default, such as ASP.NET integration with IIS or WCF components.

Another complication comes from patches. Patches that include bug fixes or security updates can be distributed to customers via Windows updates or through the Microsoft Download Center. But the .NET Framework you test your application on may have different patches than the ones customers are using. It's often difficult to determine what causes strange behavior in an application if you assume that the .NET Framework is the same for all customers.

.NET Core's modular design means that you only include the dependencies you need, and all of those dependencies go into the same folder as your application. Deploying an application is now as simple as copying a folder—what Microsofties refer to as "xcopy-deployable" (xcopy being a Windows tool for copying files and folders). Another advantage to this approach is that you can have multiple versions running side by side. This strategy is key to making the deployment experience consistent on all platforms.

1.5.3   *Clouds and containers*

In cloud systems, it's important to strive for higher density—serving more customers with less hardware. The smaller the footprint of an application, the higher the density.

The most common approach to deploying an application in cloud systems has been the virtual machine. A virtual machine allows an operating system to be installed on virtual hardware. The virtual machine is stored in a small number of files that can be easily replicated. But virtual machines have several problems:

- *Size*—A typical virtual machine file is gigabytes, if not tens of gigabytes. This makes it time-consuming to transfer them across networks, and it has significant requirements on disk space.
- *Startup times*—Starting a virtual machine means starting an operating system. For Windows, this presents a challenge, because it may take minutes to start a new machine. This can make handling sudden bursts of traffic difficult.
- *Memory*—The virtual machine needs to load an entire operating system into memory, along with the applications. This means a lot of a host's memory can be redundant and therefore wasted.
- *Inconsistency*—Although the same virtual machine can be copied to multiple hosts, the hosts have to provide the same virtualized hardware, which can be dependent on the physical hardware. There's no guarantee that a virtual machine will operate the same way, if at all, on any given host.

Containers solve the issues of virtual machines by also virtualizing the operating system— the container only holds the application and its dependencies. File sizes are many times smaller, startup times are measured in seconds, only the application is loaded in memory, and the container is guaranteed to work the same on any host.

The .NET Framework was designed to be built into Windows, and it doesn't fit well into containers. A Framework application depends on the Framework being installed. Given the clear advantages of containers, one of the design decisions of .NET Core was to make it modular. This means that your .NET Core application can be "published" so that it and all of its dependencies are in one place, which makes it easy to put into a container.

1.5.4 ASP.NET performance

ASP.NET is a set of libraries built into the .NET Framework for creating web applications. It was released in 2002 with the first version of the .NET Framework, and it has continued to evolve. Despite its success (being used by many high-profile organizations, including Stack Overflow), there was a feeling among the ASP.NET team that they were losing developers because ASP.NET performance isn't competitive, and because it only works on the Windows platform.

A company called TechEmpower runs a benchmark of web application frameworks every few months and provides a ranking in several categories. The benchmarks are run on Linux, so Windows-only frameworks are not included. For the ASP.NET team, this was a problem. There are many frameworks for writing cross-platform web applications, and their performance numbers are impressive. Some Java frameworks, like Rapidoid and Undertow, were posting astronomical numbers: Rapidoid with 3.7 million plaintext requests per second and Undertow with 2.9 million (shown in figure 1.4).

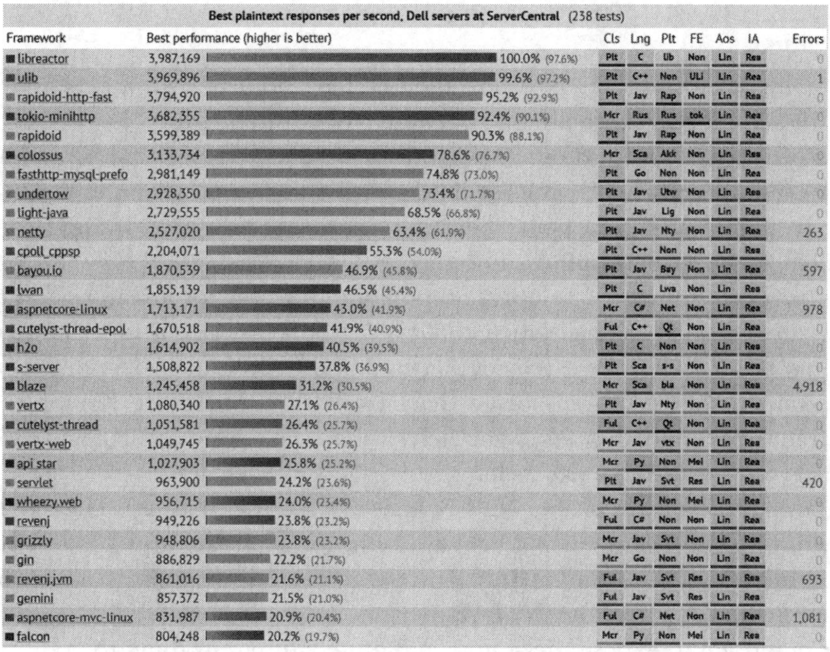

Framework	Best performance (higher is better)	Cls	Lng	Plt	FE	Aos	IA	Errors
libreactor	3,987,169 — 100.0% (97.6%)	Plt	C	Lib	Non	Lin	Rea	
ulib	3,969,896 — 99.6% (97.2%)	Plt	C++	Non	ULi	Lin	Rea	1
rapidoid-http-fast	3,794,920 — 95.2% (92.9%)	Plt	Jav	Rap	Non	Lin	Rea	0
tokio-minihttp	3,682,355 — 92.4% (90.1%)	Mcr	Rus	Rus	tok	Lin	Rea	
rapidoid	3,599,389 — 90.3% (88.1%)	Plt	Jav	Rap	Non	Lin	Rea	0
colossus	3,133,734 — 78.6% (76.7%)	Mcr	Sca	Akk	Non	Lin	Rea	
fasthttp-mysql-prefo	2,981,149 — 74.8% (73.0%)	Plt	Go	Non	Non	Lin	Rea	
undertow	2,928,350 — 73.4% (71.7%)	Plt	Jav	Utw	Non	Lin	Rea	
light-java	2,729,555 — 68.5% (66.8%)	Plt	Jav	Lig	Non	Lin	Rea	
netty	2,527,020 — 63.4% (61.9%)	Plt	Jav	Nty	Non	Lin	Rea	263
cpoll_cppsp	2,204,071 — 55.3% (54.0%)	Plt	C++	Non	Non	Lin	Rea	
bayou.io	1,870,539 — 46.9% (45.8%)	Plt	Jav	Bay	Non	Lin	Rea	597
lwan	1,855,139 — 46.5% (45.4%)	Plt	C	Lva	Non	Lin	Rea	
aspnetcore-linux	1,713,171 — 43.0% (41.9%)	Mcr	C#	Net	Non	Lin	Rea	978
cutelyst-thread-epol	1,670,518 — 41.9% (40.9%)	Ful	C++	Qt	Non	Lin	Rea	
h2o	1,614,902 — 40.5% (39.5%)	Plt	C	Non	Non	Lin	Rea	
s-server	1,508,822 — 37.8% (36.9%)	Plt	Sca	s-s	Non	Lin	Rea	
blaze	1,245,458 — 31.2% (30.5%)	Mcr	Sca	bla	Non	Lin	Rea	4,918
vertx	1,080,340 — 27.1% (26.4%)	Plt	Jav	Nty	Non	Lin	Rea	
cutelyst-thread	1,051,581 — 26.4% (25.7%)	Ful	C++	Qt	Non	Lin	Rea	
vertx-web	1,049,745 — 26.3% (25.7%)	Mcr	Jav	vtx	Non	Lin	Rea	
api star	1,027,903 — 25.8% (25.2%)	Mcr	Py	Non	Mei	Lin	Rea	
servlet	963,900 — 24.2% (23.6%)	Plt	Jav	Svt	Res	Lin	Rea	420
wheezy.web	956,715 — 24.0% (23.4%)	Mcr	Py	Non	Mei	Lin	Rea	
revenj	949,226 — 23.8% (23.2%)	Ful	C#	Non	Non	Lin	Rea	
grizzly	948,806 — 23.8% (23.2%)	Mcr	Jav	Svt	Non	Lin	Rea	
gin	886,829 — 22.2% (21.7%)	Mcr	Go	Non	Non	Lin	Rea	
revenj.jvm	861,016 — 21.6% (21.1%)	Ful	Jav	Svt	Non	Lin	Rea	693
gemini	857,372 — 21.5% (21.0%)	Ful	Jav	Svt	Res	Lin	Rea	
aspnetcore-mvc-linux	831,987 — 20.9% (20.4%)	Ful	C#	Net	Non	Lin	Rea	1,081
falcon	804,248 — 20.2% (19.7%)	Mcr	Py	Non	Mei	Lin	Rea	

Best plaintext responses per second, Dell servers at ServerCentral (238 tests)

Figure 1.4 TechEmpower benchmark (round 14), May 2017

On round 11 of the TechEmpower benchmark, ASP.NET MVC on the Mono framework was included in the testing. The results weren't good. ASP.NET on Mono produced a paltry 2,000 plaintext requests per second. But because Mono wasn't created by Microsoft, it wouldn't have received the same amount of performance tuning as the regular .NET Framework. To get a fairer comparison, the ASP.NET team decided to run a benchmark with .NET 4.6 on the same hardware as TechEmpower. The result was around 50,000 requests per second, not even close to Node.js (320,000 requests per second) or any of the other top frameworks on the TechEmpower list.

The pitifully low score wasn't exactly a surprise. As mentioned before, the ASP.NET team knew some of the hurdles that stood in the way of being competitive with frameworks like Node.js. These hurdles could only be cleared by rewriting the whole thing. One major difficulty with ASP.NET was that it needed to support customers' legacy code, including "classic ASP," which preceded .NET. The only way to free ASP.NET from the legacy code burden was to start over.

The ASP.NET team embarked on building ASP.NET Core, and many months later they celebrated crossing the 1 million requests per second mark (as you can see in figure 1.4). There is a team dedicated to pushing that number even higher, as well as to improving the performance of many other real-world scenarios.

Improving the performance of ASP.NET is indicative of a shift in Microsoft's thinking. Microsoft realizes that it has to be competitive to win developers. It also has to compete on platforms other than Windows. ASP.NET was the driving force behind the creation of .NET Core.

1.5.5   *Open source*

Historically, Microsoft has been very tight-lipped about new products and features under development. There are good reasons for this. First, the competition has less time to respond if they find out about a feature on the day it ships. Also, if a feature was targeted for a particular release date and wasn't done on time, it could be postponed without causing an issue, because customers didn't know about it. Plus, it always helps to have new stuff to announce at conferences.

But modern software developers aren't content to ask for a feature and hope it's delivered in the next release, which could be a year away. This is especially true when there may be an open source project that could fulfill their needs. As large companies warm to open source software, even the most faithful Microsoft developers turn to other frameworks and libraries to get their own projects done on time and within budget. Microsoft needed to make a change.

Exposing the source for the .NET Framework was the first step. The .NET Framework source code has been publicly available for years at https://referencesource .microsoft.com and also on GitHub. The Reference Source website makes it easy to search the source code of the .NET Framework.

It's one thing to expose the source and quite a different thing to accept external contributions. The .NET Core developers not only wanted to allow external contributions, they also wanted to include the community in the design and development. This led to a lot more transparency. Every week, the ASP.NET Core team holds a live community standup meeting at http://live.asp.net. The code for .NET Core has been available publicly on GitHub from the start, and anyone can make a pull request. Community members can also create bugs and feature requests in GitHub. .NET Core marked a significant change in direction for Microsoft regarding open source.

1.5.6   *Bring your own tools*

Because .NET Core works on many platforms, command-line functionality is crucial for .NET Core tooling. For some Linux variants, or when working with Docker containers, a terminal may be all that's available. The .NET Command-Line Interface (CLI) was designed for this purpose.

I can't make any assumptions about what kind of editor you'll use to write your code. You can use an integrated development environment like Visual Studio or a simple text editor like vi or emacs. There are also plenty of tools that feature syntax highlighting, like Notepad2 or Sublime. This book focuses on the use of the CLI so that you'll be able to try all the examples regardless of which platform you're using.

1.6   *Applying .NET Core to real-world applications*

What sets .NET Core apart from other frameworks when it comes to building real-world applications? Let's look back at the claims architecture from figure 1.1. A claims adjuster goes to the scene of an accident and enters the evidence (notes and photos, for example) into a software application that generates the estimate. In order to determine what evidence needs to be collected, the software may use complex, proprietary business logic. The adjuster needs to gather this information regardless of connectivity, so it will be helpful to have the business logic available in the mobile application.

Rewriting all the business logic in a language suitable for a mobile application introduces a maintenance issue. Both the team working on the server side and the team writing the mobile application must update their codebases with any changes to the business logic. Ownership gets split between teams, and keeping in sync becomes difficult. With Xamarin support for the .NET Standard library, web services and mobile applications alike can use the same business logic library. Claims adjusters get consistent behavior, and maintenance costs go down.

Scaling in response to demand

In the case of a natural disaster, such as a hurricane or flood, claims adjusters will be working overtime, increasing demand. The claims architecture needs to scale to meet this demand. With the improved performance of ASP.NET Core and the ability to deploy .NET Core applications to containers, adjusters can rely on the claims system to handle the workload. This is important to the insurance company, because downtime of backend systems directly affects customer experience and slows down adjusters.

1.7   Differences from the .NET Framework

.NET Core is not simply the .NET Framework for Linux and Mac. Rather than port all of the .NET Framework, Microsoft has taken the approach of waiting to see what customers want. There has to be enough customer interest in a framework feature to persuade Microsoft to allocate the resources to do a port. One of the obstacles to porting is that the teams that originally built these features have almost completely moved on. Luckily for ASP.NET customers, the ASP.NET team was the driver behind .NET Core. MVC, Web API, and SignalR are either all available in .NET Core or are on the roadmap.

1.7.1   Framework features not ported to Core

The following list identifies Framework features not currently ported to .NET Core, but I provide this with the knowledge that things can change. Some features don't apply to non-Windows platforms. There are other features that Microsoft doesn't want to carry forward into the future, either because there are better replacements or because the feature was problematic in some way (insecure, hard to maintain, and so on):

- *WPF/XAML*—The Windows Presentation Foundation is only meant for user interfaces. The .NET Standard Library doesn't include UI libraries, and .NET Core doesn't attempt to provide a cross-platform UI framework.
- *Transactions*—This library made it easy to create distributed transactions, but it relies on Windows-specific components, so it's not readily portable to .NET Core.
- *AppDomains*—These were useful for isolating assemblies so they could be unloaded without killing the process, which is great for applications that allow plugins. They rely on some Windows-specific constructs that wouldn't work on other operating systems.
- *.NET remoting*—Remote objects have been succeeded by REST services.
- *ASMX*—This was an old way of writing web services that has been replaced by Web API.
- *Linq to SQL*—This has been replaced by Entity Framework, which is touched upon in chapter 6.
- *WCF services*—Windows Communication Foundation client capabilities are available in .NET Core, but you can't create services.
- *WF*—Windows Workflow Foundation depends on XAML, WCF services, and transactions, among other .NET Framework-only features.

1.7.2   Subtle changes for .NET Framework developers

Experienced .NET Framework developers may encounter a few surprises when working in .NET Core. Writing new code should be relatively straightforward, because you're unlikely to use older constructs like `HashTable` or `ArrayList`. Visual Studio's IntelliSense will also indicate whether a type, method, property, and so on, is supported in .NET Core. In figure 1.5, you can see the auto-completion window flagging members that are different in .NET Core.

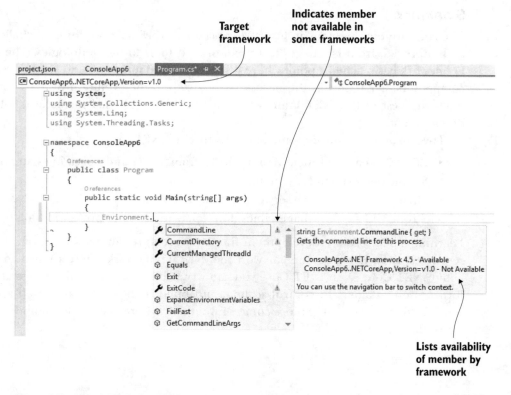

Figure 1.5 Visual Studio IntelliSense indicates whether a class or member is available in .NET Core.

.NET PORTABILITY ANALYZER
If you're attempting to convert an existing .NET application to .NET Core, the best place to start would be the .NET Portability Analyzer. It's available both as a command-line application and a Visual Studio plugin. This tool creates a detailed report with useful suggestions wherever possible. We'll explore this tool further in chapter 11.

1.7.3 Changes to .NET reflection

Reflection works differently in .NET Core than in the .NET Framework. The most noticeable difference is that a lot of the operations normally available in the `Type` class are no longer available. Some have been moved to a new class called `TypeInfo`. You'll see examples of this later in the book.

Additional resources

To find out more about .NET Core and C#, try the following resources:

- Microsoft's .NET Core Guide: https://docs.microsoft.com/en-us/dotnet/core/
- *C# in Depth, Fourth Edition*, by Jon Skeet (Manning, 2018): http://mng.bz/6yPQ
- ASP.NET Core Community Standups: http://live.asp.net

Summary

The software development industry is constantly evolving. Everything is challenged and improved, from languages to frameworks to tools to methodologies. The .NET Framework has reached a point where it's too rigid and monolithic to keep up with its competitors. .NET Core is the necessary next step in the evolution of .NET. It combines the best of the .NET Framework with the practices used in modern software development.

This chapter introduced some of the features of .NET Core:

- Libraries that can function on multiple frameworks and operating systems
- Simple deployment for containers
- High-performance web services with ASP.NET Core
- Strong CLI support that enables developers to use their preferred tools

Learning a new software development framework requires an investment of time and resources. Even if you're familiar with the .NET Framework, there's much to learn about .NET Core. With .NET Core you can write code that's portable across all platforms, use containers to control scaling, and build high-performance web applications. In this book, we'll explore some of what .NET Core is capable of, and why it's worth the investment.

Building your first
.NET Core applications

This chapter covers

- Installing the .NET Core SDK
- Using the .NET CLI
- Creating and executing a .NET Core application

In this chapter, you'll learn how to set up your development environment, create an application, and deploy that application to another machine. You'll start by installing the .NET Core SDK, which includes the .NET Command-Line Interface (CLI) that's used throughout this book. From there, you'll create a console application and an ASP.NET web application. Then you'll deploy those applications.

> **NOTE FOR EARLY ADOPTERS** If you've experimented with .NET Core in the past, you may have used DNVM, DNU, or DNX. Although these tools were useful in the beginning, they had a few problems and inconsistencies. They have been deprecated in favor of the .NET CLI.

2.1 The trouble with development environments

There's something special about development environments. They accumulate a combination of tools, files, and settings that allow your application to work perfectly during development but fail mysteriously everywhere else. Testers get frustrated when I tell them, "It works on my machine." I've been in several situations where a test was "flaky," sometimes working and sometimes not, only to discover that one of the build machines in the pool didn't have a component installed.

Making software behave consistently from development to test to production starts with the development framework. .NET Core is designed to be self-contained. It doesn't depend on Windows-specific resources like the .NET Framework—the .NET CLI is consistent on each OS. Plus, .NET Core is tailored to containers. The same container can be used for development, test, and production, reducing the friction traditionally experienced when crossing these boundaries. In the following sections, we'll explore the key features of .NET Core that produce a consistent developer experience.

2.2   Installing the .NET Core SDK

.NET Core can be installed on Windows, several Linux distros, macOS, and Docker.

An easy-to-remember URL for .NET is https://dot.net. Interestingly, you won't find much mention of the word "Core" on the .NET site. This is to clarify for newcomers to .NET that .NET Framework, .NET Standard, and .NET Core are all part of one large family. Go to the .NET site, click the Get Started button, and pick the operating system you're working on.

2.2.1   Installing on Windows operating systems

There are two methods for installing on Windows: Visual Studio and command line. Visual Studio 2017 comes with everything you'll need for .NET Core development, and the Community edition is free. It installs the .NET SDK, which has the command-line tools as well. Because the command-line tools are universal to all operating systems, this book will focus on that version. The Get Started portion on the .NET site covers both the .NET SDK and Visual Studio installations.

2.2.2   Installing on Linux-based operating systems

The process for installing .NET Core on Linux varies depending on the distro. The instructions change constantly, so by the time this book goes to print, any instructions I included here would likely be out of date. See Microsoft's .NET site (https://dot.net), click the Get Started button, choose "Linux," and pick your Linux distribution for the latest instructions.

2.2.3   Installing on macOS

.NET Core supports OS X version 10.11 and later. The best way to install is with the .pkg file available for download from the .NET site (https://dot.net). Click the Get Started button and choose "macOS."

You can also install Visual Studio for Mac, which will have the option to install the .NET Core SDK.

2.2.4 *Building .NET Core Docker containers*

When working with Docker, you only need to get the "dotnet" base image, which includes the .NET SDK. Simply run the following command using the Docker CLI:

```
docker run -it microsoft/dotnet:latest
```

> **GETTING STARTED WITH DOCKER**   If you're not familiar with Docker, I encourage you to check out *Docker in Action* by Jeff Nickoloff (Manning, 2016). You can get started with Docker by going to https://www.docker.com/get-docker and downloading the Docker Community Edition. The Docker site includes lots of easy-to-follow documentation for installing Docker and running containers.

2.3 *Creating and running the Hello World console application*

The .NET Core SDK includes a sample Hello World application, and the instructions for creating it are the same on every platform. Execute the following commands on the command line or terminal:

```
mkdir hwapp
cd hwapp
dotnet new console
```

The command `dotnet new console` creates a new Hello World console application in the current folder. When new versions of .NET Core are released, it can be helpful to run this command to see if there are any updates to the fundamental pieces of .NET Core.

The `dotnet new console` command creates two files: Program.cs and hwapp.csproj. Program.cs should look similar to the following listing.

> **Listing 2.1   Program.cs from the Hello World application**

```csharp
using System;

namespace hwapp
{
  public class Program
  {
    public static void Main(string[] args)
    {
      Console.WriteLine("Hello World");
    }
  }
}
```

This is a straightforward C# program. If you're familiar with C#, you'll know that the same code will work in other versions of .NET.

The hwapp.csproj file gets its name from the folder it was created in. The following listing shows the contents of this file.

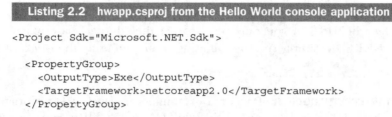

Listing 2.2   hwapp.csproj from the Hello World console application

```
<Project Sdk="Microsoft.NET.Sdk">

  <PropertyGroup>
    <OutputType>Exe</OutputType>
    <TargetFramework>netcoreapp2.0</TargetFramework>
  </PropertyGroup>

</Project>
```

The csproj file describes the project. By default, all source code files in the project folder are included, including any subfolders. .NET Framework developers may be used to seeing each source code file listed explicitly in the csproj, but since the convention for .NET projects is to keep all the files under the project folder, .NET Core by default includes everything in the project folder. The OutputType property indicates that this project is an executable application.

2.3.1   *Before you build*

You now have the Hello World code and the project description, but there's a critical step that needs to take place before you build or run your application. You need to *restore* your packages. You have a set of dependencies for your project, and each dependency is a package that may also have its own dependencies. The package-restore step expands the full tree of dependencies and determines which versions of each package to install.

The command to restore packages is dotnet restore. Try running it to see how it works. If you're adding a new package reference to your csproj, it's a helpful command for testing whether the reference is correct.

The .NET Core SDK keeps a local cache of the packages you use. If a particular version of a package isn't in the cache, it's downloaded when you do the package restore. Since .NET Core 2.0, the .NET Core SDK will perform a restore implicitly where necessary.

2.3.2   *Running a .NET Core application*

When you're using the .NET Core SDK, your application will be built automatically when needed. There's no need to worry about whether or not you're executing the latest code.

Try running the Hello World application by executing dotnet run at the command line or terminal.

2.4   *Creating an ASP.NET Core web application*

Now that you've tried the Hello World console application, let's look at a Hello World ASP.NET Core application. This application will create an HTTP service that returns "Hello World" to a GET request.

ASP.NET is the web framework for .NET, and ASP.NET Core is a new version built from the ground up for .NET Core. In this book, I'll briefly introduce ASP.NET Core. To learn more about ASP.NET Core, check out *ASP.NET Core in Action* by Andrew Lock (Manning, 2018).

First, create a new .NET Core application. Create a new folder called hwwebapp. Execute `dotnet new web` in the hwwebapp folder. Inside the folder, you'll find the following files:

- hwwebapp.csproj
- Program.cs
- Startup.cs
- wwwroot

The hwwebapp.csproj file has a package reference to Microsoft.AspNetCore.All, as shown in the following listing.

> **Listing 2.3   hwwebapp.csproj package reference to Microsoft.AspNetCore.All**

```
<Project Sdk="Microsoft.NET.Sdk.Web">

  <PropertyGroup>
    <TargetFramework>netcoreapp2.0</TargetFramework>
  </PropertyGroup>

  <ItemGroup>
    <Folder Include="wwwroot\" />        ◁  You won't use this
  </ItemGroup>                              folder in this example.

  <ItemGroup>
    <PackageReference
      Include="Microsoft.AspNetCore.All"  ◁  PackageReference references
      Version="2.0.0" />                     a NuGet package.
  </ItemGroup>

</Project>
```

2.4.1   ASP.NET Core uses the Kestrel web server

Web applications need a web server, and Kestrel is the web server that was built for ASP.NET Core. It can be started from a console application and is included as part of the Microsoft.AspNetCore.All metapackage (a package that references a bunch of other packages). In the following listing, Kestrel is included as part of the default `WebHost` builder.

> **Listing 2.4   Program.cs for an ASP.NET Core web application**

```
using Microsoft.AspNetCore;
using Microsoft.AspNetCore.Hosting;    ◁  The usings are trimmed to
                                          only what's needed.
```

```
namespace hwwebapp
{
  public class Program
  {
    public static void Main(string[] args)
    {
        BuildWebHost(args).Run();
    }

    public static IWebHost BuildWebHost(string[] args) =>          Starts the Kestrel
      WebHost.CreateDefaultBuilder(args)                           web server
        .UseStartup<Startup>()                        References the Startup
        .Build();                                     class in Startup.cs
    }
  }
}
```

2.4.2   Using a Startup class to initialize the web server

Next, let's look at the `Startup` class referenced from Program.cs. This class is used by ASP.NET to define how requests will be handled. Your web service will simply return "Hello World" in the response.

The Startup.cs file included with the template includes more than is necessary. The following listing shows a trimmed-down version of this class.

Listing 2.5   Trimmed-down Startup.cs file for a Hello World web application

```
using Microsoft.AspNetCore.Builder;
using Microsoft.AspNetCore.Hosting;
using Microsoft.AspNetCore.Http;
using Microsoft.Extensions.Logging;

namespace hwwebapp
{
  public class Startup                                         These are created by
  {                                                            dependency injection,
    public void Configure(IApplicationBuilder app,             covered in chapter 6.
      IHostingEnvironment env, ILoggerFactory loggerFactory)
    {
      loggerFactory.AddConsole();              Log messages go
                                               to the console.
      if (env.IsDevelopment())
      {
        app.UseDeveloperExceptionPage();       Exceptions are hidden from web
      }                                        pages except in development mode.

      app.Run(async (context) =>
        await context.Response.WriteAsync(     Responds to all requests
          "Hello World")                       with "Hello World"
      );
    }
  }
}
```

Whereas the `Program` class starts the web server, the `Startup` class starts the web application.

There's a lot of stuff to unpack in listing 2.5. This book doesn't delve deeply into ASP.NET Core, but anonymous methods, async/await, dependency injection, and logging are all covered in later chapters.

For those not familiar with C#

If you aren't familiar with C#, the => may be confusing. This is used to create an anonymous method—*anonymous* meaning that it has no name. The arguments for the method go on the left side of the =>, which is the `HttpContext` in listing 2.5. The method definition goes on the right side. If the method needs only one line and returns a value, you can forgo the brackets, `return`, and `;` and keep only the expression.

In this case, you want to write "Hello World" in the HTTP response and return the asynchronous `Task` object. We'll cover the subject of tasks later in the book.

Pros and cons of anonymous methods

Anonymous methods in C# can provide a huge productivity boost. In addition to making code more readable, there's another often-overlooked benefit: you don't have to figure out a name for a method. I'm surprised by how much time I spend thinking about how to name various artifacts in my code.

Some of the drawbacks to anonymous methods are evident in debugging. Anonymous methods still get names in stack traces, just not recognizable ones. It's also difficult to manually create breakpoints on or in anonymous methods from a debugger when you don't know the method name.

2.4.3 Running the Hello World web application

To run the web application, execute the `dotnet run` command at the command line, just as before. This starts the web server, which should produce output like the following:

```
Hosting environment: Production
Content root path: /hwwebapp
Now listening on: http://localhost:5000        The web address
Application started. Press Ctrl+C to shut down.  for the app
```

The output of `dotnet run` includes the web address for the Kestrel server. In this example it's http://localhost:5000. Open a browser and navigate to this address. Figure 2.1 shows the Hello World web application running in the browser.

Figure 2.1 Hello World web application in the browser

2.5   *Creating an ASP.NET Core website from the template*

In the previous section, you created a minimal ASP.NET Core web application. That may be a useful starting point for creating a service, but a website requires a lot more work. The .NET Core SDK includes a template for ASP.NET Core websites to help get you started. If you're familiar with ASP.NET development in Visual Studio, this is closer to the New Project scenario.

To use the template, start from a new folder called "hwwebsite," and in that folder, execute this command: `dotnet new mvc`. List the contents of the folder, and you'll find a lot more files than you created in the previous template.

Run the `dotnet run` command to get the web server started as before. Then visit http://localhost:5000 in your browser to see the default website.

2.6   *Deploying to a server*

Now that you've written some applications, you can try deploying them to a server. .NET Core was designed to deploy by simply copying files. It helps to know where these files come from.

In figure 2.2, the .NET CLI package contains some assemblies that are installed into the dotnet folder. They're enough to power the .NET CLI (command-line interface) but not much else. When the SDK does the restore, it determines what packages it needs to download based on your dependencies. Kestrel is an example of a dependency that isn't part of .NET Core but is necessary to run an ASP.NET application.

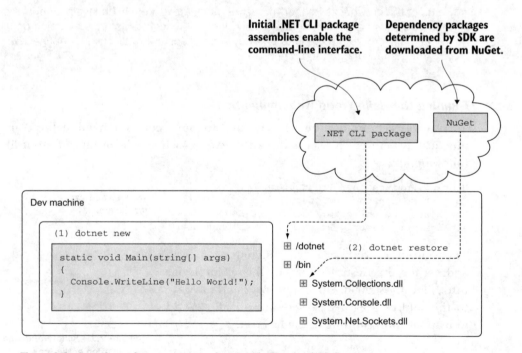

Figure 2.2   Locations of components and assembly files for .NET Core

The .NET CLI downloads these dependency packages from a package store called NuGet and stores them centrally, so you don't have to download them for every project you write.

2.6.1 Publishing an application

The .NET CLI provides a way to consolidate all the binaries needed to deploy your application into one folder. From the folder containing the Hello World console application (hwapp), execute `dotnet publish -c Release` from the command line or terminal. The console output indicates to which folder the binaries are published.

Change to the publish folder under the output folder. There should be four files:

- hwapp.deps.json
- hwapp.dll
- hwapp.pdb
- hwapp.runtimeconfig.json

Copy these files to another machine that has the .NET Core SDK installed. Then, to execute the application, run the command `dotnet hwapp.dll` from the folder containing the copied files.

In this example, only the binaries built for the project, and any included packages, are published. This is called a *framework-dependent deployment*. When you deploy the files from the publish folder, you need to have the .NET Core SDK installed on the target machine.

PUBLISHING A SELF-CONTAINED APPLICATION

There's another way to create an application that will include all of the .NET Core assemblies, so it can run on a machine that doesn't have the .NET Core SDK installed. This is called a *self-contained application*.

To create a self-contained application, you'll first need to be explicit about what runtimes your application can run on. This is done by adding the `Runtime-Identifiers` property to your project file, as shown in the following listing.

> **Listing 2.6 Add `RuntimeIdentifiers` to the hwapp.csproj file**

```
<Project Sdk="Microsoft.NET.Sdk">
  <PropertyGroup>
    <OutputType>Exe</OutputType>
    <TargetFramework>netcoreapp2.0</TargetFramework>
    <RuntimeIdentifiers>win10-x64;osx.10.11-x64;linuxmint.17.1-x64
    </RuntimeIdentifiers>
  </PropertyGroup>
</Project>
```

Now you can create a self-contained application by using the runtime identifier in the publish command, as follows:

```
dotnet publish -c Release -r linuxmint.17.1-x64
```

Listing the contents of the bin\Release\netcoreapp2.0\linuxmint.17.1-x64\publish folder will reveal a lot of files. Figure 2.3 illustrates what this publishing step looks like.

Packages are stored either in the local .NET CLI cache or in a NuGet package library. The restore process pulls all the files to the cache. The `dotnet publish` command with the runtime option collects all the files necessary, including the binaries built from your project code, and puts them into the publish folder. The full contents of this folder can then be copied to other machines or containers.

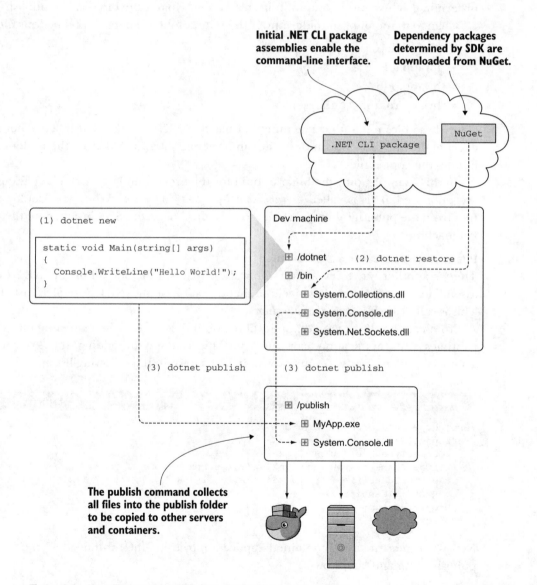

Figure 2.3   How files used by .NET Core applications are published

2.6.2 *Deploying to a Docker container*

Deploying to a Linux, macOS, or Windows machine is all the same—copy the contents of the publish folder to a folder on the target machine. If you're not deploying a self-contained application, the only prerequisite for the target machine is having the .NET Core SDK installed. For Docker, the same general theory applies, but you'll typically want to create a container with your application.

Earlier, you used Microsoft's .NET Core container by executing the following command from the Docker CLI:

```
docker run -it microsoft/dotnet:latest
```

You get the latest .NET Core container from Docker Hub by using `microsoft/dotnet:latest`.

To create a new Docker container with the application, you'll start with the .NET Core container, copy your published application's files, and tell it to run the application.

First, open a command prompt with the Docker CLI. Change to the folder containing the Hello World console application, and then create a new text file in the current folder called Dockerfile. Insert the text from the following listing.

Listing 2.7   Dockerfile for Hello World console application

```
FROM microsoft/dotnet:latest
COPY bin/Release/netcoreapp2.0/publish/ /root/
ENTRYPOINT dotnet /root/hwapp.dll
```

Save and close the Dockerfile file. Then execute the following Docker CLI command to build the container.

Listing 2.8   Command to build Hello World console application container image

```
docker build -t hwapp .
```

Now you can run the container with the following command and see that your application is working.

Listing 2.9   Running the Hello World console application Docker container

```
$ docker run -it hwapp
Hello World
```

DEPLOYING THE WEB APPLICATION

The barebones ASP.NET Core web application you created earlier (hwwebapp) will need some adjustments before it can work on Docker. First, modify the Program.cs file as shown in the following listing.

Listing 2.10   Modifying Program.cs for Docker container deployment

```
using Microsoft.AspNetCore;
using Microsoft.AspNetCore.Hosting;

namespace hwwebapp
{
  public class Program
  {
    public static void Main(string[] args)
    {
      BuildWebHost(args).Run();
    }

    public static IWebHost BuildWebHost(string[] args) =>
      WebHost.CreateDefaultBuilder(args)
        .UseUrls("http://*:5000/")          ◁┐ Add this
        .UseStartup<Startup>()                │ line.
        .Build();
  }
}
```

The added line allows URLs other than http://localhost:5000. Because the application is being deployed to a container, you'll need to test it by pinging it from outside the container.

You also need to configure Docker to open the port. To do this, you'll first need to edit the Dockerfile, as shown in the following listing

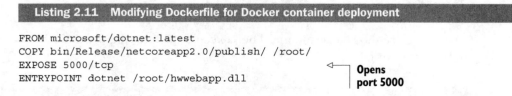

Listing 2.11   Modifying Dockerfile for Docker container deployment

```
FROM microsoft/dotnet:latest
COPY bin/Release/netcoreapp2.0/publish/ /root/
EXPOSE 5000/tcp                          ◁┐ Opens
ENTRYPOINT dotnet /root/hwwebapp.dll      │ port 5000
```

Build and run the application and Docker container with the following commands:

```
dotnet publish -c Release
docker build -t hwwebapp .
docker run -it -p 5000:5000 hwwebapp
```

To test the web application, use localhost with port 5000 in your browser: http://localhost:5000.

2.6.3   *Packaging for distribution*

.NET Core makes it easy to package your library or application so that others can use it in their applications. This is accomplished through the dotnet pack command.

Try this out on the Hello World console application. Go to the hwapp folder and run `dotnet pack -c Release`. This command will create a hwapp.1.0.0.nupkg file.

The .nupkg file produced by the `dotnet pack` command is a NuGet package. A lot of the dependencies you use in your .NET Core applications will come from NuGet packages. They're a great way of sharing code both privately and publicly. We'll cover these in more depth in chapter 12.

2.7 Development tools available for .NET Core

Microsoft typically released new versions of the .NET Framework in tandem with updates to Visual Studio. This meant that the files involved in .NET projects didn't need to be human-readable, because the IDE would take care of that work. When Microsoft started building .NET Core, they needed simple files that developers could edit directly with text editors. They relied on JSON and created a custom build system.

In the long term, maintaining two different build systems would be costly and confusing, so even though developers loved the new JSON-based .NET Core build system, the Microsoft team needed to incorporate it back into their existing build system, called MSBuild. The chief complaint against MSBuild was about the complexity of the project files. Luckily, MSBuild is flexible enough that the .NET Core team could address this concern.

The .NET Core project files use a lot of techniques to reduce the file size and complexity so that developers can more easily edit them by hand. This means you can use any text editor you want for writing your .NET Core applications, instead of needing to use Visual Studio. The range of development tools includes everything from full-featured IDEs to vi, notepad, or butterflies (see https://xkcd.com/378). For this book, you'll only need a basic text editor and a command prompt. But you can also try out some of these editors to improve your experience.

2.7.1 OmniSharp

OmniSharp is a family of open source projects whose goal is to enable building .NET in the most popular text editors. It does this with tools, editor integrations, and libraries. OmniSharp provides plugins for all kinds of text editors:

- Atom (atom.io)
- Sublime (sublimetext.com)
- Brackets (brackets.io)
- Emacs (gnu.org/software/emacs)
- Vim (vim.org)
- Visual Studio Code (code.visualstudio.com)

As an example, install the OmniSharp extension for Visual Studio Code.

OmniSharp for Visual Studio Code

Visit https://code.visualstudio.com from your browser and download Visual Studio Code. After installing it, you can run the command `code .` from a new terminal or command line window to open Visual Studio Code on the current folder.

Mac users need to take an extra step: open the Command Palette from the View menu, and type in "shell command" to find "Install 'code' command in PATH".

When you open a C# file with VS Code for the first time, it will prompt you to install an extension. The one entitled "C#" is the OmniSharp extension. This extension should be all you need to build, run, and debug .NET Core applications—assuming you've already installed the .NET SDK.

Also note that VS Code has an integrated terminal that can be configured to Windows Command Prompt, PowerShell, or Bash. You can also have multiple terminals open at the same time. This makes it easier to try out the various .NET CLI commands used throughout this book.

2.7.2 *Visual Studio for Mac*

Developers who may have worked with Xamarin Studio in the past will recognize Visual Studio for Mac as being Xamarin Studio rebranded. VS for Mac has several editions, including a free community edition.

> **BUILDING XAMARIN APPS ON WINDOWS** If you want the Xamarin Studio experience but aren't on Mac, Xamarin is an option you can choose from the Visual Studio 2017 installer.

Creating new projects in Visual Studio for Mac is done through the New Project wizard (shown in figure 2.4). You can use this instead of the `dotnet` command-line options. Also note that VS for Mac will perform restores for you.

2.7.3 *Visual Studio 2017*

Visual Studio has always been the flagship development environment for Microsoft. It only runs on Windows and has been synonymous with Windows and the .NET Framework for many years. Only in recent releases has Visual Studio started to support other languages, such as Python and JavaScript. You can use the preview .NET Core tooling in Visual Studio 2015, but it doesn't come with support. Visual Studio 2017 has a free Community Edition that includes .NET Core and Xamarin tooling. You can find it at www.visualstudio.com/downloads.

With Visual Studio, you don't need to use the `dotnet` command-line commands. For example, the New Project wizard shown in figure 2.5 replaces the `dotnet new` functionality.

Xamarin applications

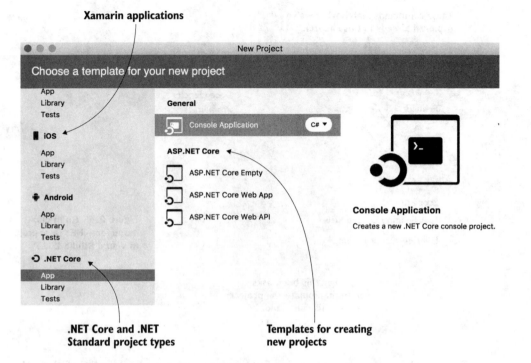

.NET Core and .NET
Standard project types

Templates for creating
new projects

Figure 2.4 Visual Studio for Mac's New Project wizard

.NET Core and .NET
Standard project types

Don't pay attention to this. It
doesn't have any bearing on your
.NET Core/Standard projects.

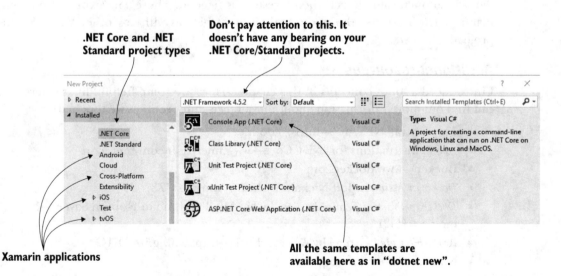

Xamarin applications

All the same templates are
available here as in "dotnet new".

Figure 2.5 Visual Studio 2017 Community edition New Project wizard

These commands match what we've explored already in this chapter.

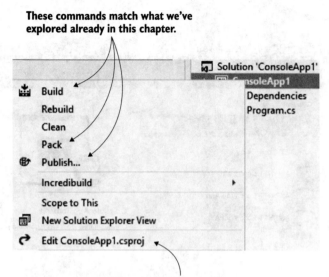

Figure 2.6 Right-click menu for a .NET Core project in Visual Studio 2017

Whenever this book asks you to manipulate the project file, use this command.

Right-click on the project in the Solution Explorer to find some of the other commonly used .NET CLI commands. Figure 2.6 shows what's available.

Note that `dotnet restore` isn't mentioned anywhere. That's because Visual Studio will automatically detect when a restore is needed. There's no explicit Run command, but you can use the traditional F5 or Ctrl-F5, as with any other Visual Studio project.

Additional resources

I introduced a lot of concepts in this chapter. Here are some helpful links where you can find out more information about the subjects and products we touched on:

- The central .NET site—https://dot.net
- Install instructions for .NET Core—www.microsoft.com/net/core
- Docker—www.docker.com
- *Docker in Action* by Jeff Nickoloff—http://mng.bz/JZSJ
- *Docker in Practice, Second Edition,* by Ian Miell and Aidan Hobson Sayers—http://mng.bz/H42I
- *ASP.NET Core in Action* by Andrew Lock—http://mng.bz/DI1O
- Node.js—https://nodejs.org
- *Node.js in Action, Second Edition,* by Alex Young, Bradley Meck, and Mike Cantelon—http://mng.bz/mK7C
- Bower package manager—https://bower.io

Summary

In this chapter you learned how to get started with .NET Core by doing the following:

- Installing the .NET Core SDK
- Learning basic .NET CLI commands
- Building both a console application and an ASP.NET Core web application
- Preparing applications for deployment and distribution

These are all fundamental skills for developing with .NET Core. Here are a few tips to keep in mind:

- The `dotnet new` command makes it easy to get a template for starting a new project. It's also nice if you need a quick reference.
- Whenever you make changes to the dependencies, you can run the `dotnet restore` command to get the packages immediately.
- Use the Yeoman generator for more customizable templates.

You'll practice more with the .NET CLI commands (`restore`, `new`, `run`, `publish`, and `pack`) throughout the book. In the next chapter, we'll get into the details of the project files and you'll learn how to build more substantial applications with .NET Core.

How to build with
.NET Core

This chapter covers

- Frameworks, runtimes, and platforms
- MSBuild fundamentals

Throughout my time as a software developer, there has been a dichotomy between the things I want to do, like write code, and the things I have to do, like build code. I didn't want to learn makefiles or MSBuild. IDEs also made it possible to skip most of that.

At least until the day when I had to do one specific thing. Then I had to either go through the steep learning curve to figure out what I needed, or copy-paste from Stack Overflow and hope for the best. Neither situation is ideal. Knowing the fundamentals of your build files not only keeps you out of sticky situations, it also lets you know what's possible. For this chapter, I recommend that you not use an IDE and instead code the exercises by hand.

3.1 Key concepts in .NET Core's build system

Even experienced .NET Framework developers will find new terminology and concepts in .NET Core. The way projects are built is essentially the same, but there are several improvements.

3.1.1   *Introducing MSBuild*

In the previous chapter, you created several projects, and the most critical component for building them was the csproj file. A csproj is a C#-specific project file containing MSBuild XML. For F# projects, the project file has an .fsproj extension; VB project files have a .vbproj extension. It's also possible to import other MSBuild files, but those files don't usually have the .*proj extensions.

> ### What happened to project.json?
> When .NET Core 1.0 was released, it used a build system based on a JSON file called project.json. For .NET Core 2.0, project.json was dropped in favor of the established MSBuild, which is used for .NET Framework projects.

3.1.2   *Creating .NET projects from the command line*

.NET Framework developers could always rely on Visual Studio to take care of a lot of the build nastiness—most .NET Framework developers don't write their own MSBuild project files. This presented a challenge for the .NET Core team, because they couldn't rely on UI tools. What they produced was a much simpler way to build .NET projects.

In this chapter, I'll show you how to use the .NET Core build system by example. Build systems are critical to writing applications, and the .NET Core team has simplified building to the point that you can learn it up front and build better projects.

3.1.3   *Clearing up the terminology*

Many words used to describe software aren't clearly defined, and they become interchangeable. For instance, what's the difference between a framework, a platform, and a runtime? Another confusing term is *dependency*. Figure 3.1 illustrates what a dependency is using a class diagram. The individual items in figure 3.1 are explained further in the following sections.

When you add a dependency to a project file, that dependency can be a package, metapackage, or another project. A package is generally a NuGet package containing files and assemblies organized by the framework those assemblies will work on. Metapackages reference a bunch of other packages and may also define a framework. An example of a metapackage that defines a framework is the .NET Standard Library. In chapter 2, you used another metapackage called Microsoft.AspNetCore.All, which doesn't define a framework—it's just a handy way of including all the ASP.NET Core packages. Each package has a set of frameworks that it targets, and each of these target frameworks contains files, including any number of assemblies. Assemblies can either be portable, like a .NET Standard assembly, or be runtime-specific.

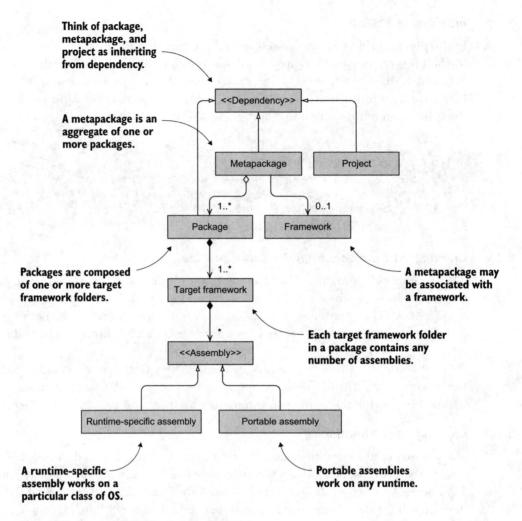

Think of package, metapackage, and project as inheriting from dependency.

A metapackage is an aggregate of one or more packages.

Packages are composed of one or more target framework folders.

A metapackage may be associated with a framework.

Each target framework folder in a package contains any number of assemblies.

A runtime-specific assembly works on a particular class of OS.

Portable assemblies work on any runtime.

Figure 3.1 Dependencies illustrated with UML

FRAMEWORKS

Frameworks, or more specifically *target frameworks*, are a NuGet concept. A target framework is a flavor and/or version of .NET, such as .NET Framework 4.5 or .NET Core 1.0. A framework is typically specified using its target framework moniker (TFM). For instance, .NET Framework 4.5 is `net45` and .NET Core 1.0 is `netcoreapp1.0`.

When working with the project file or the .NET CLI, you use TFMs. In the project file, the `TargetFramework` property is where you specify the target framework your project supports. The following listing shows an example project file for a class library project.

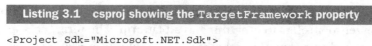

Listing 3.1   csproj showing the `TargetFramework` property

```
<Project Sdk="Microsoft.NET.Sdk">

  <PropertyGroup>
    <TargetFramework>netstandard1.4</TargetFramework>
  </PropertyGroup>

</Project>
```

From the CLI, you would use the `-f` or `--framework` option to pick the target framework you want to build, or test, or publish as follows:

```
dotnet build -f netcoreapp2.0
dotnet test -f netcoreapp2.0
```

A list of TFMs is provided in appendix A, but you can also get the current list from the online NuGet documentation.

.NET STANDARD

If your code works on multiple frameworks, it can be tedious to list all of those frameworks in your project. Listing them can also mean that when a new framework comes out that you want to support, you have to create a new version of your project. .NET Standard alleviates some of this pain by allowing you to use one TFM that many frameworks will support.

Wherever possible, you'll use the `netstandard` moniker with the lowest version number that's compatible with the sample code. This works for libraries, but console applications and web services need to use `netcoreapp`, because that provides an entry point for starting the application.

RUNTIMES

A *runtime specification* is composed of an operating system and CPU architecture, such as `win10-x64`, `osx.10.11-x64`, and `linuxmint.17.1-x86`. There's no satisfactory explanation that I've found for why this is called a *runtime*. I speculate that runtime once referred to OS, CLR type (CLR, CoreCLR, Mono), and CPU architecture. But because the CLR type isn't specific enough for generating NuGet packages, it was removed in favor of the target framework.

In figure 3.1, there are also *runtime-specific assemblies*. A runtime-specific assembly would typically be a natively compiled assembly that only works on a particular class of operating systems. There's nothing in a package that lets it indicate that it only supports certain runtimes, but the .NET CLI will check runtime support during build.

A list of runtime IDs is available in appendix A. The runtime IDs would be used either in the project file in the `RuntimeIdentifiers` property or as a CLI parameter with `-r` or `--runtime`.

PLATFORMS

Platform is the vaguest of all these terms. Whereas "framework" and "runtime" have tangible meanings in .NET Core, "platform" doesn't. Sometimes, platform is used in place of framework, and sometimes in place of runtime. You may have noticed that the .NET Portability Analyzer tool refers to everything as a platform. The term "cross-platform" is typically used to indicate something that works on multiple operating systems.

In this book, I will try to only use platform to describe an operating system. Using runtime to refer to operating systems can be confusing when you're not talking about the contents of a project file or about parameters to the .NET CLI.

3.2   CSV parser sample project

The example project you'll build in this chapter is a CSV parser. It will be as basic an implementation as possible—the code is terribly inefficient and has no error handling. But it will help you see how projects are laid out, and you'll learn some of the options available.

To get started, create a CsvParser project by executing the following commands from a command line. Be sure to start in a folder that's not within another project:

```
mkdir CsvParser
cd CsvParser
dotnet new console
```

Now create a new file called CsvReader.cs, and enter the following code.

Listing 3.2   Contents of the CsvReader.cs file

```
using System.Collections.Generic;
using System.IO;

namespace CsvParser
{
  public class CsvReader
  {
    private string[] columns;
    private TextReader source;

    public CsvReader(TextReader reader)
    {
      this.source = reader;
      var columnLine = reader.ReadLine();           ◁—— The first line is assumed to
      this.columns = columnLine.Split(',');              contain column headings.
    }

    public IEnumerable<KeyValuePair<string, string>[]> Lines
    {
      get
      {                                              ◁—— Need to specify string
        string row;                                       instead of var
        while ((row = this.source.ReadLine()) != null)
        {
          var cells = row.Split(',');                ◁——————
          var pairs = new                                   Each row is expected
            KeyValuePair<string, string>[columns.Length];   to have the same
                                                            number of columns.
```

```
        for (int col = 0; col < columns.Length; col++)
        {
          pairs[col] = new KeyValuePair<string, string>(
            columns[col], cells[col]);
        }

        yield return pairs;                    ◁━┐  yield return returns
      }                                            enumerable values
    }                                              as they are read.
  }
}
```

For those not familiar with C#

I'll explain some basic aspects of C# that will help those new to C# parse this and other code in the book.

At the top of the code is usually a `using` statement. This indicates that you want to include classes for a particular namespace without having to specify the full type name. For instance, instead of writing `System.IO.TextReader` everywhere in the code, you can add `using System.IO` and then only type `TextReader` in the code. Note that `using` isn't the same as a dependency. You can't add a `using` statement for a namespace that doesn't exist in your project's dependencies.

The `Split(',')` method in listing 3.1 is a way to split a string into an array of strings using "," as a delimiter.

`TextReader` is an abstract base class that defines the `ReadLine` method. It's only meant for reading text files and streams.

`KeyValuePair` is exactly what you think it is. The `<>` brackets used in the code indicate generics. For example, `KeyValuePair<string, string>` is a pair where the key and value are both of type `string`.

Sometimes I use `var` to declare a variable, and other times I use the explicit type, like `string`. When a variable is declared and assigned to an obvious type, the C# compiler will infer the type. If there's some ambiguity or if the variable isn't assigned at the same time as it's declared, you need to specify the type.

Now that you've got a CSV reader class, you can experiment with it from your console application. Edit the Program.cs file and add the following code.

Listing 3.3   Program.cs for CsvParser

```
using System;
using System.IO;
using System.Linq;

namespace CsvParser
{
```

```
  public class Program
  {
    public static void Main(string[] args)
    {
      var csv = @"Year,Title,Production Studio
2008,Iron Man,Marvel Studios
2008,The Incredible Hulk,Marvel Studios
2008,Punisher: War Zone,Marvel Studios
2009,X-Men Origins: Wolverine,20th Century Fox
2010,Iron Man 2,Marvel Studios
2011,Thor,Marvel Studios
2011,X-Men: First Class,20th Century Fox
";

      var sr = new StringReader(csv);
      var csvReader = new CsvReader(sr);
      foreach (var line in csvReader.Lines)
        Console.WriteLine(
          line.First(p => p.Key == "Title").Value);
    }
  }
}
```

Taken from Wikipedia's "List of films based on Marvel Comics"

A LINQ query to get only the film titles

For those not familiar with C#

In listing 3.3, the `@"` indicates a *verbatim string*. It allows you to put newlines into the string, and it ignores escape characters. It's useful for keeping long strings like this easy to read.

The `StringReader` class is a subclass of `TextReader`.

The expression `line.First(p => p.Key == "Title").Value` is built using LINQ. LINQ is a powerful C# feature that can make complex logic more readable. This expression looks for the first `KeyValuePair` with a key called `Title` and gets its value. You'll use LINQ expressions throughout the book. If you're interested in learning more, I recommend reading Jon Skeet's *C# in Depth, Fourth Edition* (Manning 2018).

If everything is typed in correctly, you should be able to run the program, as shown here:

```
> dotnet run

Iron Man
The Incredible Hulk
Punisher: War Zone
X-Men Origins: Wolverine
Iron Man 2
Thor
X-Men: First Class
```

For the preceding code, you didn't need to modify the csproj file. That's because you didn't take any dependencies outside of the `netcoreapp` framework, and there was no need to change any of the defaults. But as your application or library becomes more complex, you'll need to know how to modify the project file. In this chapter, you'll learn how to customize the project file to fit your needs.

3.3 *Introducing MSBuild*

Before .NET Core, most developers didn't need to look into the MSBuild project files. Visual Studio took care of most of the work, so the project files tended to be verbose. They could still be edited by hand, but they were far from intuitive.

To make MSBuild work cross-platform and support the promise that developers could use whatever tool they preferred, the project files for .NET Core needed to be trimmed down. This meant using conventions and lots of defaults. In this chapter, we'll explore what some of these defaults and conventions are and how you can extend beyond them.

> **MSBUILD FILES ARE CASE-SENSITIVE** Just as in normal XML files, the elements and attributes used in MSBuild files are case-sensitive. The convention is to use camel case with a capitalized first letter.

3.3.1 *PropertyGroups*

A `PropertyGroup` node in an MSBuild file can contain any number of properties. These are key-value pairs, and they're evaluated in the order that they appear in the file. This is important when thinking about properties. Properties must be defined in the right order.

To test this out, try modifying the CsvParser.csproj file (or create a new project and modify its csproj) to look like the following.

Listing 3.4   A test of how order of properties works in MSBuild

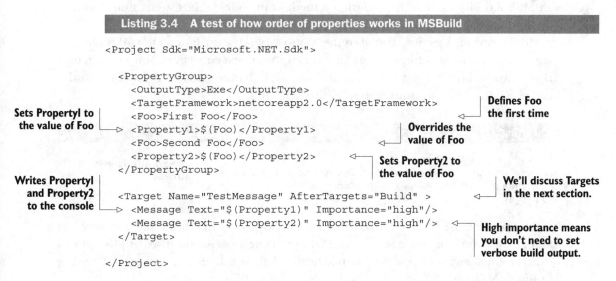

```
<Project Sdk="Microsoft.NET.Sdk">

  <PropertyGroup>
    <OutputType>Exe</OutputType>
    <TargetFramework>netcoreapp2.0</TargetFramework>
    <Foo>First Foo</Foo>
    <Property1>$(Foo)</Property1>
    <Foo>Second Foo</Foo>
    <Property2>$(Foo)</Property2>
  </PropertyGroup>

  <Target Name="TestMessage" AfterTargets="Build" >
    <Message Text="$(Property1)" Importance="high"/>
    <Message Text="$(Property2)" Importance="high"/>
  </Target>

</Project>
```

Sets Property1 to the value of Foo

Writes Property1 and Property2 to the console

Defines Foo the first time

Overrides the value of Foo

Sets Property2 to the value of Foo

We'll discuss Targets in the next section.

High importance means you don't need to set verbose build output.

> **EDITING THE PROJECT FILE FROM AN IDE** How you edit the project file is different depending on your development environment. If you're using one of the

editors supported by OmniSharp, the csproj file is likely just another file listed in the folder. In Visual Studio for Mac, control-click the project and choose Tools > Edit File. In Visual Studio 2017, right-click on the project and chose the option to edit the project file. Each editor will also have varying capabilities in terms of IntelliSense.

From the command prompt, run `dotnet build`. You should see output like this:

```
First Foo
Second Foo
```

> **Undefined properties and debugging build files**
>
> For another interesting experiment, try removing the first `Foo` property setting and build again. Only the `Second Foo` line will appear. The same thing happens if you make the first `Foo` property setting an empty element. The `Message` task won't print empty output. As a result, it's useful to add some text to the message other than just the value of a property.

3.3.2   Targets

We've already seen two targets in the previous section. One is a built-in target called `Message` that writes data to the MSBuild log. The other is a custom target that you defined in the project file. The former comes from a .NET assembly. You won't create those kinds of MSBuild targets in this book. Instead, you'll use the latter method of defining targets in the project file.

All targets must have a name. That's how they're referenced. Declaring a target in an MSBuild file is similar to declaring a method in code. Unless something calls that method, it's never used.

In the previous section, you used the `AfterTargets` attribute to tell MSBuild that after it was done executing the `Build` target it should execute yours. You can also execute a target directly from the command line. Try changing the target defined in the csproj file from the previous section to the following.

Listing 3.5   **Target declaration with no `AfterTargets` attribute set**

```
<Target Name="TestMessage">
  <Message Text="$(Property1)" Importance="high"/>        Remove AfterTargets
  <Message Text="$(Property2)" Importance="high"/>         attribute
</Target>
```

Executing `dotnet  build` from the command line won't print the messages as before. But you can run `dotnet build -t:TestMessage` to instruct MSBuild to execute the `TestMessage` target specifically. This is a handy technique for testing things in MSBuild.

3.3.3 *ItemGroups*

Build systems deal with lots of files. In MSBuild, the `ItemGroup` construct is a useful tool for holding a set of filenames. It operates like an array and exposes operations for manipulating that array. For instance, you can remove a single file or a set of files that match a wildcard from a list.

Try this out with your CsvParser by removing Program.cs from the list of files to compile during the build, as shown in the next listing.

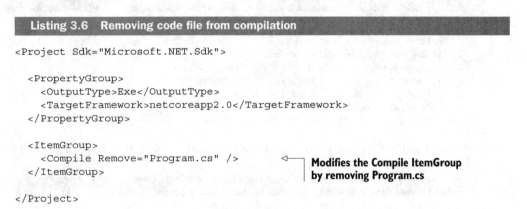

Listing 3.6 Removing code file from compilation

```
<Project Sdk="Microsoft.NET.Sdk">

  <PropertyGroup>
    <OutputType>Exe</OutputType>
    <TargetFramework>netcoreapp2.0</TargetFramework>
  </PropertyGroup>

  <ItemGroup>
    <Compile Remove="Program.cs" />          ◁─  Modifies the Compile ItemGroup
  </ItemGroup>                                    by removing Program.cs

</Project>
```

Removing Program.cs means there's no longer a class with a static `Main` method. When you run `dotnet build`, you should see an error message:

```
Build FAILED.

CSC : error CS5001: Program does not contain a static 'Main' method
                    suitable for an entry point
    0 Warning(s)
    1 Error(s)
```

MSBuild will use the `Compile` ItemGroup as the list of files to send to the compiler. This means that you can manipulate the ItemGroup to include files from other folders or to exclude files that are no longer used.

The default definition of the `Compile` ItemGroup for C# projects is something like the next listing.

Listing 3.7 Default definition for the `Compile` ItemGroup

```
<ItemGroup>
  <Compile Include="**/*.cs" />
</ItemGroup>
```

> **ITEMGROUPS CAN HAVE DUPLICATES** Don't put the `Include` from listing 3.7 into your project file, as it will add duplicate files to the `Compile` ItemGroup and the build will fail.

USING ITEMGROUP TO COPY FILES TO BUILD OUTPUT

Let's find something more interesting to do with the ItemGroup than break the build. The Program.cs file in your CSV parser example includes a test CSV string. You're going to split that test CSV into its own file.

Start by creating a new file called Marvel.csv and pasting in the contents of the verbatim string from Program.cs, as follows.

Listing 3.8   Marvel.csv—contents taken from string in Program.cs

```
Year,Title,Production Studio
2008,Iron Man,Marvel Studios
2008,The Incredible Hulk,Marvel Studios
2008,Punisher: War Zone,Marvel Studios
2009,X-Men Origins: Wolverine,20th Century Fox
2010,Iron Man 2,Marvel Studios
2011,Thor,Marvel Studios
2011,X-Men: First Class,20th Century Fox
```

Then modify Program.cs to load the file instead of using the string, as shown next.

Listing 3.9   Program.cs modified to load Marvel.csv

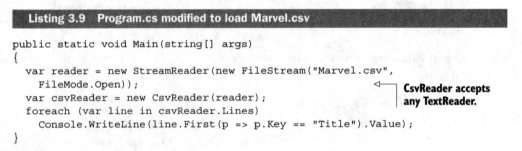

```
public static void Main(string[] args)
{
  var reader = new StreamReader(new FileStream("Marvel.csv",
    FileMode.Open));                                              ◁─┐  CsvReader accepts
  var csvReader = new CsvReader(reader);                              any TextReader.
  foreach (var line in csvReader.Lines)
    Console.WriteLine(line.First(p => p.Key == "Title").Value);
}
```

This depends on the Marvel.csv file being in the same folder as the binary for your application.

You can copy the file from your project folder by using a common MSBuild project item. Modify the csproj as follows.

Listing 3.10   Modifying a csproj to copy a file to the build output

```
<Project Sdk="Microsoft.NET.Sdk">

  <PropertyGroup>
    <OutputType>Exe</OutputType>
    <TargetFramework>netcoreapp2.0</TargetFramework>
  </PropertyGroup>                                        │ None indicates no action
                                                          │ on this file by the compiler.
  <ItemGroup>
    <None Include="Marvel.csv">                     ◁──┘
      <CopyToOutputDirectory>PreserveNewest</CopyToOutputDirectory>
    </None>                            ◁─┐  CopyToOutputDirectory is
  </ItemGroup>                            a common project item.

</Project>
```

Run `dotnet build` and look at the bin/Debug/netcoreapp2.0 folder. It will have a copy of Marvel.csv in it. When you run `dotnet run`, CsvParser will find the CSV file in the same folder and execute correctly.

EMBEDDING FILES IN THE PROJECT

.NET projects have a concept of embedding files into the assembly. This is useful if you don't want to copy a separate file with your assembly. In our example, it isn't obvious that the Marvel.csv file needs to be copied along with CsvParser.dll in order for the application to work. Let's see how to use embedding to put Marvel.csv inside the assembly.

First, change the csproj to embed the CSV instead of copying it to output, as shown in the next listing.

Listing 3.11 Embedding a file in an assembly

```
<Project Sdk="Microsoft.NET.Sdk">

  <PropertyGroup>
    <OutputType>Exe</OutputType>
    <TargetFramework>netcoreapp2.0</TargetFramework>
  </PropertyGroup>

  <ItemGroup>
    <EmbeddedResource Include="Marvel.csv" />
  </ItemGroup>

</Project>
```

Next, modify Program.cs to pick up the embedded file, as shown in the following listing.

Listing 3.12 Modifying Program.cs to read the embedded file

```
using System;
using System.IO;
using System.Linq;
using System.Reflection;            ◁─── Adds a reference to
                                         System.Reflection to
namespace CsvParser                      expose GetTypeInfo()
{
  public class Program
  {
    public static void Main(string[] args)
    {
      var stream = typeof(Program).GetTypeInfo().Assembly.
        GetManifestResourceStream(
        "CsvParser.Marvel.csv");                    ◁─── This statement gets the
      var reader = new StreamReader(stream);             stream from the assembly.
      var csvReader = new CsvReader(reader);
      foreach (var line in csvReader.Lines)
        Console.WriteLine(line.First(p => p.Key == "Title").Value);
    }
  }
}
```

FOR THOSE NOT FAMILIAR WITH C# GetTypeInfo is something called an *extension method* in C#, meaning that it isn't part of the original type. In this case, the typeof() operator returns the Type object that represents the Program class. Type doesn't have a method called GetTypeInfo. But once you've included the System.Reflection namespace, you get the GetTypeInfo extension method for Type.

FOR .NET FRAMEWORK DEVELOPERS The Type class doesn't have a property called Assembly in .NET Core. This is to optimize for native compilation. A lot of the reflection capabilities have been moved to a new class called Type-Info.

Assuming you cleaned up the files from the previous build, Marvel.csv should not show up in the build output. The file is now inside the CsvParser assembly.

3.4   *Dependencies*

There are three types of dependencies in .NET Core: target frameworks, packages, and projects. You can see a simple example of this in the following listing.

Listing 3.13   **Three types of dependencies shown in a project file**

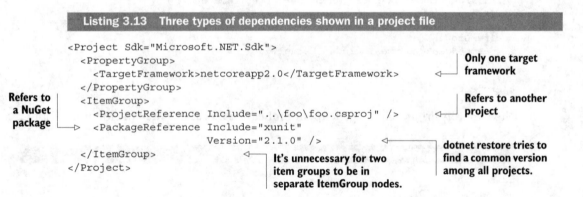

```
<Project Sdk="Microsoft.NET.Sdk">
  <PropertyGroup>
    <TargetFramework>netcoreapp2.0</TargetFramework>        Only one target
  </PropertyGroup>                                           framework
  <ItemGroup>
    <ProjectReference Include="..\foo\foo.csproj" />         Refers to another
    <PackageReference Include="xunit"                        project
                      Version="2.1.0" />
  </ItemGroup>                                               dotnet restore tries to
</Project>                                                   find a common version
                    It's unnecessary for two                among all projects.
                    item groups to be in
                    separate ItemGroup nodes.
```

Refers to a NuGet package

The TargetFramework is the moniker of the .NET framework you want to build the assembly with. You'll only use the netcoreapp and netstandard target framework monikers (TFMs) in this book. A list of the TFMs available when building from the .NET CLI is included in appendix A.

A ProjectReference is a reference to another code project. MSBuild will determine the correct order in which to build the projects. It will also print error messages if there are circular dependencies.

PackageReferences are for NuGet packages, which can come from public or private feeds, depending on your configuration. A version number is also specified. During restore, the .NET CLI will check to see what other references there are to the same package, and determine which version will work for all of them. This means that although I specified xUnit version 2.1.0, I may not get 2.1.0 specifically. If incompatibilities are detected, the restore command will write warnings or errors to the console. The ability to force a package version, like in .NET Core version 1.1 and earlier, went away in .NET Core 2.0.

METAPACKAGES Some packages have no assemblies in them; instead, they reference a set of dependencies. These packages are called *metapackages.* Microsoft.AspNetCore.All is an example. These are convenient for grouping a set of packages that are typically referenced together.

When referencing a package, that package is downloaded from an external source. This keeps the .NET Core SDK small while making it easy to reference non-Microsoft packages. The package manager used by the .NET Core SDK is called NuGet. As its website says, "NuGet is the package manager for .NET" (http://nuget.org).

How to set custom NuGet feeds

A feed is an HTTP REST API endpoint for the package store. The default feed URL for NuGet is https://api.nuget.org/v3/index.json. This feed is available automatically without configuration.

But there are cases where you may want to use different feeds. For example, you may want to use a nightly build of ASP.NET Core. You could also create your own feed for your company to share packages internally. To use other feeds, you need to create a NuGet.config file. This file can go in the folder of your project or in any of its parent folders.

Here's a sample NuGet.config file:

```xml
<?xml version="1.0" encoding="utf-8"?>
<configuration>
  <packageSources>
    <clear />
    <add key="AspNetCI"
      value="https://www.myget.org/F/aspnetvnext/api/v3/index.json"/>
    <add key="NuGet.org"
      value="https://api.nuget.org/v3/index.json" />
  </packageSources>
</configuration>
```

NuGet feeds are covered in more detail in chapter 12.

3.5 *Targeting multiple frameworks*

In the previous section, you saw that `TargetFramework` is an MSBuild property and isn't defined as an `ItemGroup`. But what if you want to build a version of the code for .NET Core and another version for the .NET Framework? Perhaps you have an existing .NET Framework application and you want to change one of the projects to .NET Core without having two copies of the code? There's a powerful MSBuild construct that can help you do this, called *conditions.*

Let's assume that you want the CsvParser to be built for the .NET Framework as well as for .NET Core. Consider the changes shown in the following listing.

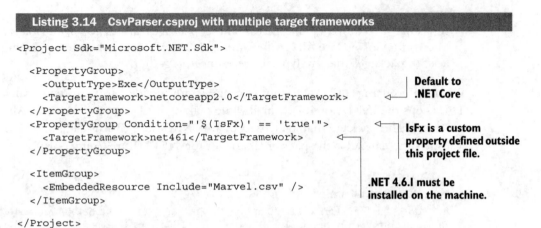

Listing 3.14   CsvParser.csproj with multiple target frameworks

```
<Project Sdk="Microsoft.NET.Sdk">

  <PropertyGroup>
    <OutputType>Exe</OutputType>
    <TargetFramework>netcoreapp2.0</TargetFramework>          ◁——  Default to
  </PropertyGroup>                                                  .NET Core
  <PropertyGroup Condition="'$(IsFx)' == 'true'">          ◁
    <TargetFramework>net461</TargetFramework>         ◁———        IsFx is a custom
  </PropertyGroup>                                                 property defined outside
                                                                   this project file.
  <ItemGroup>
    <EmbeddedResource Include="Marvel.csv" />              .NET 4.6.1 must be
  </ItemGroup>                                             installed on the machine.

</Project>
```

In listing 3.15, you use a `Condition` parameter to tell MSBuild to only evaluate the `PropertyGroup` if the condition is true. `Condition` can be applied to almost any element in an MSBuild project file. As you learned earlier, the properties are evaluated in the order of their appearance in the file, so if the `IsFx` property is set to `true`, it will override the value of the `TargetFramework` property.

If you're running on Windows, you can test this condition by specifying the property on the command line. This has to be done for both the restore and build steps. The following listing shows the commands to do this.

Listing 3.15   .NET CLI commands to specify a build property that affects dependencies

```
dotnet restore -p:IsFx=true
dotnet build -p:IsFx=true
```

MULTIPLE BUILD PROPERTIES   You can specify multiple properties on the command line by comma-separating or using multiple -p parameters.

Additional resources

To learn more about what we covered in this chapter, try the following resources:

- NuGet—http://nuget.org
- MSBuild Concepts—http://mng.bz/0Se7

Summary

In this chapter you explored the basics of MSBuild and learned how to use it to build .NET Core projects. These key concepts were covered:

- The fundamental constructs in MSBuild
- How to modify the project file to perform some common build operations

Here are some important techniques to remember from this chapter:

- Use the `Message` target with high importance to write debug messages from MSBuild.
- Targets and property values can be specified on the command line.
- Conditions in MSBuild are a powerful tool for customizing builds.
- Embedding a file in an assembly is useful when a user may forget to copy the file, and its contents don't need to be changed.

Integrated development environments (IDEs) tend to hide from developers how the underlying build mechanisms work. Most of us .NET Framework developers used Visual Studio and didn't spend much time with MSBuild. .NET Core is a bit different in that it targets the command-line experience foremost, and tooling is considered supplemental. One benefit is that MSBuild files are much easier to read and manipulate than before.

MSBuild is a special-purpose language. It helps to spend a little time getting familiar with it before diving into .NET project development. I consider it to be one of the fundamental building blocks for working with .NET. In the next chapter, we'll explore another of these building blocks: unit testing.

Unit testing with xUnit

This chapter covers

- Executing unit tests with the .NET CLI
- Writing unit tests with xUnit
- The difference between facts and theories
- Logging test output

Testing is an essential part of writing great libraries and applications, and the first line of defense for testing is the unit test. In this chapter you'll learn how to write unit tests in .NET Core, execute the tests, and add and collect logging data.

4.1 Why write unit tests?

Unit tests are written against the smallest units in a software library, such as classes. A class should have responsibility over a single piece of functionality, and that responsibility should be entirely encapsulated by the class. This is the *single responsibility principle*, and it's one of the SOLID software design principles.

> **SOLID SOFTWARE DESIGN** The SOLID design principles are part of the core principles of the agile software development methodology. They're also

48

just good practice. I recommend reading *Clean Code: A Handbook of Agile Software Craftsmanship* by Robert C. Martin (Prentice Hall, 2008) to learn more.

When developing a software application, it's common to want to build all the pieces and test the software's functionality as a whole. The problem with this approach is that it's too easy to miss corner cases or unanticipated scenarios. Unit testing gets the developer to think about each unit individually and to verify those units independently.

Unit tests also help build confidence in an application's functionality. When the unit tests achieve a high percentage of code coverage, you know that most of the code has been exercised (although you should avoid relying too much on this metric). The tests also enforce a contract for each unit, so any changes to the source code must either comply with the existing contract or explicitly change the contract.

> **REFACTORING**   Modifying the code without changing its external behavior is called *refactoring*. Unit tests are an essential part of the refactoring process.

I believe that unit testing is an essential tool for building software. You'll use unit testing throughout this book, so it's important to introduce it early. The .NET CLI seamlessly integrates with unit-testing frameworks and makes them a primary function. Unit testing is easier to learn if you start with some sample code first and build unit tests for that code.

4.2   *Business-day calculator example*

I once worked on a manufacturer/supplier collaboration application. The premise was simple: the manufacturer wanted to communicate with all of its suppliers to make sure it had supplies at the right time and in the right quantities so as not to interrupt the assembly line. In this case, it was imperative that the right dates were calculated. Most suppliers gave estimates in the form of a number of business days, so I was tasked with coming up with a way to display the estimated date of a shipment's delivery based on when the order was placed.

To my inexperienced ears, the problem sounded simple. But this was back before I knew what unit testing was for. The component I wrote didn't correctly calculate dates where suppliers had different holiday schedules than the manufacturer, and I missed this bug because I didn't have unit tests. Luckily, the manufacturer, our customer, noticed the issue before it caused an assembly-line mishap.

In this chapter, you'll write a business-day calculator and the accompanying unit tests. The concept may seem trivial, but calculating the date incorrectly can cost your customer or employer money and can cost you a contract. You'll make the library able to calculate a target date based on a start date and the number of business days. You'll focus on US holidays for now, but you'll leave the library open to work with other nations.

You'll create two projects in a folder called BusinessDays. The folder structure and project files should look like this:

- BusinessDays
  - BizDayCalc
    - BizDayCalc.csproj
  - BizDayCalcTests
    - BizDayCalcTests.csproj

First, create the three folders. At the command prompt, go to the BizDayCalc folder and execute `dotnet new classlib`. You haven't used this template before—it's for creating class libraries. Class libraries don't have an entry point and can't run on their own, but they can be referenced by other projects.

Rename the Class1.cs file to Calculator.cs, and insert the following code.

Listing 4.1   Contents of Calculator.cs

```
using System;                                            Needed for
using System.Collections.Generic;          Needed for    DateTime
                                           List<>
namespace BizDayCalc
{
  public class Calculator
  {
    private List<IRule> rules = new List<IRule>();

    public void AddRule(IRule rule)
    {
      rules.Add(rule);
    }

    public bool IsBusinessDay(DateTime date)
    {
      foreach (var rule in rules)
        if (!rule.CheckIsBusinessDay(date))      If a rule reports false,
          return false;                          it's not a business day.

      return true;
    }
  }
}
```

The `Calculator` class allows you to add a set of rules, and then it tests those rules against a given date. If any rule returns `false`, it's not a business day.

Each rule is singularly responsible for its logic. If you attempt to put all the logic together into one long string of `if` statements, you'll end up with complex code that's hard to maintain. Dividing the logic into rules also gives applications using the Biz-DayCalc library the ability to customize. For instance, you could have a rule for President's Day, which some companies may observe as a holiday and others may not. The application offers the user the freedom to choose.

A rule implements the `IRule` interface. `IRule` only has one method: `Check-IsBusinessDay`. The goal is to make implementing a rule as simple as possible. The `Calculator` class can determine how many business days fall within a given date range or work out an estimated date based on the number of business days, using only the `CheckIsBusinessDay` method.

You're going to add the code for the `IRule` interface. Create a new file called IRule.cs and insert the following code.

Listing 4.2   Contents of IRule.cs

```
using System;

namespace BizDayCalc
{
  public interface IRule
  {
    bool CheckIsBusinessDay(DateTime date);
  }
}
```

So far you haven't defined any actual business logic. For many companies, weekends aren't considered business days, so define a rule that checks the day of the week. Create a new file called WeekendRule.cs and add the following code.

Listing 4.3   Contents of WeekendRule.cs

```
using System;

namespace BizDayCalc
{
  public class WeekendRule : IRule
  {
    public bool CheckIsBusinessDay(DateTime date)
    {
      return
        date.DayOfWeek != DayOfWeek.Saturday &&
        date.DayOfWeek != DayOfWeek.Sunday;
    }
  }
}
```

You'll build more of this library throughout this chapter. You have enough now to start creating unit tests.

4.3   *xUnit—a .NET Core unit-testing framework*

xUnit is a unit-testing framework. Each unit-testing framework is different, but they can all interface with the .NET CLI to execute tests.

The .NET CLI command to run tests is `dotnet test`, and you'll be using it throughout this chapter. Other unit-testing frameworks will also work with `dotnet test`, but each framework has different ways of writing unit tests. xUnit worked with .NET Core very early on, so it's a favorite of early adopters. Plus, there's a xUnit template for dotnet new built into the CLI.

xUnit takes advantage of features available in .NET that older .NET unit-testing frameworks don't. This makes for a more powerful testing framework that's easier to code, and it incorporates recent advances in unit testing.

> **XUNIT PHILOSOPHY**   xUnit.net on GitHub has a great explanation of why xUnit was built in an article titled "Why did we build xUnit 1.0?" (http://mng.bz/XrLK).

4.4   Setting up the xUnit test project

Go to the parent folder, BusinessDays, and create a new subfolder called BizDayCalcTests. Inside the subfolder, run `dotnet new xunit`. Modify the BizDayCalcTests.csproj file as shown in the following listing.

Listing 4.4   Modifying BizDayCalcTests.csproj to reference the BizDayCalc project

```
<Project Sdk="Microsoft.NET.Sdk">

  <PropertyGroup>
    <TargetFramework>netcoreapp2.0</TargetFramework>
    <IsPackable>false</IsPackable>
  </PropertyGroup>

  <ItemGroup>
    <PackageReference Include="Microsoft.NET.Test.Sdk"
                      Version="15.3.0" />
    <PackageReference Include="xunit" Version="2.2.0" />
    <PackageReference Include="xunit.runner.visualstudio"     xUnit test runner, so you
                      Version="2.2.0" />                      can use dotnet test
    <ProjectReference
                      Include="../BizDayCalc/BizDayCalc.csproj" />
  </ItemGroup>                                                References the
                                                              BizDayCalc class library
</Project>
```

You'll learn how to use the xUnit CLI runner in the next section.

4.5   Evaluating truth with xUnit facts

The first test you'll write is for the WeekendRule.cs file. Rename the UnitTest1.cs file to WeekendRuleTest.cs, and modify the code to look like the following.

Listing 4.5   WeekendRuleTest.cs using Fact

```
using System;
using BizDayCalc;
using Xunit;

namespace BizDayCalcTests
{
```

```
public class WeekendRuleTest
{
  [Fact]
  public void TestCheckIsBusinessDay()          ←—— Fact is a type
  {                                                    of xUnit test.
    var rule = new WeekendRule();
    Assert.True(rule.CheckIsBusinessDay(new DateTime(2016, 6, 27)));
    Assert.False(rule.CheckIsBusinessDay(new DateTime(2016, 6, 26)));
  }
}
}
```

For those not familiar with C#

[Fact] is an attribute, and it indicates that the method is a unit test. Attributes can be applied on classes, members of classes, or even whole assemblies, and they provide information about an item. The full type name of [Fact] is Xunit.FactAttribute, and it's part of the xUnit library. By convention, C# will assume the Attribute suffix.

Execute dotnet test to run the test. You should see output similar to the following.

```
Starting test execution, please wait...
[xUnit.net 00:00:00.7711235]    Discovering:  BizDayCalcTests
[xUnit.net 00:00:00.9131241]    Discovered:   BizDayCalcTests
[xUnit.net 00:00:00.9663611]    Starting:     BizDayCalcTests
[xUnit.net 00:00:01.1293488]    Finished:     BizDayCalcTests

Total tests: 1. Passed: 1. Failed: 0. Skipped: 0.
Test Run Successful.
```

How does dotnet test work?

There's no built-in support for xUnit in .NET Core. Yet the dotnet test command is so simple, it feels like xUnit is integrated somehow.

The magic is down to the xunit.runner.visualstudio package. If you were to peek at the code in the package, you'd find assemblies with entry points. The dotnet test command is essentially running another application and passing it parameters. This makes it easy for testing frameworks to work with .NET Core.

Also note that the .NET Core test runner operates in both a console mode and a design-time mode. The design-time mode is used by IDEs such as Visual Studio. In the IDE, the test runner operates slightly differently.

Now that you've successfully run a unit test, let's explore this test a bit. The first thing to notice is [Fact]. It indicates that the test is always true. Also note that the Assert class, which is a common pattern in unit-testing frameworks, has methods like True and False instead of IsTrue and IsFalse. xUnit generally leaves out verbs in the method names.

It's also important to note what isn't in this code. There's no attribute on the `WeekendRuleTest` class that indicates it's a test class. xUnit avoids the use of such devices to make the code cleaner. The presence of test methods is enough to tell xUnit that it's a test class.

4.6   *Running tests from development environments*

Most development environments integrate testing into the editor. For example, OmniSharp adds links to each method in Visual Studio Code (see figure 4.1).

Although VS Code allows you to run an individual unit test, it doesn't have a way to run all the tests in an integrated fashion. You can run all the tests by running the `dotnet test` command from the integrated terminal. In that case, the output from the tests goes to the Output pane in the editor.

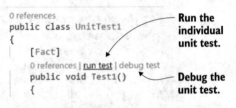
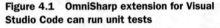

Figure 4.1   OmniSharp extension for Visual Studio Code can run unit tests

> **RUNNING TESTS FROM VS CODE**   See chapter 8 for information on how to use VS Code tasks to run tests.

Visual Studio for Mac runs tests through the Run menu. If you try to start a test project with or without debugging, VS for Mac will recognize that it's a test project and collect the results from the tests in the Tests pane.

Visual Studio 2017 has more complete integration with .NET Core testing. Figure 4.2 shows a typical testing process.

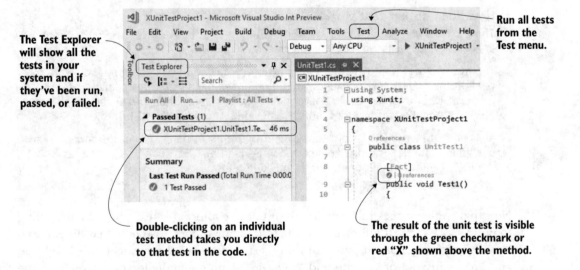

Figure 4.2   Visual Studio 2017 test integration

4.7 When it's impossible to prove all cases, use a theory

The test you wrote for `WeekendRule` is actually not a good example of a "fact." There are many different inputs that you can use when testing this class, and it's not possible to test them all. That's why xUnit has *theories*. A theory is a test that's true only for a particular set of data.

Add a few theories, as shown in the next listing.

Listing 4.6 WeekendRuleTest.cs using `Theory`

```
using System;
using BizDayCalc;
using Xunit;

namespace BizDayCalcTests
{
  public class WeekendRuleTest
  {
    [Fact]
    public void TestCheckIsBusinessDay()
    {
      var rule = new WeekendRule();
      Assert.True(rule.CheckIsBusinessDay(new DateTime(2016, 6, 27)));
      Assert.False(rule.CheckIsBusinessDay(new DateTime(2016, 6, 26)));
    }
    [Theory]                                    ← Marks as a theory
    [InlineData("2016-06-27")] // Monday        ← The data to pass to
    [InlineData("2016-03-01")] // Tuesday         the test method
    [InlineData("2017-09-20")] // Wednesday
    [InlineData("2017-09-17")] // Sunday        ← This test method
    {                                             takes a parameter.
      var rule = new WeekendRule();
      Assert.True(rule.CheckIsBusinessDay(DateTime.Parse(date)));
    }

    [Theory]
    [InlineData("2016-06-26")] // Sunday
    [InlineData("2016-11-12")] // Saturday
    public void IsNotBusinessDay(string date)
    {
      var rule = new WeekendRule();
      Assert.False(rule.CheckIsBusinessDay(DateTime.Parse(date)));
    }
  }
}
```

Run `dotnet test` to execute the tests. Notice that you now have six tests—each `[InlineData]` for your theory is an individual test. You can only test a small subset of possible dates, so these tests fit better as theories than as facts. Also note that one of these tests fails with an error, as you can see here:

```
Failed   BizDayCalcTests.WeekendRuleTest.IsBusinessDay(date: "2017-09-17")
Error Message:
```

```
 Assert.True() Failure
Expected: True
Actual:   False
Stack Trace:
   at BizDayCalcTests.WeekendRuleTest.IsBusinessDay(String date) in
   /chapter4/BusinessDays/BizDayCalcTests/WeekendRuleTest.cs:line 25
```

Notice that the failure message includes the parameters to the test method. This is very helpful for determining which inputs break the theory. In this case, you can remove the `InlineData` for "2017-09-17".

`InlineData` also allows you to specify multiple parameters, which can shorten the test code. The following listing shows an example of `InlineData` with multiple parameters.

Listing 4.7   WeekendRuleTest.cs using `InlineData` with multiple parameters

```
public class WeekendRuleTest
{
  [Theory]
  [InlineData(true,  "2016-06-27")]
  [InlineData(true,  "2016-03-01")]
  [InlineData(false, "2016-06-26")]
  [InlineData(false, "2016-11-12")]
  public void IsBusinessDay(bool expected, string date)
  {
    var rule = new WeekendRule();
    Assert.Equal(expected, rule.CheckIsBusinessDay(DateTime.Parse(date)));
  }
}
```

In the preceding code, you have only four tests specified, but already the attributes take up a lot of space. If you were to include `InlineData` to test every weekend in a given year, you'd end up with a large stack of attributes. In these cases, where you need many test cases for your theories, or if you want the test cases to generate data that isn't easily specified statically in an attribute, use `MemberData`. The following listing shows an example of `MemberData`.

Listing 4.8   WeekendRuleTests.cs using `[MemberData]`

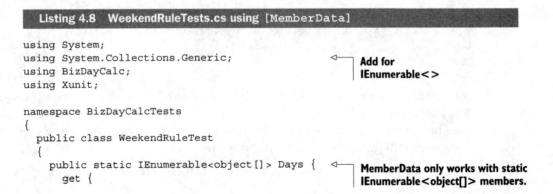

```
using System;
using System.Collections.Generic;          ◁——  Add for
using BizDayCalc;                                 IEnumerable< >
using Xunit;

namespace BizDayCalcTests
{
  public class WeekendRuleTest
  {
    public static IEnumerable<object[]> Days {   ◁——  MemberData only works with static
      get {                                            IEnumerable<object[]> members.
```

```
            yield return new object[] {true,   new DateTime(2016,  6, 27)};
            yield return new object[] {true,   new DateTime(2016,  3,  1)};
            yield return new object[] {false,  new DateTime(2016,  6, 26)};
            yield return new object[] {false,  new DateTime(2016, 11, 12)};
        }
    }

    [Theory]
    [MemberData(nameof(Days))]
    public void TestCheckIsBusinessDay(bool expected, DateTime date)
    {
        var rule = new WeekendRule();
        Assert.Equal(expected, rule.CheckIsBusinessDay(date));
    }
  }
}
```

> ### For those not familiar with C#
>
> `yield return` can be used in C# properties that return `IEnumerable` (or `IEnumerator`). Instead of creating a `List` or array and returning it immediately, `yield return` lets you return each individual item as it's accessed through the enumerator.

In the previous code listings, you had to pass a string in `[InlineData]` because a new `DateTime` isn't a constant expression and therefore can't be used as an argument to an attribute. With `[MemberData]` you can use a static property instead and create the `DateTime` objects inside. `[MemberData]` can only be used on static properties.

4.8 Shared context between tests

xUnit creates a new object of your test class for every test method it executes. That includes each invocation of a theory. This allows tests to be executed in any order and in parallel. xUnit will execute tests in random order.

Sometimes you have some setup or cleanup code that's common to a set of tests. This is called *shared context*. xUnit has a few different approaches to shared context, depending on the level at which you want to share context.

4.8.1 Using the constructor for setup

The constructor of a test class can be used to share common setup code for all the test methods in a class. To see this in action, first create a new rule in the business-day calculator. In the BizDayCalc folder, create a new file called HolidayRule.cs with the following code.

Listing 4.9 Contents of HolidayRule.cs

```
using System;

namespace BizDayCalc
{
```

```
public class HolidayRule : IRule
{
  public static readonly int[,] USHolidays = {          ◁━━  A two-dimensional
    { 1, 1 },    // New Year's day                            array
    { 7, 4 },    // Independence day
    { 12, 24 }, // Christmas eve
    { 12, 25 }  // Christmas day
  };

  public bool CheckIsBusinessDay(DateTime date)
  {
    for (int day = 0; day <=
      USHolidays.GetUpperBound(0); day++)       ◁━━  GetUpperBound gets the highest
    {                                                 index in the given dimension.
      if (date.Month == USHolidays[day, 0] &&
          date.Day   == USHolidays[day, 1])
        return false;
    }
    return true;
  }
}
}
```

This is a new rule that adds U.S. holidays that are the same from year to year.

Instead of writing tests against the `HolidayRule` directly, use the `Calculator` class in your test. In the BizDayCalcTests folder, create a new file called USHoliday-Test.cs with the following code.

> **Listing 4.10   Contents of USHolidayTest.cs**

```
using System;
using System.Collections.Generic;
using BizDayCalc;
using Xunit;

namespace BizDayCalcTests
{
  public class USHolidayTest
  {
    public static IEnumerable<object[]> Holidays {
      get {
        yield return new object[] { new DateTime(2016, 1, 1) };
        yield return new object[] { new DateTime(2016, 7, 4) };
        yield return new object[] { new DateTime(2016, 12, 24) };
        yield return new object[] { new DateTime(2016, 12, 25) };
      }
    }

    private Calculator calculator;

    public USHolidayTest()                  ◁━━  The constructor
    {                                            creates the context.
      calculator = new Calculator();
```

```
      calculator.AddRule(new HolidayRule());
    }

    [Theory]
    [MemberData(nameof(Holidays))]
    public void TestHolidays(DateTime date)
    {
      Assert.False(calculator.IsBusinessDay(date));
    }

    [Theory]
    [InlineData("2016-02-28")]
    [InlineData("2016-01-02")]
    public void TestNonHolidays(string date)
    {
      Assert.True(calculator.IsBusinessDay(DateTime.Parse(date)));
    }
  }
}
```

In the preceding test, the `calculator` field is instantiated in the constructor and used by both test methods. The `TestHolidays` theory will execute four times, and the `TestNonHolidays` theory will execute twice. A `USHolidayTest` object will be created for each test execution, so the constructor will be called six times. You can verify this by placing a `Console.WriteLine` in the constructor, as follows.

Listing 4.11 `USHolidayTest` with `Console.WriteLines`

```
public USHolidayTest()
{
  calculator = new Calculator();
  calculator.AddRule(new HolidayRule());
  Console.WriteLine("In USHolidayTest constructor");
}

[Theory]
[InlineData("2016-02-28")]
[InlineData("2016-01-02")]
public void TestNonHolidays(string date)
{
  Assert.True(calculator.IsBusinessDay(DateTime.Parse(date)));
  Console.WriteLine($"In TestNonHolidays {date}");        ◁── $"... {date}" is a shortcut for
}                                                              inserting values into strings.

[Theory]
[MemberData(nameof(Holidays))]
public void TestHolidays(DateTime date)
{
  Assert.False(calculator.IsBusinessDay(date));
  Console.WriteLine(
    $"In TestHolidays {date:yyyy-MM-dd}");                ◁── :yyyy-MM-dd is used to
}                                                              format the DateTime.
```

In the output you'll see that the constructor is called before each test method invocation. Here's an example of this output:

```
In USHolidayTest constructor
In TestNonHolidays 2016-02-28
In USHolidayTest constructor
In TestNonHolidays 2016-01-02
In USHolidayTest constructor
In TestHolidays 2016-01-01
In USHolidayTest constructor
In TestHolidays 2016-07-04
In USHolidayTest constructor
In TestHolidays 2016-12-24
In USHolidayTest constructor
In TestHolidays 2016-12-25
```

4.8.2   *Using Dispose for cleanup*

Just as common setup code can be added to the constructor, common cleanup code can be added to the `Dispose` method. xUnit uses the dispose pattern because it's a well-known .NET pattern that's more intuitive than creating an explicit teardown method. If you're already familiar with the dispose pattern, skip the next section.

THE DISPOSE PATTERN

The dispose pattern is a common .NET pattern used to clean up resources. .NET has a garbage collector built in that will free memory that you're no longer using. However, there are cases where you need to free other resources explicitly, such as closing file handles or network sockets. Consider the following code, taken from chapter 3.

> **Listing 4.12   CSV parsing code from chapter 3**

```
public static void Main(string[] args)
{
  var sr = new StreamReader(new FileStream("Marvel.csv",
    FileMode.Open));
  var csvReader = new CsvReader(sr);
  foreach (var line in csvReader.Lines)
    Console.WriteLine(line.First(p => p.Key == "Title").Value);
}
```

This code creates a new `FileStream` that's passed into a `StreamReader`. It opens a file handle, an operating system resource for manipulating files, but it never explicitly closes it. The file handle will be closed when the process ends, so it's not an issue for this scenario. But if your program is opening many files, it should explicitly close them.

The code from listing 4.12 can be modified as follows.

> **Listing 4.13   CSV parsing code from chapter 3 modified to close the CSV file**

```
public static void Main(string[] args)
{
  using (var sr = new StreamReader(new FileStream("Marvel.csv",
```

```
    FileMode.Open)))
  {
    var csvReader = new CsvReader(sr);
    foreach (var line in csvReader.Lines)
      Console.WriteLine(line.First(p => p.Key == "Title").Value);
  }
}
```

The `using` statement is a helpful C# tool for indicating that the `sr` object is "disposable" and explicitly defines when it should be disposed of. The `using` statement is nice, because if an exception is thrown inside a `using` block, the disposal will still be performed.

A `using` can only be used on a type that implements the `IDisposable` interface. This interface has one method: `Dispose()`. Note that although `using` will explicitly call the `Dispose` method, the .NET garbage collector won't. The specifics of garbage collection and disposal are beyond the scope of this book.

USING THE DISPOSE PATTERN IN XUNIT UNIT TESTS

The business-day calculator library doesn't need any cleanup code in its unit tests. But if you were writing unit tests for the CSV parser created in chapter 3, you might want some cleanup code. The following listing shows how you could use the dispose pattern in a unit test of the CSV parser library.

Listing 4.14 CSV parser library unit test using dispose pattern

```
using System;
using System.Collections.Generic;
using System.IO;
using System.Linq;
using CsvParser;
using Xunit;

namespace CsvParserTests
{
  public class CsvReaderTest : IDisposable        ◁──┐ Implements the
  {                                                   │ IDisposable interface
    private StreamReader streamReader;
    private CsvReader csvReader;

    public CsvReaderTest()
    {
      streamReader = new StreamReader(new FileStream("Marvel.csv",
        FileMode.Open));
      csvReader = new CsvReader(streamReader);
    }

    public void Dispose()
    {
      streamReader.Dispose();        ◁──┐ Your Dispose must call the
    }                                    │ StreamReader's Dispose.
```

```
    [Fact]
    public void VerifyNumberOfLines()
    {
      Assert.Equal(7, csvReader.Lines.Count());      ◁─┐  Count() is a LINQ
    }                                                    extension method.
  }
}
```

Here you open a file in the constructor so that it can be used by each test method. You
then close that file in the `Dispose` method, which will keep you from leaking open
file handles. Just as the constructor is called before each test method invocation, the
`Dispose` method is called after each test method invocation.

4.8.3   *Sharing context with class fixtures*

The constructor in a test class lets you share the setup code for each of the test methods. But there are cases where you want a setup operation to be performed once and
reused for the entire test class. xUnit's solution to this is called a *class fixture*.

   The business-day calculator allows you to add many rules, so you want to test the
case where many rules are applied. It might be an expensive operation to create a calculator that has all the rules if you have to load those rules from a file or a database. In
this case, you can create a class fixture so that the setup and cleanup operations are
only performed once for the whole test class.

   The business-day calculator will operate differently depending on the region it's
in. For example, the weekend rule in the United States only needs to check if the day
of the week is Saturday or Sunday. But in China, weekends can be moved adjacent to
national holidays. A region would therefore have a collection of applicable rules,
much like your calculator.

   The following listing shows an example of a class fixture that tests the rules for the
United States region.

Listing 4.15   Example class fixture for the business-day calculator
---

```
using BizDayCalc;

namespace BizDayCalcTests
{
  public class USRegionFixture
  {
    public Calculator Calc { get; private set; }      ◁─┐  A property with a public
                                                          getter and private setter
    public USRegionFixture()
    {
      Calc = new Calculator();
      Calc.AddRule(new WeekendRule());
      Calc.AddRule(new HolidayRule());
    }
  }
}
```

Now create a test that uses the preceding class fixture. Create a new file named USRegionTest.cs and copy the code from `USHolidayTest`. The following listing shows how to modify the test code to use the fixture.

Listing 4.16 Contents of USRegionTest.cs

```csharp
using System;
using BizDayCalc;
using Xunit;

namespace BizDayCalcTests
{
  public class USRegionTest
    : IClassFixture<USRegionFixture>          ⟵  Tells xUnit that this test uses a class fixture
  {
    private USRegionFixture fixture;

    public USRegionTest(USRegionFixture fixture)   ⟵  xUnit creates the object and passes it to the test's constructor.
    {
      this.fixture = fixture;
    }

    [Theory]
    [InlineData("2016-01-01")]
    [InlineData("2016-12-25")]
    public void TestHolidays(string date)
    {
      Assert.False(fixture.Calc.IsBusinessDay(     ⟵  Using the Calculator object from the fixture
        DateTime.Parse(date)));
    }

    [Theory]
    [InlineData("2016-02-29")]
    [InlineData("2016-01-04")]
    public void TestNonHolidays(string date)
    {
      Assert.True(fixture.Calc.IsBusinessDay(
        DateTime.Parse(date)));
    }
  }
}
```

To identify exactly how often the class fixture object is created, add a `Console.WriteLine` to the fixture's constructor (be sure to add `using System` at the top). You should see it constructed only once, before any of the tests execute.

> **CLASS FIXTURE CLEANUP** You can add cleanup code to class fixtures by using the same dispose pattern described earlier in this chapter.

4.8.4 Sharing context with collection fixtures

Class fixtures share context for one test class, but you may instead need to share context among multiple test classes. The way to handle this in xUnit is with a *collection fixture.* Creating a collection fixture is simple enough that I always create one when creating a class fixture.

The first step is to add a second, empty class for the collection fixture that uses the class fixture. The following listing shows how to do that with the USRegionFixture class.

```
using BizDayCalc;
using Xunit;

namespace BizDayCalcTests
{
  public class USRegionFixture
  {
    public Calculator Calc { get; private set; }

    public USRegionFixture()
    {
      Calc = new Calculator();
      Calc.AddRule(new WeekendRule());
      Calc.AddRule(new HolidayRule());
    }
  }

  [CollectionDefinition("US region collection")]      The name of
  public class USRegionCollection                     the collection
    : ICollectionFixture<USRegionFixture>         The class fixture is what
  {                                               the test classes will use.
  }
}
```

To use the collection fixture in a test class, you need to refer to the collection by name. The test class doesn't need to implement the IClassFixture interface. Besides those two changes, the test class works just as if you were using a class fixture.

The following listing shows the USRegionTest class modified to use the collection fixture.

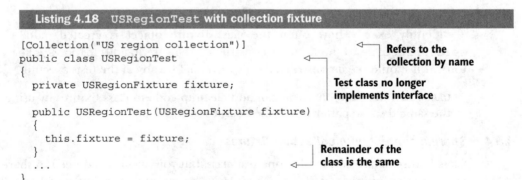

```
[Collection("US region collection")]          Refers to the
public class USRegionTest                      collection by name
{
  private USRegionFixture fixture;          Test class no longer
                                            implements interface
  public USRegionTest(USRegionFixture fixture)
  {
    this.fixture = fixture;
  }                                         Remainder of the
  ...                                       class is the same
}
```

The collection fixture class doesn't have any setup or cleanup code of its own. That's done in the class fixture.

4.9 *Getting output from xUnit tests*

Using `Console.WriteLine` to get output from a test is problematic. xUnit typically runs tests in parallel, so console output will overlap between tests. Also, if you're using a build automation system or IDE like Visual Studio, these tools will typically provide the output from the test cases that fail. If a test passes, you don't normally want to see any output from it, but if it fails, the output is useful in diagnosing the failure. `Console.WriteLine` won't work in these situations.

There's a better way to write test output. xUnit provides an interface called `ITestOutputHelper` that has a `WriteLine` method on it that you can use to write test output. Try this out on the `USRegionTest` test class.

First, modify the BizDayCalcTests.csproj file to disable the other two tests, as follows.

Listing 4.19 Exclude other tests besides USRegionTest.cs

```
<ItemGroup>
  <Compile Remove="USHolidayTest.cs" />
  <Compile Remove="WeekendRuleTest.cs" />
</ItemGroup>
```

Now modify `USRegionTest` to use `ITestOutputHelper`.

Listing 4.20 `USRegionTest` using `ITestOutputHelper`

```
using System;
using BizDayCalc;
using Xunit;
using Xunit.Abstractions;              ◁─ ITestOutputHelper is
                                          in Xunit.Abstractions.
namespace BizDayCalcTests
{
  [Collection("US region collection")]
  public class USRegionTest
  {
    private readonly USRegionFixture fixture;
    private readonly ITestOutputHelper output;

    public USRegionTest(
      USRegionFixture fixture,
      ITestOutputHelper output)         ◁─ xUnit will provide the
    {                                      ITestOutputHelper object.
      this.fixture = fixture;
      this.output = output;
    }

    [Theory]
    [InlineData("2016-01-01")]
    [InlineData("2016-12-25")]
    public void TestHolidays(string date)
```

```
    {
      output.WriteLine($@"TestHolidays(""{date}"")");
      Assert.False(fixture.Calc.IsBusinessDay(
        DateTime.Parse(date)));
    }

    [Theory]
    [InlineData("2016-02-29")]
    [InlineData("2016-01-04")]
    public void TestNonHolidays(string date)
    {
      output.WriteLine($@"TestNonHolidays(""{date}"")");
      Assert.True(fixture.Calc.IsBusinessDay(
        DateTime.Parse(date)));
    }
  }
}
```

← **$@"…" combines string replacement with verbatim**

When you have an `ITestOutputHelper` parameter on your constructor, xUnit will detect that and provide an implementation. It doesn't matter how many other parameters are on the constructor or in what order they appear. The output helper will know automatically which test you're running and will correlate the output written for that test.

If you run `dotnet test`, you won't see the test output because all the tests pass. To see the output, try changing `Assert.False` to `Assert.True` in `TestHolidays`, which should produce output like the following.

Listing 4.21   Test output appears only when tests fail

```
BizDayCalcTests.USRegionTest.TestHolidays(date: "2016-01-01") [FAIL]
  Assert.True() Failure
  Expected: True
  Actual:   False
  Stack Trace:
    C:\dev\BusinessDays\BizDayCalcTests\USRegionTest.cs(28,0):
      at BizDayCalcTests.USRegionTest.TestHolidays(String date)
  Output:
    TestHolidays("2016-01-01")
  Assert.True() Failure
BizDayCalcTests.USRegionTest.TestHolidays(date: "2016-12-25") [FAIL]
  Expected: True
  Actual:   False
  Stack Trace:
    C:\dev\BusinessDays\BizDayCalcTests\USRegionTest.cs(28,0):
      at BizDayCalcTests.USRegionTest.TestHolidays(String date)
  Output:
    TestHolidays("2016-12-25")
```

Logged test output

4.10 *Traits*

Traits allow you to assign any number of properties to a test. You can use this to organize tests into categories so you can exercise specific areas of your code. The following listing shows how you can apply traits to the `USRegionTest` class.

Listing 4.22 USRegionTest.cs with traits

```
[Theory]
[InlineData("2016-01-01")]
[InlineData("2016-12-15")]
[Trait("Holiday", "true")]                          ◁─┐ Trait is a
public void TestHolidays(string date)                  │ name/value pair.
{
  output.WriteLine($@"TestHolidays(""{date}"")");
  Assert.False(fixture.Calc.IsBusinessDay(DateTime.Parse(date)));
}

[Theory]
[InlineData("2016-02-28")]
[InlineData("2016-01-02")]                            ┌ Key and value
[Trait("Holiday", "false")]                        ◁─┘ are both strings.
public void TestNonHolidays(string date)
{
  output.WriteLine($@"TestNonHolidays(""{date}"")");
  Assert.True(fixture.Calc.IsBusinessDay(DateTime.Parse(date)));
}
```

With the traits set, you can specify command-line parameters to xUnit for the traits
you want, as follows.

```
dotnet test --filter Holiday=true

Total tests: 4. Passed: 4. Failed: 0. Skipped: 0.
```

See appendix B for more information about specifying traits and other command-line
options.

Additional resources

To learn more about xUnit, try these resources:

- xUnit.Net on GitHub—http://xunit.github.io
- xUnit—https://github.com/xunit/xunit

Summary

In this chapter you learned about unit testing in .NET Core with xUnit, and we covered some of xUnit's features. These key concepts were covered:

- Facts and theories
- Providing theory data in different ways
- Sharing context between test cases
- Logging and viewing data from unit tests

These are some important techniques to remember from this chapter:

- Use the dispose pattern to clean up resources.
- The dispose pattern also works on class fixtures.
- Use `ITestOutputHelper` to correlate logs with individual tests.

Unit testing is a great way to improve the reliability of your code. Having a suite of tests helps you build features with confidence and identify breaking changes as your code evolves. An essential part of any development platform is the ability to unit test.

In this chapter, we focused on xUnit because it's supported on .NET Core and is popular with early adopters. In the next few chapters, you'll do more interesting things with .NET Core while using your xUnit testing skills.

Working with relational databases

This chapter covers

- Accessing databases with .NET Standard `System.Data` classes
- Using the SQLite in-memory database
- Transforming data between objects and tables
- Unit testing data-access code

Widget Corporation needs to keep better track of their supply chain, so they hire you to transform their paper-based process into software. You find that each part used in the manufacturing process comes from a different supplier, and that Widget Corp. is having trouble ordering the right supplies at the right time.

To solve this problem, you decide to use a relational database. The database will persist data, making it resilient to shutdown or power failure. It will enforce relationships between data, so that no one can add an order without indicating the supplier or part. It also makes the data queryable, which allows anyone to determine what parts are running out and need to be ordered soon. The employees of Widget Corp. shouldn't have to learn the SQL commands to enter the data into the database manually. You'll need to create software that makes it easy for them.

Now you get to apply your .NET Core skills. .NET Core is a great choice for database applications because of the powerful built-in data-access classes. In this chapter, you'll explore the low-level data-access capability that's built into the .NET Standard—encapsulated in the System.Data namespace. But before you start, you need a database.

5.1   *Using SQLite for prototyping*

If you're not already familiar with SQLite, it's an embedded SQL database engine. It supports both in-memory and file-based options. No installation required—simply reference the NuGet package and you have a database. Microsoft provides a SQLite client library for .NET Standard, which allows you to use SQLite in your .NET Core applications.

The best way to learn about SQLite is to start using it. Start by creating a new console application. The following command-line command creates the new project:

```
dotnet new console -o SqliteConsoleTest
```

-o creates a new folder for the project with the name given.

Edit the SqliteConsoleTest.csproj file as follows.

Listing 5.1   Including the SQLite dependency in the project file

```
<Project Sdk="Microsoft.NET.Sdk">

  <PropertyGroup>
    <OutputType>Exe</OutputType>
    <TargetFramework>netcoreapp2.0</TargetFramework>
  </PropertyGroup>

  <ItemGroup>
    <PackageReference Include="Microsoft.Data.Sqlite"
                      Version="2.0.0" />
  </ItemGroup>

</Project>
```

Adds a reference to Microsoft.Data.Sqlite

Open the Program.cs file and add the following code.

Listing 5.2   SQLite test code

```
using System;
using Microsoft.Data.Sqlite;

namespace SqliteConsoleTest
{
  public class Program
  {
    public static void Main(string[] args)
    {
      using (var connection = new SqliteConnection(
        "Data Source=:memory:"))
      {
        connection.Open();
```

Creates a connection to the database

Specifies in-memory database in the connection string

"SELECT 1;" is the SQL command you want to execute.

```
            var command = new SqliteCommand(
              "SELECT 1;", connection);
            long result = (long)command.ExecuteScalar();
            Console.WriteLine($"Command output: {result}");
          }
        }
      }
    }
```

You want to issue a command to the database.

You expect the result of the command to be a scalar (single value).

End of the using block disposes of the connection object

If you've never worked with relational databases before, there are a lot of new concepts in listing 5.2. Let's explore these a bit more.

The first concept is the connection. The database is typically a separate entity from your program. It manages its own memory, disk, network, and CPU resources. SQLite is a rare exception in that it runs inside your process. You wouldn't want to use it in a production environment because your application and your database would be competing for resources within the same process.

Because the database is typically separate, you need to connect to it to do anything. Most database providers, which are part of the client libraries, manage a pool of database connections for you, keyed off of the connection string. The connection string contains the information that the provider needs to know to establish a connection to the database or the data file.

The contents of a connection string are usually spelled out in the database documentation, but this documentation can be lengthy and perhaps a little intimidating. When you need a connection string, I recommend https://connectionstrings.com as a must-have in your developer tool belt. It's a great, quick reference and covers every database you can think of.

Once you're connected to the database, you perform all of your operations through commands. You don't explicitly specify what type of command you're issuing in listing 5.2. It uses the default value Text, which means a SQL statement or statements.

> **DON'T KNOW SQL?** Don't worry if you're new to SQL. This chapter sticks to simple SQL statements and provides explanations. To get deeper into SQL, check out Ben Brumm's *SQL in Motion* video courses from Manning Publications.

The SQL command you're executing in listing 5.2 is a query. Typically, you'd query data from a table, but in this case you're querying a constant value: 1. If you expect only one value to come back from a query, you tell the command object to execute the command as a scalar, and the return value for ExecuteScalar is an object. The data provider will typically map the databases data types to .NET data types for you. The value 1 matches the long value type most closely, so you can cast the returned object to a long using the (long) syntax.

Execute dotnet run to run the application. The command output should be 1.

As you can see, SQLite is quick and easy to set up. Plus, it works great with .NET Core. The "SELECT 1;" query verifies that the SQLite engine is working. Next, let's explore how you can build a solution for Widget Corp.

5.2   *Planning the application and database schema*

Before you design your application, you first must understand what Widget Corp. needs. Their primary concern is that inventory is counted by hand and recorded on paper, so the values are inaccurate and outdated. Sometimes this results in parts being ordered too late and causes disruptions in the manufacturing process. Other times, it results in too many parts being ordered, which takes up valuable warehouse space and can sometimes lead to disposing of unused parts when a design change requires a different part. Widget Corp. needs to be able to order parts at the right times, which is easier if the inventory numbers are accurate.

You also need to get the floor personnel to want to use your system. That means it should be less complicated or less work than what they're currently doing.

Ordering can be automated, requiring intervention only when parts are no longer needed. Getting the inventory count can be reduced to checking shipments and marking orders as fulfilled (either by mobile app or web). You won't try to handle late, incomplete, or incorrect order fulfillment in this example.

5.2.1   *Tracking inventory*

There are three things you need to track Widget Corp.'s inventory accurately:

- The current, accurate inventory counts
- An adjustment every time an order is fulfilled
- An adjustment every time a part is removed from inventory

Widget Corp. does a full inventory check every month. That gives your software a targeted release date so that you can take advantage of a count that's already occurring. The supervisor at the loading dock is in charge of handling incoming shipments, so instead of supervisors recording incoming shipments on paper, you could provide a simple mobile app where they could mark an order as fulfilled when it comes in. You expect there to be several incoming shipments per week.

All suppliers mark their parts with barcodes, so you can provide a mobile app that allows a factory worker to scan the barcode of a part before it's used or discarded. In the current system, a warehouse manager keeps track of everything going in and out. This manager becomes a bottleneck when there are many simultaneous requests. By allowing each factory worker unhindered access to the warehouse, they can get the parts they need more quickly. The barcode system also means that parts can be located closer to their stations, rather than in a central warehouse.

Relational databases like SQLite organize data into *tables*. There are other constructs besides tables, but they're not necessary for this example. A database design is called a *schema*. To create a schema, you'll need to design your tables, the columns for those tables, and how they relate to each other.

Let's start with a table that holds data about the type of part and a table that holds the inventory counts. These are shown in tables 5.1 and 5.2.

Table 5.1 The `PartType` table for storing each type of part used by Widget Corp

Data type	Description
int	Unique ID for part
varchar	Name of the part

Each of the parts that Widget Corp. uses has a unique name. Although you could use those names directly in all the other tables, that would result in the data being repeated everywhere. If the name of the part were to change, you'd have to change it everywhere that part name is used in the database. Plus, it's a waste of storage space. By adding an `Id` column, you're allowing other tables to reference the part with only an integer. Each row of the PartType table will have a unique `Id`.

Table 5.2 The `InventoryItem` table for storing inventory data

Name	Data type	Description
PartTypeId	int	The type of part
Count	int	Total number of units available
OrderThreshold	int	If supply drops below this number, order more

The `InventoryItem` table is an example of a table that refers to a part. Instead of storing the name of the part directly, it references the `PartType` table's `Id` column. Notice that `InventoryItem` doesn't have its own `Id` column. This is because you only want one count per part. Therefore, the `PartTypeId` can be treated as the unique `Id` of the `InventoryItem` table.

You'll use a simple mechanism for determining when to place an order for new parts. In the `InventoryItem` table, the `OrderThreshold` column indicates that when the `Count` is at or below the threshold, a new order will be placed.

5.2.2 Creating tables in SQLite

Try creating a table in SQLite to see how it works. You can create the tables using SQL statements.

Because the creation of the tables isn't part of the application you're building, you can split that process out into a separate step. Instead of modifying the console application from the previous section, create a new set of projects using the following commands:

```
cd ..
mkdir CreateTablesTest
cd CreateTablesTest
dotnet new classlib -o WidgetScmDataAccess          Data-access
                                                    project
dotnet new xunit -o SqliteScmTest          Unit-test project to exercise
                                           the data-access project
```

`WidgetScmDataAccess` will have the data-access logic for the application. `Sqlite-ScmTest` will be the unit-test project. The test project will create the tables in SQLite and populate them with example data.

Data-access projects usually don't create or alter the database schema—they're concerned with the data itself. The responsibility of creating the schema typically falls outside of the data access project. To create the schema in an in-memory database, you'll have the unit test project do that work on startup.

In chapter 4 you learned about using class fixtures in xUnit as a means to share context between tests. A class fixture serves as a great place to initialize a SQLite database for testing. Add a new file to the SqliteScmTest project called SampleScmData-Fixture.cs, and add the following code.

Listing 5.3   Contents of SampleScmDataFixture.cs

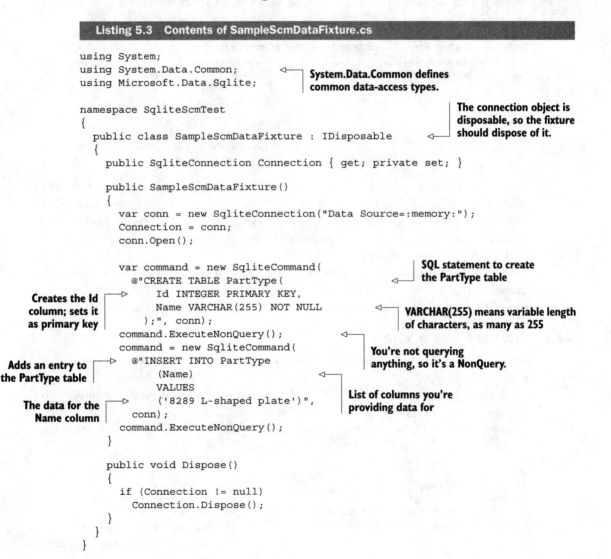

```csharp
using System;
using System.Data.Common;                    ◁─── System.Data.Common defines
using Microsoft.Data.Sqlite;                        common data-access types.

namespace SqliteScmTest                                      The connection object is
{                                                            disposable, so the fixture
  public class SampleScmDataFixture : IDisposable   ◁─────── should dispose of it.
  {
    public SqliteConnection Connection { get; private set; }

    public SampleScmDataFixture()
    {
      var conn = new SqliteConnection("Data Source=:memory:");
      Connection = conn;
      conn.Open();

      var command = new SqliteCommand(           SQL statement to create
        @"CREATE TABLE PartType(            ◁─── the PartType table
          Id INTEGER PRIMARY KEY,
          Name VARCHAR(255) NOT NULL         ◁─── VARCHAR(255) means variable length
        );", conn);                               of characters, as many as 255
      command.ExecuteNonQuery();            ◁───
      command = new SqliteCommand(
        @"INSERT INTO PartType               You're not querying
          (Name)                             anything, so it's a NonQuery.
          VALUES
          ('8289 L-shaped plate')",    ◁─── List of columns you're
        conn);                              providing data for
      command.ExecuteNonQuery();
    }

    public void Dispose()
    {
      if (Connection != null)
        Connection.Dispose();
    }
  }
}
```

Annotations:
- Creates the Id column; sets it as primary key
- Adds an entry to the PartType table
- The data for the Name column

In this example, the data fixture executes a SQL statement that creates the `PartType` table. The statement includes specifications for each column in the format "[Name] [Type] [Constraints]", and the types vary for each database. Often, database types are more specific than the value types in a programming language. For example, a database cares a lot about how much space data will take up. When designing a database schema, you have to consider this, as it will have an impact on what types you'll use.

There are two different constraints used in listing 5.2: `NOT NULL` and `PRIMARY KEY`. `NOT NULL` ensures that the column can't have a `null` value. You'll get an error if you try to insert a `null` value into the `Name` column. `PRIMARY KEY` is actually a combination of `NOT NULL` and `UNIQUE`. `UNIQUE` indicates that each row in the table must have a distinct value for the `Id` column. Notice, though, that you don't insert a value for `Id`, and the code still works. In this case, SQLite automatically adds a value for `Id`. In other databases, like SQL Server, this doesn't happen automatically unless the column is indicated as an identity column.

> **RETURN VALUE OF EXECUTENONQUERY** Although `ExecuteNonQuery` means the command isn't a query, that doesn't mean data doesn't get returned. The return value of `ExecuteNonQuery` is an integer indicating the number of rows affected by the command. You can also use this method if you're executing a command that has output parameters or return values mapped to parameters. We won't go into these uses in this book.

This class fixture creates the `PartType` table and inserts a single row. It exposes one property called `Connection` of type `Microsoft.Data.SqliteConnection`, which inherits from `System.Data.Common.DbConnection`.

The `System.Data.Common` namespace has some fundamental common types for interacting with data stores, and most data-access client libraries implement the abstract classes and interfaces from that namespace. A data-access library should stick to the `System.Data.Common` namespace as much as possible so that different databases can be used, such as SQLite for development and test and SQL Server for production. Because `SqliteConnection` inherits from `DbConnection`, you can use that connection object in your data-access library.

Now modify UnitTest1.cs to use `SampleScmDataFixture`. To do this, try the following code.

Listing 5.4   Modifying UnitTest1.cs to use `SampleScmDataFixture`

```
using Xunit;

namespace SqliteScmTest
{
  public class UnitTest1 : IClassFixture<SampleScmDataFixture>
  {
    private SampleScmDataFixture fixture;

    public UnitTest1(SampleScmDataFixture fixture)
    {
```

```
        this.fixture = fixture;
    }

    [Fact]
    public void Test1()
    {
        Assert.True(true);
    }
  }
}
```

As long as one test is run, the class fixture is used.

The test method in this class doesn't do anything interesting, but its presence is enough to trigger the constructor of the test class, and therefore the constructor and `Dispose` method of `SampleScmDataFixture`. Before executing the test, edit the project file as follows.

Listing 5.5   Dependencies to add to the SqliteScmTest.csproj

```
<ItemGroup>
  <PackageReference Include="Microsoft.NET.Test.Sdk" Version="15.3.0" />
  <PackageReference Include="xunit" Version="2.2.0" />
  <PackageReference Include="xunit.runner.visualstudio" Version="2.2.0" />
  <PackageReference Include="Microsoft.Data.Sqlite"
                    Version="2.0.0" />
  <PackageReference Include="System.Data.Common"
                    Version="4.3.0" />
  <PackageReference Include="System.Runtime.Serialization.Primitives"
                    Version="4.3.0" />
</ItemGroup>
```

Add dependency on SQLite

System.Data.Common is not part of .NET Standard.

Now you can run `dotnet test`. If the test is successful, the creation of the table and row insert was done correctly.

5.3   *Creating a data-access library*

You've created the test harness for your data-access library, including a database schema and some sample data. Now you'll add some code to the `WidgetScmData-Access` library created in the previous section.

The first thing to think about is a class to hold the data for each part. Add a Part-Type.cs file to the WidgetScmDataAccess folder with the following code.

Listing 5.6   Code for the `PartType` class that will hold the data for each part

```
namespace WidgetScmDataAccess
{
  public class PartType
  {
    public int Id { get; internal set; }
    public string Name { get; set; }
  }
}
```

Don't allow modifying the Id outside of this library.

The next thing you need is a way to *hydrate* the `PartType` objects. *Hydrate* is the term commonly used for the process of setting all the members of an object. The data-access library reads the values from a row in the `PartType` table and sets the properties of the `PartType` object representing that row. There are many ways to do this, but the one you'll use is a single *context* class—*context* meaning that the class understands how to work with all the objects and tables that are related to each other in a certain context.

Your context class will take a `DbConnection` object and populate a list with all the part type data from the source table. For this example, as shown in listing 5.7, you're only interested in retrieving the data, not creating, updating, or deleting it. You'll also cache all the part data. This isn't something you'd do lightly in a real application where parts can change, but it keeps your sample code simple.

Listing 5.7   Code for the `ScmContext` class that will get data from the data store

```
using System.Collections.Generic;
using System.Data.Common;

namespace WidgetScmDataAccess
{
  public class ScmContext
  {
    private DbConnection connection;

    public IEnumerable<PartType> Parts { get; private set; }

    public ScmContext(DbConnection conn)
    {
      connection = conn;
      ReadParts();
    }

    private void ReadParts()
    {
      using (var command = connection.CreateCommand())
      {
        command.CommandText = @"SELECT Id, Name
          FROM PartType";
        using (var reader = command.ExecuteReader())
        {
          var parts = new List<PartType>();
          Parts = parts;
          while (reader.Read())
          {
            parts.Add(new PartType() {
              Id = reader.GetInt32(0),
              Name = reader.GetString(1)
            });
          }
        }
      }
    }
  }
}
```

Annotations:
- **Explicitly lists columns instead of using SELECT *** → `command.CommandText = @"SELECT Id, Name FROM PartType";`
- **Output of command has multiple rows** → `using (var reader = command.ExecuteReader())`
- **Moves to next row, returns false if no more rows** → `while (reader.Read())`
- **Shortcut notation in C# to set properties on initialization** → `parts.Add(new PartType() {`
- **Reads the Id column as a 32-bit integer (int or Int32 in C#)** → `Id = reader.GetInt32(0),`
- **Reads the Name column as a string** → `Name = reader.GetString(1)`

This is the first time you've encountered the use of `ExecuteReader`. It returns an object that implements the `System.Data.Common.DbDataReader` class. A data reader is good for queries that return one or more rows of data. In this case, the SQL statement indicates that you want all the rows from the `PartType` table with the columns arranged `Id` first, then `Name`. The reader has an internal cursor that starts off before the first row, so your first call to `Read()` will move the cursor to the first row if there is one. If no rows were returned by the query, `Read()` returns `false`.

Once you've moved the cursor to a row, you can extract data from each column. In listing 5.7, you use `GetInt32(0)` and `GetString(1)` for the `Id` and `Name` columns respectively. The SQL statement laid out the order explicitly, so you can use that order when extracting the values. `GetInt32(0)` will get the value from the first column (using zero-based numbering) and attempt to cast it to a 32-bit integer. The data reader will throw an `InvalidCastException` if the provider doesn't interpret the database type as a 32-bit integer. In other words, it only casts; it doesn't attempt to convert the value. You couldn't, for example, call `GetString(0)` on the `Id` column because the database type for that column isn't interpreted as a string.

Other ways to get the column values

Instead of using the `Get` methods on `DbDataReader`, you can use the indexer. An indexer is a shortcut in C# that allows you to apply an index to an object as if it were an array. For example, the code to get the `Id` could look like this: `Id = (int)reader[0]`. The `DbDataReader` has an indexer that will get the column value from the current row and return it as an `object`. You can then cast it. The `GetInt32` method only does a cast anyway, so the statements are roughly equivalent.

If you don't like syncing to your query's column order, you can also pass the name of the column into the indexer. That would look like this: `Id = (int)reader["Id"]`. Note that this searches for the column (first case-sensitive then case-insensitive). Be careful not to make assumptions about case-insensitive search, as it's affected by the language. You'll learn about languages and localization in chapter 10.

LIMIT ACCESS TO YOUR INTERNAL COLLECTIONS   By exposing the `Parts` property in listing 5.7 as an `IEnumerable<T>` instead of a `List<T>`, you're indicating to developers who use this property that you intend this collection to be treated as read-only. Because the data type behind it is a `List`, a developer could simply cast `Parts` as a `List` and make modifications, so there's no enforcement. But you could change the underlying collection type as long as it implements `IEnumerable`, so those who cast it to a `List` do so at their own risk.

EXPLICITLY SPECIFY COLUMNS   Specifying the columns in the query is preferred to using a `SELECT *`, which returns all the columns but doesn't guarantee their order. It's also easy to forget to update the code if the columns in the table are changed.

Now it's time to test this code. Start by modifying the project file of the Widget-ScmDataAccess project to match the following listing.

Listing 5.8 Modifying WidgetScmDataAccess.csproj to include `System.Data.Common`

```
<Project Sdk="Microsoft.NET.Sdk">

  <PropertyGroup>
    <TargetFramework>netstandard1.2</TargetFramework>       ◁──  Try to use the lowest
  </PropertyGroup>                                                possible .NET Standard
                                                                 version you can.
  <ItemGroup>
    <PackageReference Include="System.Data.Common"
                      Version="4.3.0" />
  </ItemGroup>

</Project>
```

Remove the Class1.cs file in this project, because it's not used.

Now switch back to the SqliteScmTest project and add a test. First, modify the project file to reference the data-access library by adding this line: `<ProjectReference Include="../WidgetScmDataAccess/WidgetScmDataAccess.csproj" />`. Then modify the UnitTest1.cs file to include `Test1`, as follows.

Listing 5.9 Modify UnitTest1.cs to test for the part created in `SampleScmDataFixture`

```
using System.Linq;                                    ◁──  Needed for Count()
using Xunit;                                                and First()
using WidgetScmDataAccess;        ◁──  Add using for
                                       library project
namespace SqliteScmTest
{
  public class UnitTest1 : IClassFixture<SampleScmDataFixture>
  {
    private SampleScmDataFixture fixture;
    private ScmContext context;

    public UnitTest1(SampleScmDataFixture fixture)
    {
      this.fixture = fixture;
      this.context = new ScmContext(fixture.Connection);
    }

    [Fact]
    public void Test1()
    {
      var parts = context.Parts;                        There's only one part type,
      Assert.Equal(1, parts.Count());        ◁──────┘   and you know its contents.
      var part = parts.First();
      Assert.Equal("8289 L-shaped plate", part.Name);
    }
  }
}
```

From here, you can run `dotnet test` to get the test going. When xUnit starts the test, the fixture object will create the `PartType` table and add a row. Then the `ScmContext` object will use the connection exposed by the fixture to get all the rows from the `PartType` table and create a `PartType` object for each one. `System.Linq` exposes an extension method called `Count()` that can count how many elements are in an `IEnumerable`. The `First()` method is another `System.Linq` extension method that gets the first item in the collection.

With a relatively small amount of work, you've created a mock data store and a rudimentary data-access library. But you've only added the `PartType` table. You've yet to add inventory items to your database. To do that, you'll need to explore relationships in databases and how they correlate to your .NET code.

5.3.1 Specifying relationships in data and code

The `PartType` table only has two columns: `Id` and `Name`. The `InventoryItem` table you'll create next references the `Id` column from `PartType` in a one-to-one relationship. As mentioned before, I chose this approach because you have several tables that refer to parts, and you don't want to copy the name of the part into each row of each table. It also gives you the flexibility to add more attributes to parts later on.

Figure 5.1 shows the database schema for your application. The line connecting the `PartType` and `InventoryItem` tables indicates that there is a foreign-key relationship. The rest of the tables and relationships will become clear later in the chapter.

In SQLite, you can specify foreign keys when you create the table. Add the `InventoryItem` table to your fixture by modifying SampleScmDataFixture.cs as follows.

Listing 5.10   Code to create tables in `SampleScmDataFixture`

```
public class SampleScmDataFixture : IDisposable
{
  private const string PartTypeTable =
     @"CREATE TABLE PartType(
         Id INTEGER PRIMARY KEY,
         Name VARCHAR(255) NOT NULL
       );";
  private const string InventoryItemTable =
    @"CREATE TABLE InventoryItem(
        PartTypeId INTEGER PRIMARY KEY,
        Count INTEGER NOT NULL,
        OrderThreshold INTEGER,
      FOREIGN KEY(PartTypeId) REFERENCES PartType(Id)    ⟵┘ Foreign key relationships
      );";                                                     can be defined in the table.

  public SampleScmDataFixture()
  {
    var conn = new SqliteConnection("Data Source=:memory:");
    Connection = conn;
    conn.Open();
                                                          A short way to create
    (new SqliteCommand(PartTypeTable, conn)).ExecuteNonQuery();    an object and call a
    (new SqliteCommand(InventoryItemTable, conn)).                 method on it
      ExecuteNonQuery();                                      ⟵
```

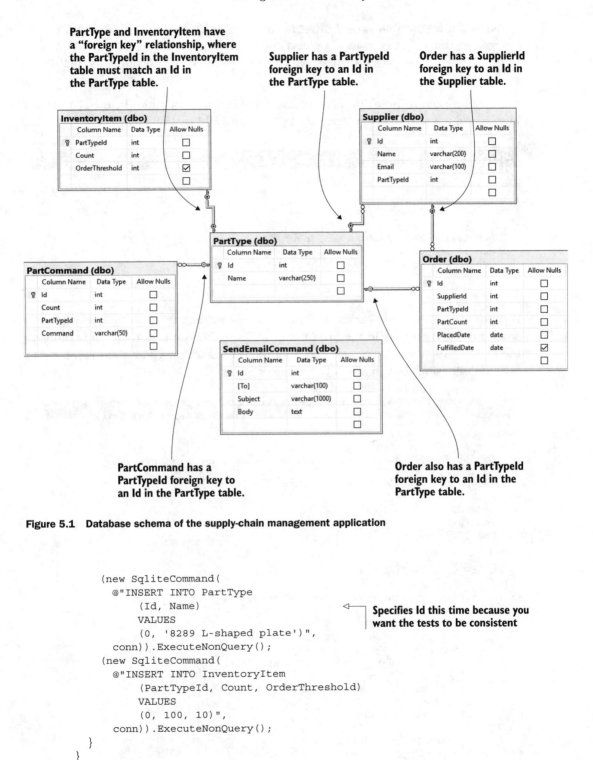

Figure 5.1 Database schema of the supply-chain management application

```
        (new SqliteCommand(
          @"INSERT INTO PartType
              (Id, Name)
              VALUES
              (0, '8289 L-shaped plate')",          ←──  Specifies Id this time because you
          conn)).ExecuteNonQuery();                        want the tests to be consistent
        (new SqliteCommand(
          @"INSERT INTO InventoryItem
              (PartTypeId, Count, OrderThreshold)
              VALUES
              (0, 100, 10)",
          conn)).ExecuteNonQuery();
      }
    }
```

CALLING A METHOD ON A NEW OBJECT In listing 5.10, you use shorthand for creating the `SqliteCommand` objects and executing a method on them. You don't use the objects for anything else in the code, so we don't need to declare a variable.

You need a class to hold the rows of the `InventoryItem` table. In the data-access library, add a new class called `InventoryItem` and add the following code.

Listing 5.11 `InventoryItem` class

```
namespace WidgetScmDataAccess
{
  public class InventoryItem
  {
    public int PartTypeId { get; set; }
    public int Count { get; set; }
    public int OrderThreshold { get; set; }
  }
}
```

You already have a `ReadParts` method in the `ScmContext` class. Now you need to add a new method to read the inventory. You'll use the same approach of reading all the items in the constructor and exposing them through an `IEnumerable` property. Add the following code to `ScmContext`.

Listing 5.12 Adding code to the `ScmContext` class for inventory items

```
public class ScmContext
{
  public IEnumerable<InventoryItem> Inventory { get; private set; }

  public ScmContext(DbConnection conn)
  {
    connection = conn;
    ReadParts();
    ReadInventory();
  }

  private void ReadInventory()
  {
    using (var command = connection.CreateCommand())
    {
      command.CommandText = @"SELECT
          PartTypeId, Count, OrderThreshold
        FROM InventoryItem";
      using (var reader = command.ExecuteReader())
      {
        var items = new List<InventoryItem>();
        Inventory = items;
        while (reader.Read())
        {
          items.Add(new InventoryItem() {
            PartTypeId = reader.GetInt32(0),
```

```
        Count = reader.GetInt32(1),
        OrderThreshold = reader.GetInt32(2)
      });
    }
   }
  }
 }
}
```

Finally, modify the test to verify that the inventory items show up. Alter the `Test1` method in `UnitTest1` as follows.

Listing 5.13 Test method to verify `InventoryItem` objects are populated correctly

```
[Fact]
public void Test1()
{
  var parts = context.Parts;
  Assert.Equal(1, parts.Count());
  var part = parts.First();
  Assert.Equal("8289 L-shaped plate", part.Name);
  var inventory = context.Inventory;
  Assert.Equal(1, inventory.Count());
  var item = inventory.First();
  Assert.Equal(part.Id, item.PartTypeId);
  Assert.Equal(100, item.Count);
  Assert.Equal(10, item.OrderThreshold);
}
```

You've defined a relationship between the `PartType` and `InventoryItem` tables, but you haven't yet created a relationship in the code. When you use an `InventoryItem` object, you probably want to know what the name of the part is, and there are many ways to get the `PartType` object. The following listing shows how you can use a LINQ expression to get the `PartType`.

Listing 5.14 Using a LINQ expression to populate the `PartType` of an `InventoryItem`

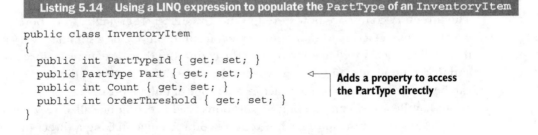

```
public class InventoryItem
{
  public int PartTypeId { get; set; }
  public PartType Part { get; set; }       ◁─ Adds a property to access
  public int Count { get; set; }              the PartType directly
  public int OrderThreshold { get; set; }
}

using System.Linq;                  ◁─ Adds a using
public class ScmContext                for LINQ
{
  public ScmContext(DbConnection conn)
  {
    connection = conn;
    ReadParts();
```

```
        ReadInventory();
    }

    private void ReadInventory()
    {
        var command = connection.CreateCommand();
        command.CommandText = @"SELECT
            PartTypeId, Count, OrderThreshold
          FROM InventoryItem";
        var reader = command.ExecuteReader();
        var items = new List<InventoryItem>();
        Inventory = items;
        while (reader.Read())
        {
            var item = new InventoryItem() {
                PartTypeId = reader.GetInt32(0),
                Count = reader.GetInt32(1),
                OrderThreshold = reader.GetInt32(2)
            };
            items.Add(item);
            item.Part = Parts.Single(p =>
                p.Id == item.PartTypeId);
        }
    }
}
```

Single ensures that there's only one PartType.

Assumes Parts is already populated

There are many different ways to hydrate objects with relationships. For example, you could have the Part property on InventoryItem only retrieve the PartType object when it's first asked for (using the get on the property). You could also use a technique called *lazy-loading*, where the PartType table would only be queried when a part was needed. This means the InventoryItem class would need to keep a reference to the context class. The InventoryItem class couldn't be defined in a different assembly, because that would create a circular reference. These are things to keep in mind when designing your application.

5.3.2   Updating data

The inventory counts are now stored in the InventoryItem table. In response to an event, such as a factory worker getting parts from inventory, or a shipment arriving at the loading dock, you'll need to update the count. But there are many factory workers and many shipments, and they all work at the same time. Modifying the count directly can be dangerous if two or more actors attempt it simultaneously.

To handle this situation, many applications used a technique called *eventual consistency*. In this case, instead of each inventory count change making a direct update to the InventoryItem table, you can record the decrease or increase in a separate table that acts like a queue. A single-threaded processor can then process those records serially. This is called eventual consistency because the inventory count will eventually catch up to reality, but there's a possibility that the count you retrieve is stale. Importance is placed on the availability of the inventory numbers rather than their accuracy.

CAP THEOREM Choosing availability over consistency is a tradeoff I make because of the CAP theorem. *CAP* stands for consistency, availability, and partition-tolerance, and the theorem states that you can only have two of the three at the same time in a service. We won't get into partition-tolerance in this book, but it's generally considered not optional if you want a distributed service that scales. That leaves the choice between consistency and availability. An argument can be made for both sides when it comes to keeping inventory numbers. If you're curious, you should look up the CAP theorem, sometimes called Brewer's theorem, after the computer scientist who created it.

The way you'll achieve eventual consistency is through a technique called Command Query Responsibility Segregation (CQRS). In this technique, queries are performed against one object (the `InventoryItem` table) while updates are performed against different objects. Updates will be stored in a command object you'll call `PartCommand` (see table 5.3).

Table 5.3 The `PartCommand` table contains all the commands made to modify the inventory.

Name	Data type	Description
Id	int	Unique ID for the inventory modification
PartTypeId	int	Type of part
PartCount	int	Number of parts to add or remove from inventory
Command	varchar	"Add" or "Remove"

Each row in the `PartCommand` table records an action against the part inventory: the inventory for a particular part is increased or decreased by a count. It's therefore not important in what order the commands are processed (although there is the possibility of a negative count). It's more important that a command is executed only once. If you need an accurate part count, you can wait until all the commands are processed—after business hours or on weekends, for example.

With this approach, a single-threaded processor will read the commands and update the inventory count. It's easier to guarantee consistency with a single-writer, multiple-reader system than it is with a multiple-writer, multiple-reader system, which is what you would have if you didn't use commands and updated the inventory table directly.

Add a new file to `WidgetScmDataAccess` called PartCommand.cs with the following code. This class will be used to add rows to or remove them from the `Part-Command` table.

Listing 5.15 Contents of `PartCommand` class

```
namespace WidgetScmDataAccess
{
  public class PartCommand
  {
    public int Id { get; set; }
```

```
    public int PartTypeId { get; set; }
    public PartType Part { get; set; }
    public int PartCount { get; set; }
    public PartCountOperation Command { get; set; }
}

public enum PartCountOperation
{
    Add,
    Remove
}
}
```

Enumerations are used
for discrete sets of values.

`PartCountOperation` is an enumeration, which makes it easier to work with in code. Otherwise, you'd need to use a string or an integer, and define somewhere what the acceptable values were for that field. C# enum types are backed by integers, so you can choose to store the command in the database as either an integer (0 or 1) or a string ("Add" or "Remove"). I prefer to store the string, because other applications may read the same database (such as reporting software) and not understand the integer.

> **DATABASE NORMALIZATION** You could alternatively create a `PartCount-Operation` table with an `Id` column and a foreign key relationship to the `Command` column in `PartCommand`. This is much like how you created the `PartType` table. The goal here is to reduce redundant data (like multiple copies of the strings "Add" and "Remove") and improve data integrity (by enforcing that only "Add" and "Remove" can be used). This is called *normalization*.

A factory worker pulls items from inventory, so in your application you'll create a `Part-Command` object that captures this action. It will need to be saved to the database, but we'll skip creating the table, because you're familiar with that code by now. The full code for creating all the tables is included in the companion GitHub repo for this book.

Let's move on to creating the new row in the `PartCommand` table. Add the `CreatePartCommand` method to the `ScmContext` class using the following code.

Listing 5.16   Method to add a part command to the database

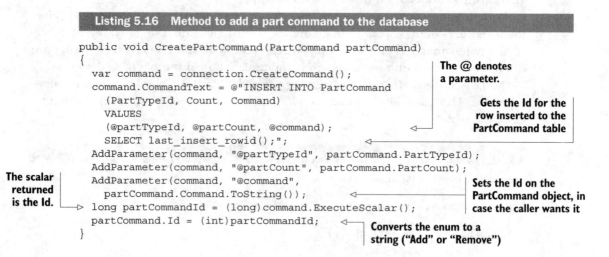

```
public void CreatePartCommand(PartCommand partCommand)
{
    var command = connection.CreateCommand();
    command.CommandText = @"INSERT INTO PartCommand
      (PartTypeId, Count, Command)
      VALUES
      (@partTypeId, @partCount, @command);
      SELECT last_insert_rowid();";
    AddParameter(command, "@partTypeId", partCommand.PartTypeId);
    AddParameter(command, "@partCount", partCommand.PartCount);
    AddParameter(command, "@command",
      partCommand.Command.ToString());
    long partCommandId = (long)command.ExecuteScalar();
    partCommand.Id = (int)partCommandId;
}
```

The @ denotes
a parameter.

Gets the Id for the
row inserted to the
PartCommand table

The scalar
returned
is the Id.

Sets the Id on the
PartCommand object, in
case the caller wants it

Converts the enum to a
string ("Add" or "Remove")

In the SQL statement, you use parameters instead of adding the values directly into the command text string. You didn't do this when inserting rows in your test code because it's test code. The `ScmContext` class is intended for use in production. Whenever you add values to a SQL statement, you should use parameters. We'll get into some of the reasons why later in this chapter.

Another odd thing in listing 5.16 is the statement `SELECT last_insert_rowid()`. This function is part of SQLite. When inserting a row into the `PartCommand` table, SQLite automatically populates the `Id` column. You use the `last_insert_rowid()` function to get the value that SQLite used for that `Id` column.

The `CreatePartCommand` code also makes use of a helper method called `AddParameter`, which creates a `DbParameter` and adds it to the `DbCommand` object. The following listing shows the code for this method.

Listing 5.17 `AddParameter` method creates `DbParameter` objects

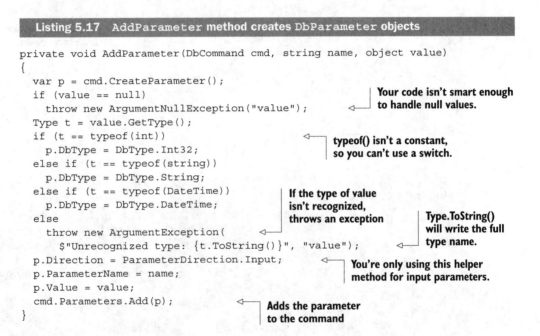

```
private void AddParameter(DbCommand cmd, string name, object value)
{
  var p = cmd.CreateParameter();
  if (value == null)                                    Your code isn't smart enough
    throw new ArgumentNullException("value");           to handle null values.
  Type t = value.GetType();
  if (t == typeof(int))                                 typeof() isn't a constant,
    p.DbType = DbType.Int32;                            so you can't use a switch.
  else if (t == typeof(string))
    p.DbType = DbType.String;
  else if (t == typeof(DateTime))          If the type of value
    p.DbType = DbType.DateTime;            isn't recognized,
  else                                     throws an exception    Type.ToString()
    throw new ArgumentException(                                  will write the full
      $"Unrecognized type: {t.ToString()}", "value");            type name.
  p.Direction = ParameterDirection.Input;        You're only using this helper
  p.ParameterName = name;                        method for input parameters.
  p.Value = value;
  cmd.Parameters.Add(p);            Adds the parameter
}                                    to the command
```

The `AddParameter` method doesn't handle `null` values, but it's reasonable that a parameter passed to a command could have a `null` value, because certain columns allow `null` values. The problem is that you can't call a method, such as `GetType()`, on a `null` value. You need to specify a `DbType` that matches the column's type, so in listing 5.17 you're using the .NET type of the `value` parameter to infer a `DbType`. If you had an overload of the `AddParameter` method that took a `DbType` parameter, you wouldn't have to throw the exception for a `null` value.

Your single-threaded, eventually consistent processor will read the commands from the `PartCommand` table and make updates to the `InventoryItem` table. The following listing has the code to retrieve all the `PartCommand` objects in order by `Id`.

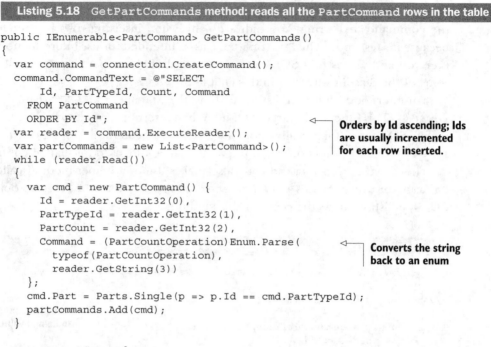

Listing 5.18   GetPartCommands method: reads all the PartCommand rows in the table

```csharp
public IEnumerable<PartCommand> GetPartCommands()
{
  var command = connection.CreateCommand();
  command.CommandText = @"SELECT
      Id, PartTypeId, Count, Command
    FROM PartCommand
    ORDER BY Id";
  var reader = command.ExecuteReader();
  var partCommands = new List<PartCommand>();
  while (reader.Read())
  {
    var cmd = new PartCommand() {
      Id = reader.GetInt32(0),
      PartTypeId = reader.GetInt32(1),
      PartCount = reader.GetInt32(2),
      Command = (PartCountOperation)Enum.Parse(
        typeof(PartCountOperation),
        reader.GetString(3))
    };
    cmd.Part = Parts.Single(p => p.Id == cmd.PartTypeId);
    partCommands.Add(cmd);
  }

  return partCommands;
}
```

Orders by Id ascending; Ids are usually incremented for each row inserted.

Converts the string back to an enum

Parsing enumerations

The Enum.Parse() method takes a string and attempts to match it to one of the enum values. The Enum class doesn't have a generic method like T Parse<T> (string), which would be less verbose, but there is a bool TryParse<T> (string, out T) method. That's a better method to use if Command has an unrecognized value or is null. To use it, instead of setting Command in the initialization of the PartCommand object, add the following code:

```csharp
PartCountOperation operation;
if (Enum.TryParse<PartCountOperation>(reader.GetString(3), out operation))
  cmd.Command = operation;
```

Getting data in order

Integer identity columns like your Id columns typically start at 0 and increment for each row inserted. The count never decrements for rows deleted, so don't rely on it as a count of rows in the table.

Identity columns are also not reliable as a way of ordering the rows, especially if there are multiple simultaneous inserts to the table. You could try using a timestamp

> to order the rows, but you should use the database to generate the timestamp instead of the application. If the application runs on multiple machines, there's no guarantee that the clocks are synced. Also, you're limited by the precision of the timestamp.
>
> What you should really be thinking about is whether order really matters, or whether you can make your application robust enough to handle commands out of order.

5.3.3 Managing inventory

You can now add rows to and retrieve rows from the `PartCommands` table. But you still haven't handled updating the `InventoryItem` table.

Add another method to the `ScmContext` class with the following code.

Listing 5.19 Method to update the part count in the `InventoryItem` table

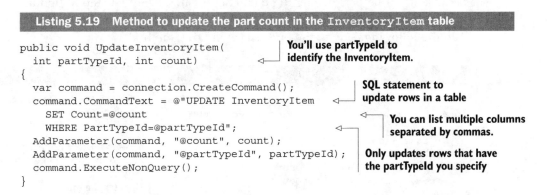

```
public void UpdateInventoryItem(              You'll use partTypeId to
  int partTypeId, int count)                  identify the InventoryItem.
{
  var command = connection.CreateCommand();          SQL statement to
  command.CommandText = @"UPDATE InventoryItem        update rows in a table
    SET Count=@count                                  You can list multiple columns
    WHERE PartTypeId=@partTypeId";                    separated by commas.
  AddParameter(command, "@count", count);
  AddParameter(command, "@partTypeId", partTypeId);   Only updates rows that have
  command.ExecuteNonQuery();                          the partTypeId you specify
}
```

After `PartCommand` has been applied to the inventory, you need to delete the record from the table so you don't process it again. Add another method to `ScmContext` to delete the row, as follows.

Listing 5.20 Method to delete the `PartCommand` row from the table

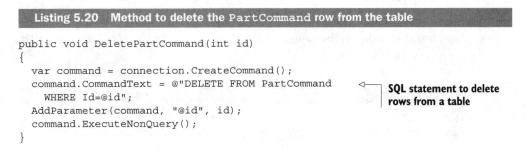

```
public void DeletePartCommand(int id)
{
  var command = connection.CreateCommand();
  command.CommandText = @"DELETE FROM PartCommand         SQL statement to delete
    WHERE Id=@id";                                        rows from a table
  AddParameter(command, "@id", id);
  command.ExecuteNonQuery();
}
```

Next, create a new class called `Inventory` to manage the inventory, as shown in the next listing.

Listing 5.21 Creating the `Inventory` class

```
using System;                     You'll be using these
using System.Linq;                namespaces later.
```

```
namespace WidgetScmDataAccess
{
  public class Inventory
  {
    private ScmContext context;
    public Inventory(ScmContext context)
    {
      this.context = context;
    }

    public void UpdateInventory() {}
  }
}
```

◁── **Must have the context to get and update data**

◁── **This method will be filled in later.**

The `UpdateInventory` method is the one you want to execute in a single thread, because it will be performing the database updates. The first step in `UpdateInventory` is to go through all the `PartCommand` objects and update the inventory counts. Add the following code to the `UpdateInventory` method.

Listing 5.22   Updates the inventory counts based on the `PartCommands`

```
foreach (var cmd in context.GetPartCommands())
{
  var item = context.Inventory.Single(i =>
    i.PartTypeId == cmd.PartTypeId);
  if (cmd.Command == PartCountOperation.Add)
    item.Count += cmd.PartCount;
  else
    item.Count -= cmd.PartCount;

  context.UpdateInventoryItem(item.PartTypeId,
    item.Count);
  context.DeletePartCommand(cmd.Id);
}
```

◁── **Gets all the PartCommands from the table**

◁── **Gets the InventoryItem for the part mentioned in the command**

Updates the count

◁── **Deletes the PartCommand so you don't duplicate it**

Now test this code. In the SqliteScmTest project, open UnitTest1.cs and add a new test method with the following code.

Listing 5.23   Test if the part commands correctly update the inventory count

```
[Fact]
public void TestPartCommands()
{
  var item = context.Inventory.First();
  var startCount = item.Count;
  context.CreatePartCommand(new PartCommand() {
    PartTypeId = item.PartTypeId,
    PartCount = 10,
    Command = PartCountOperation.Add
  });
  context.CreatePartCommand(new PartCommand() {
```

```
    PartTypeId = item.PartTypeId,
    PartCount = 5,
    Command = PartCountOperation.Remove
  });
  var inventory = new Inventory(context);
  inventory.UpdateInventory();
  Assert.Equal(startCount + 5, item.Count);
}
```

⟵ **InventoryItem object is updated with database**

In this test, you're adding 10 items to the inventory and removing 5 items. You want to make sure both commands are processed correctly.

5.3.4 *Using transactions for consistency*

There's a nasty flaw in listing 5.23 that could cause you some sleepless nights and cause Widget Corp. not to trust the inventory count. What would happen if the deletion of the row from the PartCommand table failed, or if it never executed because of a process crash, hardware failure, power outage, or some other disastrous event? When the application starts up again, it would process the same PartCommand it's already processed. The inventory count would be wrong, and the only way you'd know is if you stopped everything, did a full count, and compared the numbers.

You need something that can guarantee that if a failure occurs while you're updating InventoryItem or deleting from PartCommand, both of these commands will be undone. The term for this is a *transaction*. A transaction groups several actions and ensures that either all of those actions occur or none of them do.

ACID transactions

Database transactions are atomic, consistent, isolated, and durable (ACID):

- *Atomic*—This refers to the all-or-nothing approach. If any part of the transaction fails, the whole transaction fails, and the database is unchanged.
- *Consistent*—All changes are valid, meaning that they don't violate constraints, foreign key relationships, and so on.
- *Isolated*—It shouldn't matter if transactions are executed concurrently, meaning there shouldn't be any incomplete state from one transaction that affects another.
- *Durable*—Once the transaction is committed, the database will remain changed even in the event of a crash, hardware issue, or other disaster.

SQLite is a *transactional* database, though the durability part doesn't apply if you're using an in-memory database like you are here.

To get a transaction, you'll need a DbTransaction object, which is created from the DbConnection object. Because you don't expose the connection used inside ScmContext, you'll need to provide a method to get a transaction object. Add the following code to ScmContext.

Listing 5.24   Method to get a `DbTransaction` object from the `ScmContext` object

```
public DbTransaction BeginTransaction()
{
  return connection.BeginTransaction();
}
```

Now add transactions to the `UpdateInventory` method of the `Inventory` class. Modify the code as follows.

Listing 5.25   Update the inventory counts based on the `PartCommands`

```
foreach (var cmd in context.GetPartCommands())
{
  var item = context.Inventory.Single(i =>
    i.PartTypeId == cmd.PartTypeId);
  var oldCount = item.Count;                      ◁── Stores the old count in case
  if (cmd.Command == PartCountOperation.Add)          the transaction fails
    item.Count += cmd.PartCount;
  else
    item.Count -= cmd.PartCount;                            Creates a new
                                                            database transaction
  var transaction = context.BeginTransaction();   ◁──
  try {                                                  UpdateInventoryItem
    context.UpdateInventoryItem(item.PartTypeId,         needs to use the same
      item.Count, transaction);                   ◁──    transaction object.
    context.DeletePartCommand(cmd.Id, transaction);  ◁──
    transaction.Commit();                     ◁──          Deletes the
  }                                      Commits the transaction  PartCommand under
  catch {                                if there are no errors   the transaction as well
    transaction.Rollback();                    ◁──      Rolls back the transaction
    item.Count = oldCount;          ◁──                 if an error occurred
    throw;                       Sets the item count
  }                              back to its old value
}
```

TRANSACTION ROLLBACKS DON'T AFFECT OBJECTS `DbTransaction` only applies to the database, so you have to manually restore the `InventoryItem` object back to its original state. Therefore, you need to set the `Count` property back to its original value.

In listing 5.25 you pass the `DbTransaction` object to the `UpdateInventoryItem` and `DeletePartCommand` methods so they can be used on the `DbCommand` objects. Update those methods with the following code.

Listing 5.26   Update `DeletePartCommand` and `UpdateInventoryItem`

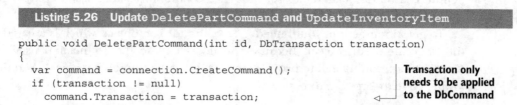

```
public void DeletePartCommand(int id, DbTransaction transaction)
{
  var command = connection.CreateCommand();            Transaction only
  if (transaction != null)                             needs to be applied
    command.Transaction = transaction;          ◁──    to the DbCommand
```

```
  command.CommandText = @"DELETE FROM PartCommand
    WHERE Id=@id";
  AddParameter(command, "@id", id);
  command.ExecuteNonQuery();
}

public void UpdateInventoryItem(int partTypeId, int count,
  DbTransaction transaction)
{
  var command = connection.CreateCommand();
  if (transaction != null)
    command.Transaction = transaction;
  command.CommandText = @"UPDATE InventoryItem
    SET Count=@count
    WHERE PartTypeId=@partTypeId";
  AddParameter(command, "@count", count);
  AddParameter(command, "@partTypeId", partTypeId);
  command.ExecuteNonQuery();
}
```

> **Transaction only needs to be applied to the DbCommand**

To test this out, try throwing an exception from `DeletePartCommand` or `Update-Inventory` just before the call to `Commit()`. You should see in both the `Inventory-Item` object and the database that the part count hasn't changed. You can rest assured that at least this operation is resilient.

Now that you have the inventory handled, let's move on to handling orders.

5.4 *Ordering new parts from suppliers*

Widget Corp. orders parts from its suppliers via email. For this example, let's assume that each supplier only supplies one part. In the real world, suppliers offer multiple parts and at different prices, which becomes too complicated for this example.

Given these restrictions, your `Supplier` table looks like table 5.4.

Table 5.4 Supplier table containing the names, email addresses, and part types of each supplier

Name	Data type	Description
Id	int	Unique ID for the supplier
Name	varchar	Supplier name
Email	varchar	Email to order parts from
PartTypeId	int	Type of part this supplier provides

We established earlier that there's an order threshold in the `InventoryItem` table that tells the application when to order new parts. When the threshold is exceeded (when the part count goes below the threshold), the application should send an email to the supplier. You only want to send one email at a time until the order is fulfilled. Otherwise, you could end up with duplicate orders and receive too many parts.

To handle this, you'll create two records in the database: one for the order and one for the command to send an email. The tables for these are outlined in tables 5.5 and 5.6 respectively.

Table 5.5   `Order` **table contains all the orders made to suppliers**

Name	Data type	Description
Id	int	Unique order ID
SupplierId	int	ID of the supplier to which this order was sent
PartTypeId	int	The type of part ordered
PartCount	int	Number of parts ordered
PlacedDate	date	The date on which the order was placed
FulfilledDate	date	The date the order was fulfilled

Table 5.6   `SendEmailCommand` **table contains commands to send order emails**

Name	Data type	Description
Id	int	Unique ID for the email
To	varchar	Email address to send to
Subject	varchar	Subject line of email
Body	varchar	Body of email

The same single-threaded processor we use to update the inventory will create the orders. After processing all the `PartCommand` objects, it checks each item to see if the part count is below the threshold. If there are no outstanding orders for an item, it creates new records in the `Order` and `SendEmailCommand` tables. Another processor is responsible for sending the emails.

5.4.1   *Creating an Order*

An order consists of two things, a row in the `Order` table and a row in the `Send-EmailCommand` table, so you should create these records as part of a transaction. Start by defining the `Order` class, as shown in the next listing.

Listing 5.27   `Order` class

```
using System;

namespace WidgetScmDataAccess
{
  public class Order
  {
```

```
      public int Id { get; set; }
      public int SupplierId { get; set; }
      public Supplier Supplier { get; set; }
      public int PartTypeId { get; set; }
      public PartType Part { get; set; }
      public int PartCount { get; set; }
      public DateTime PlacedDate { get; set; }
   }
}
```

Listing 5.28 shows how you'll create the records in the Order and SendEmail-Command tables. The CreateOrder method, shown in the following listing, takes an Order object with all the properties filled in (except the Id property).

Listing 5.28 The CreateOrder method

```
public void CreateOrder(Order order)
{
   var transaction = connection.BeginTransaction();
   try {
      var command = connection.CreateCommand();
      command.Transaction = transaction;
      command.CommandText = @"INSERT INTO [Order]          Order is a special keyword
         (SupplierId, PartTypeId, PartCount,              in SQLite, so you have to
         PlacedDate) VALUES (@supplierId,                 surround it with brackets.
         @partTypeId, @partCount, @placedDate);
         SELECT last_insert_rowid();";
      AddParameter(command, "@supplierId", order.SupplierId);
      AddParameter(command, "@partTypeId", order.PartTypeId);
      AddParameter(command, "@partCount", order.PartCount);
      AddParameter(command, "@placedDate", order.PlacedDate);
      long orderId = (long)command.ExecuteScalar();
      order.Id = (int)orderId;                            Sets the Id in case the caller
                                                          of CreateOrder needs it
      command = connection.CreateCommand();
      command.Transaction = transaction;
      command.CommandText = @"INSERT INTO SendEmailCommand
         ([To], Subject, Body) VALUES
         (@To, @Subject, @Body)";
      AddParameter(command, "@To",                        The Supplier property
         order.Supplier.Email);                           must be populated.
      AddParameter(command, "@Subject",
         $"Order #{orderId} for {order.Part.Name}");
      AddParameter(command, "@Body", $"Please send {order.PartCount}" +
         $" items of {order.Part.Name} to Widget Corp");
      command.ExecuteNonQuery();
                                                          The Part property
      transaction.Commit();                               must be populated.
   }
   catch {
      transaction.Rollback();
      throw;
   }
}
```

To is another SQLite keyword.

SEE COMPANION REPO FOR TABLE CREATION CODE   In listing 5.28, I'm making the assumption that the `Order` and `SendEmailCommand` tables already exist. You should already be pretty familiar with creating tables, but if you don't want to type all of that code, the full source code for this book is available on GitHub at http://mng.bz/F146.

SQL injection

Let's consider briefly what could happen if you weren't using parameters to construct the SQL statement. The code for setting the command text would look like this:

```
command.CommandText = $@"INSERT INTO SendEmailCommand
  ([To], Subject, Body) VALUES
  ('{order.Supplier.Email}', '{order.Part.Name}', '{body}')";
```

What if the part name had a single quote character in it like "John's bearing"? This would cause the command text to be an invalid SQL string, and your application would be unable to place orders for this part. By using a parameter, you don't have to worry about this.

Hackers search for weaknesses like SQL statements built as strings. The technique is called *SQL injection*, and it puts you at risk of compromising or losing all your data. As a best practice, always use parameters when writing SQL statements.

Also check out a great XKCD comic on this subject at https://xkcd.com/327.

Notice that in order to send the email, you need to have the `Supplier` and `Part` properties filled in on the `Order` object. One issue that could occur is that the caller of `CreateOrder` doesn't specify one of these properties. This would result in a `NullReferenceException`, which would cause the transaction to roll back.

Test this out. In the SqliteScmTest project, add a new test to UnitTest1.cs with the following code. This code shows how you can execute `CreateOrder`, encounter an exception that causes a rollback, and verify that the order record wasn't created.

Listing 5.29   Unit test to verify that `CreateOrder` is transactional

```
[Fact]
public void TestCreateOrderTransaction()
{
  var placedDate = DateTime.Now;
  var supplier = context.Suppliers.First();
  var order = new Order()                      ← Supplies the part and supplier IDs, but not the objects
  {
    PartTypeId = supplier.PartTypeId,
    SupplierId = supplier.Id,
    PartCount = 10,
    PlacedDate = placedDate
  };
  Assert.Throws<NullReferenceException>(() =>    ← You expect the code you're calling to throw a NullReferenceException.
    context.CreateOrder(order));                 ← xUnit catches and checks that it's a NullReferenceException.
```

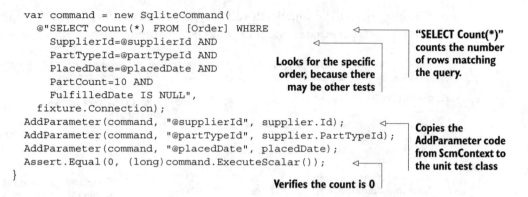

```
var command = new SqliteCommand(
  @"SELECT Count(*) FROM [Order] WHERE
    SupplierId=@supplierId AND
    PartTypeId=@partTypeId AND
    PlacedDate=@placedDate AND
    PartCount=10 AND
    FulfilledDate IS NULL",
  fixture.Connection);
AddParameter(command, "@supplierId", supplier.Id);
AddParameter(command, "@partTypeId", supplier.PartTypeId);
AddParameter(command, "@placedDate", placedDate);
Assert.Equal(0, (long)command.ExecuteScalar());
}
```

"SELECT Count(*)" counts the number of rows matching the query.

Looks for the specific order, because there may be other tests

Copies the AddParameter code from ScmContext to the unit test class

Verifies the count is 0

In this test, the PartType and Supplier objects aren't set in the Order object. You know from the code in listing 5.29 that the first INSERT command will work but the second will fail. The test verifies that the transaction successfully rolls back the first change.

SIMPLER TRANSACTIONS WITH SYSTEM.TRANSACTIONS

In the .NET Framework, there's another way to create transactions that doesn't involve explicitly setting the transaction on each command. This is particularly helpful if you're using an external library that's performing database work but that doesn't let you pass in a DbTransaction object. This functionality is built into a library called System.Transactions.

> **LIMITED SUPPORT OF SYSTEM.TRANSACTIONS** System.Transactions was only added to .NET Core as of version 2.0. SQLite currently doesn't support it as I'm writing this book. However, it's likely to be supported soon.

System.Transactions is part of .NET Core but not of .NET Standard, so you'll have to modify WidgetScmDataAccess.csproj as follows.

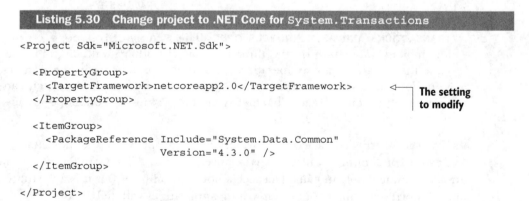

Listing 5.30 Change project to .NET Core for System.Transactions

```
<Project Sdk="Microsoft.NET.Sdk">

  <PropertyGroup>
    <TargetFramework>netcoreapp2.0</TargetFramework>
  </PropertyGroup>

  <ItemGroup>
    <PackageReference Include="System.Data.Common"
                      Version="4.3.0" />
  </ItemGroup>

</Project>
```

The setting to modify

The code for using a System.Transactions transaction is a little simpler than for the DbTransaction method: create a TransactionScope and use the using block and dispose pattern to automatically roll back in case of a failure. The following listing shows how the `CreateOrder` method could be rewritten to use `TransactionScope`.

Listing 5.31   `CreateOrder` rewritten to use `TransactionScope`

```
using System.Transactions;                          ◁──  Adds the System.Transactions
                                                         namespace
public void CreateOrderSysTx(Order order)
{                                                        Creates an ambient
  using (var tx = new TransactionScope())         ◁──┘  transaction
  {
    var command = connection.CreateCommand();     ◁──  Commands that are run
    command.CommandText = @"INSERT INTO [Order]         within the transaction scope
      (SupplierId, PartTypeId, PartCount,               automatically participate.
      PlacedDate) VALUES (@supplierId,
      @partTypeId, @partCount, @placedDate);
      SELECT last_insert_rowid();";
    AddParameter(command, "@supplierId", order.SupplierId);
    AddParameter(command, "@partTypeId", order.PartTypeId);
    AddParameter(command, "@partCount", order.PartCount);
    AddParameter(command, "@placedDate", order.PlacedDate);
    long orderId = (long)command.ExecuteScalar();
    order.Id = (int)orderId;

    command = connection.CreateCommand();
    command.CommandText = @"INSERT INTO SendEmailCommand
      ([To], Subject, Body) VALUES
      (@To, @Subject, @Body)";
    AddParameter(command, "@To", order.Supplier.Email);
    AddParameter(command, "@Subject",
      $"Order #{orderId} for {order.Part.Name}");
    AddParameter(command, "@Body", $"Please send {order.PartCount}" +
      $" items of {order.Part.Name} to Widget Corp");
    command.ExecuteNonQuery();

    tx.Complete();                      ◁──  Tells the TransactionScope
  }                                          that everything is good
}
```

TRANSACTIONS AND ASYNCHRONOUS CODE The `TransactionScope` creates an ambient transaction on the thread. If you call other methods from your code that create database operations, they'll also participate in the transaction. You can also use `TransactionScope` in `async` methods, which can move to different threads, by specifying the `TransactionScopeAsync-FlowOption`.

As I warned earlier, data-access providers have to opt in to take advantage of the `TransactionScope`. Because this is relatively new to .NET Core 2.0, it may not be available immediately in your data-access library of choice. But it is a useful feature, and it's worth knowing about when writing applications with .NET Core.

DISTRIBUTED TRANSACTIONS NOT SUPPORTED IN .NET CORE In the .NET Framework, `System.Transactions` was capable of enlisting operations on multiple databases into a single transaction. This is not available in .NET Core. In order to support multiple databases, `System.Transactions` will promote a transaction from local to distributed. Distributed transactions are managed by a Windows component called the Distributed Transaction Coordinator (DTC), but there's no equivalent on other operating systems. `System.Transactions` in .NET Core only supports local transactions, meaning all transactions for the same database.

5.4.2 Checking if parts need to be ordered

After processing all of the `PartCommand` records and updating the `InventoryItem` table, the next step of `UpdateInventory` is to determine what part counts have dropped below the order threshold. Orders need to be created for those parts unless you already have outstanding orders for them.

To determine if you have an outstanding order, add a property to `Order` that indicates if and when the order was fulfilled, as shown in the next listing.

Listing 5.32   `Order` class

```
using System;

namespace WidgetScmDataAccess
{
  public class Order
  {
    public int Id { get; set; }
    public int SupplierId { get; set; }
    public Supplier Supplier { get; set; }
    public int PartTypeId { get; set; }
    public PartType Part { get; set; }
    public int PartCount { get; set; }
    public DateTime PlacedDate { get; set; }
    public DateTime? FulfilledDate { get; set; }   ⟵  FulfilledDate
  }                                                     can be null.
}
```

In the `Inventory` class's `UpdateInventory` method, append the following code to the end of the method.

Listing 5.33   Code to add in `UpdateInventory`

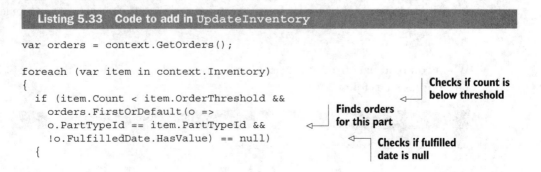

```
var orders = context.GetOrders();

foreach (var item in context.Inventory)
{
  if (item.Count < item.OrderThreshold &&        ⟵  Checks if count is
    orders.FirstOrDefault(o =>                         below threshold
    o.PartTypeId == item.PartTypeId &&           ⟵  Finds orders
    !o.FulfilledDate.HasValue) == null)              for this part
  {                                              ⟵  Checks if fulfilled
                                                     date is null
```

```
    OrderPart(item.Part, item.OrderThreshold);    ◁──┐  Orders the same number
  }                                                   │  of parts as the threshold
}
```

We haven't yet defined the `ScmContext.GetOrders` or `Inventory.OrderPart` methods. `OrderPart` provides a reference for what logic the `Inventory.Update-Inventory` method uses. `GetOrders` will get all the orders in the `Ordertable`, and you can then use a LINQ query on the returned collection to check whether orders already exist for inventory items that have counts lower than the threshold. `First-OrDefault` will return either the first item in the collection that matches the query, or `null` if nothing matches. The query looks for the `PartTypeId` and checks that the order is still unfulfilled (`FulfilledDate` is null).

The number of parts to order could be complicated. For this example, you're using the order threshold, since it's easier. Also remember that if an order isn't fulfilled, it's considered outstanding. That's why you allowed `FulfilledDate` to be null in the `Order` table. But that also means you have to handle `null` values in your code.

HANDLING NULL VALUES

Notice in listing 5.33 that `FulfilledDate` has a property called `HasValue`. Let's explore this a bit more. First, go back and look at the code in listing 5.33. The `FulfilledDate` property has the type `DateTime?`, where the "?" indicates that it's a nullable type. `HasValue` is a Boolean property indicating whether the value is `null`.

> ### What is a nullable type?
>
> C#, like many C-based languages, has two types of variables: *reference* and *value*. A reference type is a pointer to a memory location, whereas value types directly contain the values of the variables. Examples of value types include `int`, `bool`, and `double`. A struct in C# is also a value type, and `DateTime` is a struct.
>
> Value types can't be assigned to the `null` value because `null` refers to an empty reference (pointer) value. In cases like our example, where the `FulfilledDate` might not contain a value, if you can't set it to `null`, then you have to pick a value that represents `null`. This can be problematic for other developers using the library if they don't understand the convention.
>
> Luckily, C# has the concept of nullable types. This creates a wrapper around a value type that indicates whether that value has been set. The `?` is actually a shorthand that makes it much easier to read the code. For more information on nullable types and other interesting bits of C#, see Jon Skeet's *C# in Depth, Fourth Edition* (Manning, 2018).

When you read data from the `Order` table, you need to special-case the `Fulfilled-Date` property as follows.

Listing 5.34 Reading the `Order` records from the table

```
public IEnumerable<Order> GetOrders()
{
```

```
var command = connection.CreateCommand();
command.CommandText = @"SELECT
    Id, SupplierId, PartTypeId, PartCount, PlacedDate, FulfilledDate
  FROM [Order]";
var reader = command.ExecuteReader();
var orders = new List<Order>();
while (reader.Read())
{
  var order = new Order() {
    Id = reader.GetInt32(0),
    SupplierId = reader.GetInt32(1),
    PartTypeId = reader.GetInt32(2),
    PartCount = reader.GetInt32(3),
    PlacedDate = reader.GetDateTime(4),
    FulfilledDate = reader.IsDBNull(5) ?
      default(DateTime?) : reader.GetDateTime(5)
  };
  order.Part = Parts.Single(p => p.Id == order.PartTypeId);
  order.Supplier = Suppliers.First(s => s.Id == order.SupplierId);
  orders.Add(order);
}

return orders;
}
```

Checks if it's null in the table with ternary operator

default() gives you a Nullable<DateTime> with HasValue false.

TERNARY OPERATOR   The line that populates the `FulfilledDate` property in listing 5.34 uses something called a *ternary operator*. If you haven't seen this in other programming languages before, it's basically a shorthand for doing an `if/else` within an expression, where `if` and `else` both return a value of the same type. The syntax is `<bool> ? <then> : <else>`. Try not to confuse the ternary operator with the nullable type operator.

FILLING IN THE ORDER OBJECT

The only method you haven't yet completed is `OrderPart`. You've seen before that not populating all the properties in the `Order` object will cause an exception. `Order-Part` is a helper method to hydrate the `Order` object and create the order, as shown in the following listing.

Listing 5.35   `OrderPart` helper method to hydrate the `Order` object and create the order

```
public void OrderPart(PartType part, int count)
{
  var order = new Order() {
    PartTypeId = part.Id,
    PartCount = count,
    PlacedDate = DateTime.Now
  };
  order.Part = context.Parts.Single(p => p.Id == order.PartTypeId);
  order.Supplier = context.Suppliers.First(
    s => s.PartTypeId == part.Id);
  order.SupplierId = order.Supplier.Id;
  context.CreateOrder(order);
}
```

Note that you'll need to have data in the Supplier table first.

Now test out this whole process. In the SqliteScmTest project, add another test to UnitTest1.cs with the following code.

> **Listing 5.36   Test that `UpdateInventory` creates an `Order` when part count is zero**

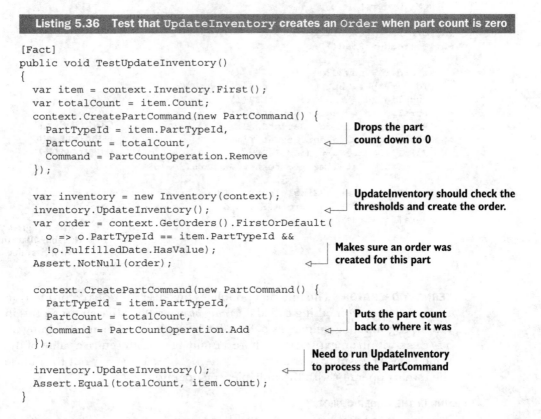

```
[Fact]
public void TestUpdateInventory()
{
  var item = context.Inventory.First();
  var totalCount = item.Count;
  context.CreatePartCommand(new PartCommand() {
    PartTypeId = item.PartTypeId,                    ⟵  Drops the part
    PartCount = totalCount,                              count down to 0
    Command = PartCountOperation.Remove
  });

  var inventory = new Inventory(context);          ⟵  UpdateInventory should check the
  inventory.UpdateInventory();                         thresholds and create the order.
  var order = context.GetOrders().FirstOrDefault(
    o => o.PartTypeId == item.PartTypeId &&
    !o.FulfilledDate.HasValue);                     ⟵  Makes sure an order was
  Assert.NotNull(order);                                created for this part

  context.CreatePartCommand(new PartCommand() {
    PartTypeId = item.PartTypeId,
    PartCount = totalCount,                         ⟵  Puts the part count
    Command = PartCountOperation.Add                    back to where it was
  });
                                                    ⟵  Need to run UpdateInventory
  inventory.UpdateInventory();                          to process the PartCommand
  Assert.Equal(totalCount, item.Count);
}
```

This test doesn't check for the `SendEmailCommand` record, but that's easy enough to add. In a real application, the `UpdateInventory` method would execute on a regular interval. New `PartCommand` records can be created at any time. The interval on which the `SendEmailCommand` records are processed can be separate, giving Widget Corp. a chance to evaluate them before the emails are sent.

Additional resources

To learn more about what we covered in this chapter, try the following resources:

- Ben Brumm, *SQL in Motion*—http://mng.bz/i433
- ADO.NET Overview—http://mng.bz/f0lM

Summary

In this chapter you learned about working with relational data in .NET Core and we covered some useful data-access features.

These are the key concepts from this chapter:

- `System.Data.Common` classes are database-agnostic, allowing you to prototype with SQLite or another lightweight database, yet still use a full-featured database in production.
- In-memory databases make unit testing data-access code predictable.
- Transactions allow multiple changes to be made in an all-or-nothing fashion, so data can be kept consistent.

You also used a few techniques that you should keep in mind when writing data-access code:

- Use identity columns in database tables to simplify your code.
- Use nullable types to allow `null`s in value types that don't support `null`.
- Use specific fields in your `SELECT` statements rather than using `SELECT *` to guarantee the order and number of fields, so your code doesn't break when the database schema changes.

As you can see from this chapter, even a simple data model can turn into a lot of code. Most of the projects I've worked on have had relational databases. There are many ways to access databases from .NET, and libraries wax and wane in popularity—this chapter focused on the low-level way to access data in .NET. It provides a solid foundation; we'll build a better understanding of the high-level data-access libraries in the next chapter.

Simplify data access with object-relational mappers

This chapter covers

- Implementing a data-access layer with an object-relational mapper (ORM)
- Comparing a micro-ORM (Dapper) with a full-featured ORM (Entity Framework Core)
- Using Microsoft.Extensions libraries to build a data-access layer

Your implementation of supply chain management software was a success, and now Widget Corporation would like to expand its capabilities. They want touchscreens for their assembly-line workers; daily, weekly, and monthly reports; and a bunch of other new features. The head of your consulting company decides that this should be a product that you can sell to other customers, so she starts hiring new team members to help you build it.

The low-level data-access layer you built worked great when there was only one client and one database. Now you've got to think about appealing to customers with all kinds of databases. Your team members also find that the code for interacting with the relational database is tedious and subject to human error. They suggest using an ORM, but there are so many choices, and you're not sure which one to use.

> **What is object-relational mapping?**
> An object-relational mapper (ORM) performs the conversion between objects and relational database entities. It understands certain strategies for mapping tables to objects and vice versa. It also converts programming language data types such as strings and integers to and from database types like VARCHAR and Blob. Complex ORMs handle things like database functions, stored procedures, and mapping object hierarchies to tables.

This chapter intends to arm you with experience of .NET Core ORMs so you're better able to make decisions about what works best in your application. We'll look at two different kinds of ORMs: full-featured ORMs and micro-ORMs. Both have advantages and disadvantages, but both automate some of the boilerplate code needed to convert between objects and relational databases. The full-featured ORM we'll look at is called Entity Framework Core, which is a part of .NET Core. But first, let's explore a library called Dapper, which has been ported to .NET Standard, to see what a micro-ORM is capable of in .NET Core.

6.1 Dapper

Stack Overflow and the rest of Stack Exchange are powered by a custom ORM library called Dapper. Dapper is considered a *micro-ORM* because it doesn't write SQL queries for you like many full-featured ORMs. It only tries to simplify the process of converting between objects and relational data.

In the previous chapter, you created a data-access layer for your supply chain management application. You'll continue with that example and convert your existing code to use Dapper. I suggest copying the code to a new folder called DapperTest.

Go to the DapperTest\WidgetScmDataAccess folder and edit the project file so it looks like the following.

> **Listing 6.1 Modify WidgetScmDataAccess.csproj to add Dapper dependency**

```
<Project Sdk="Microsoft.NET.Sdk">

  <PropertyGroup>
    <TargetFramework>netstandard1.3</TargetFramework>        ◁───┐ Dapper uses .NET
  </PropertyGroup>                                                  Standard 1.3.

  <ItemGroup>
    <PackageReference Include="System.Data.Common"
                      Version="4.3.0" />
```

```
    <PackageReference Include="Dapper"
                      Version="1.50.2" />
  </ItemGroup>

</Project>
```
◁──── **Dapper started supporting .NET Standard as of version 1.50.**

How to tell which versions of the .NET Standard are supported by a package

To determine which versions (there can be more than one) of the .NET Standard a package supports, find the package on nuget.org. That site contains a section called Dependencies that you can expand to see what frameworks the package depends on. Dapper lists .NET Framework 4.5.1, .NET Standard 1.3, and .NET Standard 2.0. It lists two different versions of .NET Standard because it may have more features in 2.0 than in 1.3.

If your package isn't on nuget.org, you can still determine what frameworks it supports by looking inside the package. Change the .nupkg extension to .zip, or find the package in your NuGet cache (see appendix D). If the package contains a folder called lib, the folders in there will match the target framework monikers (see chapter 3 or appendix A) of the supported framework. If you don't see a lib folder, the package is probably a metapackage, and you'll have to chase down its dependencies to see what frameworks they support.

In chapter 5 you used a `DbCommand` to execute SQL commands and a `DbDataReader` to read the rows of output from that command into objects. Recall the `ReadParts` method from that chapter, and compare it to how the same can be achieved with Dapper. Both are shown in the following listing.

Listing 6.2 `ReadParts` from chapter 5 compared with the Dapper version

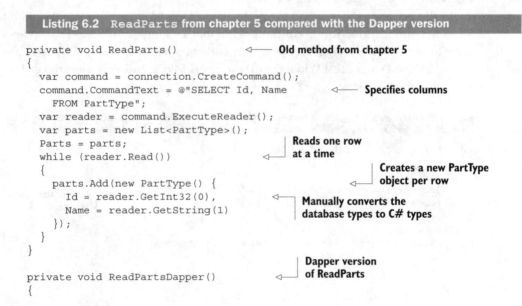

```
private void ReadParts()                    ◁──── Old method from chapter 5
{
  var command = connection.CreateCommand();
  command.CommandText = @"SELECT Id, Name    ◁──── Specifies columns
    FROM PartType";
  var reader = command.ExecuteReader();
  var parts = new List<PartType>();
  Parts = parts;                             ┐ Reads one row
  while (reader.Read())                      ◁┘ at a time
  {                                                    ┐ Creates a new PartType
    parts.Add(new PartType() {               ◁─────────┘ object per row
      Id = reader.GetInt32(0),               ◁──┐ Manually converts the
      Name = reader.GetString(1)                │ database types to C# types
    });
  }
}

private void ReadPartsDapper()              ┐ Dapper version
{                                           ◁┘ of ReadParts
```

```
Parts = connection.Query<PartType>(
    "SELECT * FROM PartType");
}
```

Query is an extension method from the Dapper library.

No need to order columns

A single line of code in Dapper replaces the whole `ReadParts` method. Let's unpack listing 6.2 a bit to understand how.

The `connection` field from `ScmContext` is a standard `DbConnection` object. Dapper defines a set of extension methods that apply to `DbConnection`, one of which is `Query`. `Query` is a generic method, meaning you use C# generics to specify that the rows returned from the SQL query will fit into `PartType` objects. Dapper uses reflection to determine the properties of the `PartType` class as well as their names and types, and maps them to the columns returned by the SQL query. Dapper only tries to match columns and properties by name, so anything that doesn't match is skipped. That's why you don't have to specify columns in the SQL query. `Query` returns an `IEnumerable` of the class you specified in the generic type parameter (the type specified in angle brackets).

You can use `Query` to get the inventory and suppliers. Let's look at how that changes the constructor of `ScmContext` in the next listing.

Listing 6.3 `ScmContext` class rewritten to use Dapper

```
using System;
using System.Collections.Generic;
using System.Data;
using System.Data.Common;
using System.Linq;
using Dapper;

namespace WidgetScmDataAccess
{
  public class ScmContext
  {
    private DbConnection connection;
    public IEnumerable<PartType> Parts { get; private set; }
    public IEnumerable<InventoryItem> Inventory { get; private set; }
    public IEnumerable<Supplier> Suppliers { get; private set; }

    public ScmContext(DbConnection conn)
    {
      connection = conn;
      Parts = conn.Query<PartType>("SELECT * FROM PartType");
      Inventory = conn.Query<InventoryItem>("SELECT * FROM InventoryItem");
      foreach (var item in Inventory)
        item.Part = Parts.Single(p => p.Id == item.PartTypeId);
      Suppliers = conn.Query<Supplier>("SELECT * FROM Supplier");
      foreach (var supplier in Suppliers)
        supplier.Part = Parts.Single(p => p.Id == supplier.PartTypeId);
    }
  }
}
```

Some of these usings are only needed later.

Used for Single extension method

Adds Dapper library

Dapper won't auto-populate class properties like Part.

Both the `Supplier` and `InventoryItem` classes reference `PartType` objects. The Dapper `Query` method will populate the value of `PartTypeId` for `Supplier` and `InventoryItem`, but it has no way of magically locating the `PartType` objects you read earlier. That's why you need to set the `Part` property explicitly on these objects. Although Dapper can't do everything, it saves a lot of the boilerplate of executing the command, reading the rows, and mapping columns to properties.

6.1.1 *Inserting rows with Dapper*

Dapper can also map an object's properties to the parameters in an `INSERT` SQL statement. Try creating an order with both `System.Data` and Dapper. You'll simplify it to just adding the row to the `Order` table and leave out the `SendEmailCommand` and transactions for this example. The following listing shows both approaches.

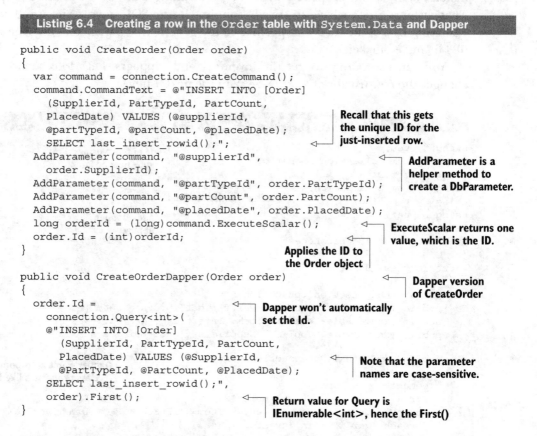

Listing 6.4   Creating a row in the `Order` table with `System.Data` and Dapper

```
public void CreateOrder(Order order)
{
  var command = connection.CreateCommand();
  command.CommandText = @"INSERT INTO [Order]
    (SupplierId, PartTypeId, PartCount,
    PlacedDate) VALUES (@supplierId,             Recall that this gets
    @partTypeId, @partCount, @placedDate);       the unique ID for the
    SELECT last_insert_rowid();";                just-inserted row.
  AddParameter(command, "@supplierId",                         AddParameter is a
    order.SupplierId);                                         helper method to
  AddParameter(command, "@partTypeId", order.PartTypeId);      create a DbParameter.
  AddParameter(command, "@partCount", order.PartCount);
  AddParameter(command, "@placedDate", order.PlacedDate);
  long orderId = (long)command.ExecuteScalar();      ExecuteScalar returns one
  order.Id = (int)orderId;                           value, which is the ID.
}                                       Applies the ID to
                                        the Order object
public void CreateOrderDapper(Order order)                    Dapper version
{                                                             of CreateOrder
  order.Id =
    connection.Query<int>(            Dapper won't automatically
    @"INSERT INTO [Order]             set the Id.
      (SupplierId, PartTypeId, PartCount,
      PlacedDate) VALUES (@SupplierId,          Note that the parameter
      @PartTypeId, @PartCount, @PlacedDate);    names are case-sensitive.
    SELECT last_insert_rowid();",
    order).First();             Return value for Query is
}                               IEnumerable<int>, hence the First()
```

Both methods use the same SQL statement, with the exception of the slight alteration to the parameter names, because Dapper uses a case-sensitive comparison on the property names of the `Order` object. Both methods assign the integer return value to the `Id` property. But where the `System.Data` approach needs eight C# statements (counting the semicolons), the Dapper approach only needs one.

6.1.2 Applying transactions to Dapper commands

The `CreateOrder` method from chapter 5 inserted a row into two different tables as part of a transaction: the row in the `Orders` table marks that an order was placed, and the row in the `SendEmailCommand` table signals another system to send an email to the supplier. You need to create either both records or neither of them (in case of a failure), so you created a `DbTransaction` object on the `DbConnection` and applied that transaction object to each `DbCommand`. In Dapper, you do basically the same thing.

The following listing shows how you can rewrite the `CreateOrder` method to use Dapper.

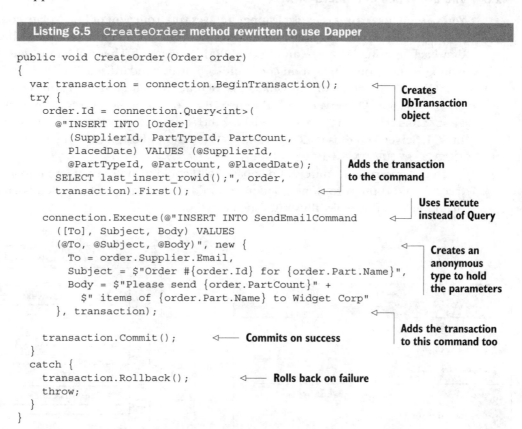

```
Listing 6.5  CreateOrder method rewritten to use Dapper

public void CreateOrder(Order order)
{
  var transaction = connection.BeginTransaction();        ◁─┐ Creates
  try {                                                       DbTransaction
    order.Id = connection.Query<int>(                         object
      @"INSERT INTO [Order]
        (SupplierId, PartTypeId, PartCount,
        PlacedDate) VALUES (@SupplierId,
        @PartTypeId, @PartCount, @PlacedDate);      ┌── Adds the transaction
      SELECT last_insert_rowid();", order,          │   to the command
      transaction).First();                         ◁─┘

                                                    ┌── Uses Execute
    connection.Execute(@"INSERT INTO SendEmailCommand  ◁─┘ instead of Query
      ([To], Subject, Body) VALUES
      (@To, @Subject, @Body)", new {          ◁─┐ Creates an
        To = order.Supplier.Email,                anonymous
        Subject = $"Order #{order.Id} for {order.Part.Name}",  type to hold
        Body = $"Please send {order.PartCount}" +              the parameters
          $" items of {order.Part.Name} to Widget Corp"
      }, transaction);                        ◁─┐ Adds the transaction
                                                  to this command too
    transaction.Commit();      ◁── Commits on success
  }
  catch {
    transaction.Rollback();    ◁── Rolls back on failure
    throw;
  }
}
```

What is an anonymous type?

In listing 6.5 you can only supply one object to the Dapper `Execute` method, and that object should have properties matching the parameters in the SQL statement. You could create a class for this, but it would only be used in this one place. C# provides a mechanism for this, called *anonymous types*. An anonymous type is a read-only class with a name you don't care about. They're most commonly used in LINQ expressions, but they're also useful for other situations.

The syntax of an anonymous type is new { Property1 = value1, Property2 = value2 }. This overloads the new operator to create an instance of a new anonymous type.

You don't need to return a SendEmailCommand, so you don't need to get the last_insert_rowid() from the insert command, which means you can use Execute instead of Query. Think of Execute as equivalent to the ExecuteNonQuery method from the DbCommand class. It executes the SQL statements and returns the number of rows affected.

6.1.3   *The drawback of a micro-ORM*

You've seen how easy it is to use Dapper. It saves you from a lot of boilerplate code and maintains great performance. Depending on your application, however, there's a drawback to using Dapper—and micro-ORMs in general. The problem is that you're writing SQL in your application code, and SQL isn't standardized.

SQL isn't the same for every database. SQLite will have different syntax and capabilities than SQL Server and PostgreSQL. For example, in SQLite you used last_insert_rowid() to get the ID for the row inserted by the previous statement. In SQL Server, you'd use SCOPE_IDENTITY(), and in PostgreSQL you'd use INSERT INTO ... RETURNING id.

In order to support different databases, you could turn ScmContext into an interface. To add support for a new database, you'd then create a new implementation of that interface. Figure 6.1 illustrates such a design.

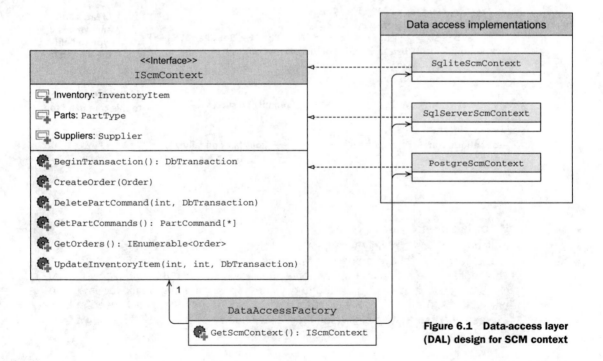

Figure 6.1   Data-access layer (DAL) design for SCM context

In figure 6.1, there are three implementations of the `IScmContext` interface, indicated by the dotted lines. When you call the `GetScmContext` method, you'll get back an `IScmContext` object, and the `GetScmContext` method is responsible for choosing which implementation class to instantiate. As a user of `DataAccessFactory`, you don't care which implementation was chosen or how that implementation works. Because all your code uses `IScmContext`, `DataAccessFactory` can create a `SqliteScmContext` object for unit testing and a `SqlServerScmContext` object for production.

The following listing shows the contents of the `DataAccessFactory` class.

Listing 6.6   Implementation of `DataAccessFactory`

```
using Scm.Dal.SQLite;                          ◁──┐  Tightly coupled to all
using Scm.Dal.SqlServer;                           │  implementations
using Scm.Dal.PostgreSql;

enum DatabaseType {              ◁──┐  Enumerates all
  Sqlite,                           │  supported databases
  SqlServer,
  PostgreSql
}
                                                            Caller must set connection
static class DataAccessFactory                              string before calling
{                                                           GetScmContext
  internal static string ConnectionString {get; set;}  ◁──┘
  internal static IScmContext GetScmContext(          ◁──┐  Caller must know what
    DatabaseType dbType)                                 │  database they want
  {
    switch (dbType)
    {
      case DatabaseType.Sqlite:
        return new SqliteScmContext(ConnectionString);
      case DatabaseType.SqlServer:
        return new SqlServerScmContext(ConnectionString);
      case DatabaseType.PostgreSql:
        return new PostgreSqlScmContext(ConnectionString);
      default:
        throw new ArgumentException(
          $"Unrecognized Database type {dbType}", "dbType");
    }
  }
}
```

`DataAccessFactory` uses the factory design pattern, which allows you to create a new object that implements an interface without knowing the specific implementation type. The factory design pattern solves the problem of determining which implementation object to create, but it introduces an interesting set of other problems. One is that the factory class must know all the implementations of a given interface. Also, adding new interfaces to the factory means adding new methods. Developers using the `DataAccessFactory` NuGet package will find it odd that they have to download the Oracle implementation even though they're using SQL Server. Also, in order to add support for a new database, you'd have to publish a new version of the package.

Design patterns

For many common problems in software development, you'll find libraries with solutions ready to use. For instance, if you want to parse arguments from the command line, you'll find a range of packages to help you. Standardizing on a single package within a team means that you don't have five different ways of reading command-line arguments to maintain and learn.

There are also problems commonly encountered when writing software that can't be solved by external libraries. These problems have been solved before, so it's not necessary to come up with a new, clever solution. By choosing from a well-known set of *design patterns*, you not only save time in development, but you also have a standard language you can use to communicate with other developers.

In our example, the common problem is that you want your data-access code to create a context class for the database without tying yourself to a particular implementation. The factory design pattern solves this problem by exposing a method that returns an object that implements your interface (or inherits from our base class). This encapsulates the code for creating the object, which may be complex, reducing duplicate code and allowing you to handle information that's not important to the calling code (like the connection string). Also, seeing "factory" in the name of a class will clue other developers to the use of the factory pattern, making it easier for them to understand how the code works.

If you want to overcome these limitations and separate the `IScmContext` implementations into different packages, then the factory pattern won't be suitable for your needs. A better way to handle this situation is to use dependency injection.

6.1.4   *A brief introduction to dependency injection*

Dependency injection (DI) is a design principle for creating objects. When you create a new object, A, it may rely on another object, B, to perform its functions. Instead of A controlling the creation of B, it allows the host or creator of A to supply an object, B. Thus, the inversion of control.

   The factory pattern is also a design principle for creating objects. To understand why the DI pattern is superior to the factory pattern, let's explore the factory pattern in more depth. A factory has a clearly defined set of methods that return objects that implement a given interface. The implementation can be chosen in many ways, including with configuration and method parameters—allowing the host to indicate which implementation to use. `DataAccessFactory` from listing 6.6 is a typical implementation of a factory.

   The advantage of the factory pattern is that you can let the host choose which implementation of `IScmContext` to use. An xUnit test can choose SQLite, and your production website can choose PostgreSQL. The disadvantage is that you have to include all implementations in your list of dependencies. Adding a new implementation, like MySql, would mean another dependency and a modification to the factory class.

The new operator creates the tight coupling. If you could remove that, you could pass in the Type object for the implementation. The following listing shows how you could modify the factory class to remove the new operator.

Listing 6.7   Factory modified to use Type object

```
using System;
using System.Linq;
using System.Reflection;

static class DataAccessFactory {
  internal static Type scmContextType = null;
  internal static Type ScmContextType {
    get { return scmContextType; }
    set {
      if (!value.GetTypeInfo().ImplementedInterfaces.
          Contains(typeof(IScmContext))) {
        throw new ArgumentException(
          $"{value.GetTypeInfo().FullName} doesn't implement IScmContext");
      }
      scmContextType = value;
    }
  }
  internal static IScmContext GetScmContext() {
    if (scmContextType == null) {
      throw new ArgumentNullException("ScmContextType not set");
    }
    return Activator.CreateInstance(scmContextType)
      as IScmContext;
  }
}
```

Annotations:
- **Host must set the implementation type before calling GetScmContext** (points to `internal static Type ScmContextType {`)
- **Checks that the type actually implements IScmContext** (points to the `if` check)
- **An alternative to new that creates an object of the passed-in Type** (points to `return Activator.CreateInstance(scmContextType)`)
- **as is similar to a typecast.** (points to `as IScmContext;`)

In listing 6.7, you've removed the tight coupling by requiring that the host pass in the implementation type. This code uses the Type object, but there are many other ways of using reflection to get the type. Instead of holding the dependencies in the factory, the host is injecting the dependency—hence the "dependency injection" name of this pattern.

One problem with listing 6.7 is that you don't pass in the connection string for types that need it. This code assumes there's a default constructor, which isn't a safe assumption. The way to solve this problem is to require the host to create the implementation object, as follows.

Listing 6.8   Factory modified to make the host supply the implementation object

```
using System.Collections.Generics;

static class DataAccessFactory
{
```

```
internal static Dictionary<Type, object> implementations =
  new Dictionary<Type, object>();

internal static void AddImplementation<T>(T t) where T : class {
  implementations.Add(typeof(T), t);
}
internal static T GetImplementation<T>() where T : class {
  return implementations[typeof(T)] as T;
}
}
```

Let's unpack listing 6.8 by first looking at the `Dictionary`. It maps types to objects—this factory class is really only a wrapper around the `Dictionary`. The `Add-Implementation` method uses C# generics to check that the object passed in the parameter implements or is a child type of the generic parameter, T. There's also a constraint (`where T : class`) to make sure nobody tries to use a value type or struct.

> **MAKE A GENERAL-PURPOSE FACTORY** You don't add the generic constraint `where T : IScmContext`. That would mean that you could only use this class for `IScm-Context` types, and only one implementation is needed for the application. Removing the constraint makes this more general-purpose, which means it should probably be called something other than `DataAccessFactory`.

To use this factory, a host, H, that uses a class, A, will create the implementation object, B, for `IScmContext` and add it to the `DataAccessFactory`. When A needs to use object B, it gets it from `DataAccessFactory`.

You've now modified your factory to the point where it's no longer a factory. It instead fits the DI (or inversion of control) pattern. The host is responsible for creating the implementation object, so it will provide the connection string if needed.

Removing the tight coupling is the biggest advantage of DI. The pattern also makes the inversion of control easy enough that you can use it in other places and thereby make your code easier to unit test.

6.1.5   *Dependency injection in .NET Core*

There are many DI libraries to choose from when writing .NET Framework applications, and some of those libraries will certainly port to .NET Standard to expand their platform reach. The ASP.NET Core team couldn't wait that long and built their own DI library. You'll use that DI library to build your data-access layer.

Figure 6.2 shows how the classes and packages lay out if you move from the factory pattern to the DI pattern. Each implementation of `IScmContext` is separated into its own package that's included only if the host decides to use it.

You're going to implement your data-access layer using DI. Use the following commands to set up a new set of projects:

```
cd ..
mkdir DapperDi
cd DapperDi
dotnet new classlib -o ScmDataAccess
dotnet new classlib -o SqliteDal
dotnet new xunit -o SqliteScmTest
```

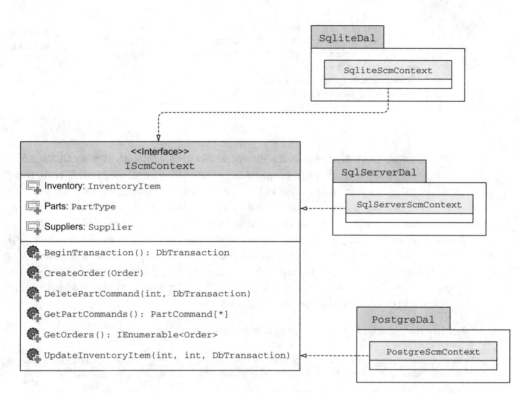

Figure 6.2   Data-access layer for SCM context using DI instead of the factory pattern

The ScmDataAccess and SqliteDal folders will have Class1.cs files in them. They won't cause any harm, but you don't need them, so feel free to remove them. In ScmDataAccess, copy the InventoryItem.cs, Order.cs, PartCommand.cs, PartType.cs, SendEmail-Command.cs, and Supplier.cs files from the previous examples. You'll need to change the namespace from WidgetScmDataAccess to ScmDataAccess because you're turning this into a product rather than a custom solution for Widget Corp.

Add a new file to ScmDataAccess called IScmContext.cs with the contents from the following listing.

Listing 6.9   Contents of the `IScmContext` interface

```
using System.Collections.Generic;
using System.Data.Common;

namespace ScmDataAccess
{
  public interface IScmContext
  {
    IEnumerable<PartType> Parts { get; }
    IEnumerable<InventoryItem> Inventory { get; }
    IEnumerable<Supplier> Suppliers { get; }
```

```
  PartCommand[] GetPartCommands();
  void DeletePartCommand(int id, DbTransaction transaction);
  void UpdateInventoryItem(int partTypeId, int count,
    DbTransaction transaction);
  void CreateOrder(Order order);
  DbTransaction BeginTransaction();
  IEnumerable<Order> GetOrders();
  }
}
```

⟵ **Array instead of IEnumerable**

BE MINDFUL THAT ENUMERABLES PROVIDE DATA AS SOON AS IT'S AVAILABLE You used GetPartCommands in chapter 5, but I didn't point out that it returns an array of PartCommand objects. By contrast, GetOrders returns an IEnumerable<Order>. The reason for this difference is that you're deleting the rows from the PartCommand table as you iterate through the list. You want the full list before you do that so that deleting the rows doesn't interfere with any locks taken during the read of the PartCommand table. IEnumerable collections can start providing objects before all of them are read. It should be clear from the API signature that all PartCommand objects are read into memory, and you do that by specifying the array.

Modify the ScmDataAccess.csproj file as follows.

Listing 6.10   ScmDataAccess.csproj contents

```
<Project Sdk="Microsoft.NET.Sdk">

  <PropertyGroup>
    <TargetFramework>netstandard1.2</TargetFramework>
  </PropertyGroup>

  <ItemGroup>
    <PackageReference Include="System.Data.Common"
                      Version="4.3.0" />
  </ItemGroup>

</Project>
```

⟵ **.NET Standard 1.2 is required for System.Data.Common.**

Now build the SqliteDal project. Change SqliteDal.csproj as follows.

Listing 6.11   SqliteDal.csproj contents

```
<Project Sdk="Microsoft.NET.Sdk">

  <PropertyGroup>
    <TargetFramework>netstandard1.3</TargetFramework>
  </PropertyGroup>

  <ItemGroup>
    <PackageReference Include="Microsoft.Data.Sqlite"
                      Version="1.1.0" />
    <PackageReference Include="Dapper"
```

⟵ **Uses .NET Standard 1.3 because you're using Dapper**

```
                            Version="1.50.2" />
    <ProjectReference Include="../ScmDataAccess/ScmDataAccess.csproj" />
  </ItemGroup>

</Project>
```

Create a file called SqliteScmContext.cs. This class will be the implementation of the IScmContext interface for the Sqlite database. Implement it as follows.

Listing 6.12 SqliteScmContext class—a SQLite implementation of IScmContext

```
using System;
using System.Collections.Generic;
using System.Data.Common;
using System.Linq;
using Dapper;
using Microsoft.Data.Sqlite;
using ScmDataAccess;

namespace SqliteDal {
  public class SqliteScmContext : IScmContext {                   There can be multiple
    private SqliteConnection connection;                          instances of SQLite
    public IEnumerable<PartType> Parts { get; private set; }           in memory.
    public IEnumerable<InventoryItem> Inventory { get; private set; }
    public IEnumerable<Supplier> Suppliers { get; private set; }

    public SqliteScmContext(SqliteConnection conn) {
      connection = conn;                                     Open can safely be
      conn.Open();                                           called multiple times.
      Parts = conn.Query<PartType>("SELECT * FROM PartType");
      Inventory = conn.Query<InventoryItem>("SELECT * FROM InventoryItem");
      foreach (var item in Inventory)
        item.Part = Parts.Single(p => p.Id == item.PartTypeId);
      Suppliers = conn.Query<Supplier>("SELECT * FROM Supplier");
      foreach (var supplier in Suppliers)
        supplier.Part = Parts.Single(p => p.Id == supplier.PartTypeId);
    }

    public PartCommand[] GetPartCommands() {
      return connection.Query<PartCommand>("SELECT * FROM PartCommand")
        .ToArray();                                ToArray reads all the values from
    }                                              the IEnumerable into an array.

    public void DeletePartCommand(int id, DbTransaction transaction) {
      connection.Execute(@"DELETE FROM PartCommands
        WHERE Id=@Id", new { Id = id }, transaction);   Uses an anonymous type
    }                                                   for the Id parameter

    public void UpdateInventoryItem(int partTypeId, int count,
      DbTransaction transaction) {
      connection.Execute(@"UPDATE InventoryItem
        SET Count=@Count
        WHERE PartTypeId=@PartTypeId",
        new { Count = count, PartTypeId = partTypeId},
```

```
          transaction);
      }

      public void CreateOrder(Order order) {                    ◁─── Same CreateOrder
        var transaction = connection.BeginTransaction();              method from earlier
        try {
          order.Id = connection.Query<int>(
            @"INSERT INTO [Order]
            (SupplierId, PartTypeId, PartCount,
            PlacedDate) VALUES (@SupplierId,
            @PartTypeId, @PartCount, @PlacedDate);
            SELECT last_insert_rowid();", order,
            transaction).First();

          connection.Execute(@"INSERT INTO SendEmailCommand
            ([To], Subject, Body) VALUES
            (@To, @Subject, @Body)", new {
              To = order.Supplier.Email,
              Subject = $"Order #{order.Id} for {order.Part.Name}",
              Body = $"Please send {order.PartCount}" +
                $" items of {order.Part.Name} to Widget Corp"
            }, transaction);

          transaction.Commit();
        }
        catch {
          transaction.Rollback();
          throw;
        }
      }

      public DbTransaction BeginTransaction() {              foreach will get all Order
        return connection.BeginTransaction();               objects in the IEnumerable,
      }                                                          just like ToArray.

      public IEnumerable<Order> GetOrders() {
        var orders = connection.Query<Order>("SELECT * FROM [Order]");
        foreach (var order in orders) {
          order.Part = Parts.Single(p => p.Id == order.PartTypeId);
          order.Supplier = Suppliers.Single(s => s.Id == order.SupplierId);
        }

        return orders;
      }
    }
  }
```

USE YIELD RETURN TO START PROCESSING DATA SOONER The GetOrders method uses foreach to supply the values for the Part and Supplier properties. Because foreach enumerates through all the Order objects, the entire result set from the SQL query has to be read. This can be a performance issue if there are a lot of orders. Instead of return orders at the end, you could put a yield return order inside the foreach loop to return the Order objects to the caller one at a time.

Now test this code out. The test project, SqliteScmTest, is going to act as the host. You'll use DI to mark SqliteScmContext as the implementation for IScmContext. The following listing shows how to add the DI libraries to SqliteScmTest.csproj.

Listing 6.13   Adding DI to SqliteScmTest.csproj

```
<Project Sdk="Microsoft.NET.Sdk">

  <PropertyGroup>
    <TargetFramework>netcoreapp2.0</TargetFramework>
  </PropertyGroup>

  <ItemGroup>
    <PackageReference Include="Microsoft.NET.Test.Sdk" Version="15.0.0" />
    <PackageReference Include="xunit" Version="2.2.0" />
    <PackageReference Include="xunit.runner.visualstudio" Version="2.2.0" />
    <PackageReference Include="Microsoft.Data.Sqlite"
                      Version="1.1.0" />
    <PackageReference
      Include="Microsoft.Extensions.DependencyInjection.Abstractions"
      Version="2.0.0" />
    <PackageReference
      Include="Microsoft.Extensions.DependencyInjection"
      Version="2.0.0" />
    <ProjectReference Include="../SqliteDal/SqliteDal.csproj" />
  </ItemGroup>

</Project>
```

Abstract types for DI → (points to `Microsoft.Extensions.DependencyInjection.Abstractions`)

Implementation of DI abstractions ← (points to `Microsoft.Extensions.DependencyInjection`)

As in the previous examples, you'll create a class fixture for your xUnit tests. The fixture is also responsible for initializing the DI settings. The full code is available online, but the important bits are shown in the next listing.

Listing 6.14   SampleScmDataFixture class using DI

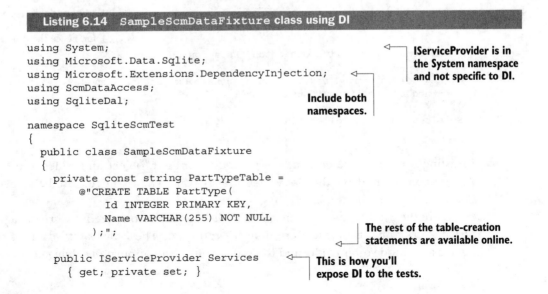

```
using System;
using Microsoft.Data.Sqlite;
using Microsoft.Extensions.DependencyInjection;
using ScmDataAccess;
using SqliteDal;

namespace SqliteScmTest
{
  public class SampleScmDataFixture
  {
    private const string PartTypeTable =
        @"CREATE TABLE PartType(
             Id INTEGER PRIMARY KEY,
             Name VARCHAR(255) NOT NULL
          );";

    public IServiceProvider Services
      { get; private set; }
```

IServiceProvider is in the System namespace and not specific to DI.

Include both namespaces.

The rest of the table-creation statements are available online.

This is how you'll expose DI to the tests.

```
public SampleScmDataFixture()
{
  var conn = new SqliteConnection(
    "Data Source=:memory:");                       Connection string specifies
  conn.Open();                                     an in-memory database
  (new SqliteCommand(PartTypeTable, conn)).ExecuteNonQuery();

  var serviceCollection = new ServiceCollection();    The rest of the table-creation
  IScmContext context = new SqliteScmContext(conn);   code is available online.
  serviceCollection.AddSingleton<IScmContext>(
    context);                                       Creates a singleton
  Services = serviceCollection.BuildServiceProvider();  instance of
}                                                      SqliteScmContext to
}                                                      implement IScmContext
}
```

In listing 6.14 you're using a singleton `SqliteScmContext` object. *Singleton* means that every time you use the `Services` property to get an implementation of `IScmContext`, you'll get the same instance.

Each `SqliteConnection` creates its own in-memory database, so if you want to share that database between tests, you'll use a singleton. But what if you don't want one test's changes to the database to interfere with another test? xUnit runs the tests in parallel and in random order, so it could cause problems if you're expecting a test to be anything other than atomic. In this case, you can have a new `SqliteScmContext` object created every time. The following listing shows how to rewrite the constructor of `SampleScmDataFixture` to use transient objects instead of a singleton.

Listing 6.15   Creating transient objects instead of using a singleton

```
public SampleScmDataFixture()
{
  var serviceCollection = new ServiceCollection();    Transient objects need to
  serviceCollection.AddTransient<IScmContext>(        be created when asked
    provider => {                                     for, hence the delegate.
    var conn = new SqliteConnection("Data Source=:memory:");
    conn.Open();
    (new SqliteCommand(PartTypeTable, conn)).ExecuteNonQuery();
    return new SqliteScmContext(conn);
  });
  Services = serviceCollection.BuildServiceProvider();
}
```

In listing 6.14 you created a new `SqliteScmContext` object and called the `AddSingleton` method on the `ServiceCollection`. When you retrieved the `IScmContext` implementation later, you got that object back.

With the `AddTransient` method in listing 6.15, you need to create a new `SqliteScmContext` object every time it's retrieved. The only way to do that is to invoke a method you provide, and to do that you use an anonymous delegate.

You're now all set to create a test and try it out. Modify the UnitTest1.cs file as follows.

Listing 6.16 Test SCM data-access layer using Dapper, SQLite, and DI

```
using System;
using System.Linq;                                            This namespace is part
using ScmDataAccess;                                          of the Abstractions
using Microsoft.Extensions.DependencyInjection;        ◁──┘  dependency.
using Xunit;

namespace SqliteScmTest
{
  public class UnitTest1 : IClassFixture<SampleScmDataFixture>
  {
    private SampleScmDataFixture fixture;
    private IScmContext context;

    public UnitTest1(SampleScmDataFixture fixture)
    {
      this.fixture = fixture;                              Extension of
      this.context = fixture.Services.                    IServiceProvider in the
        GetRequiredService<IScmContext>();          ◁──┘  Abstractions dependency
    }

    [Fact]
    public void Test1()
    {
      var orders = context.GetOrders();              Verifies that there
      Assert.Equal(0, orders.Count());          ◁──┘ are no orders
      var supplier = context.Suppliers.First();
      var part = context.Parts.First();
      var order = new Order() {
          SupplierId = supplier.Id,
          Supplier = supplier,
          PartTypeId = part.Id,
          Part = part,
          PartCount = 10,
          PlacedDate = DateTime.Now
      };                                          Creates
      context.CreateOrder(order);            ◁──┘ an order
      Assert.NotEqual(0, order.Id);
      orders = context.GetOrders();              Verifies that the
      Assert.Equal(1, orders.Count());      ◁──┘ order was created
    }
  }
}
```

BE MINDFUL OF USING SINGLETONS IN UNIT TESTS The constructor doesn't change, regardless of whether the host has set a singleton or a transient for the implementation of IScmContext. You simply ask for the implementation, and it uses whatever was specified by the host to get the object. However,

`Test1` would need to change to support singletons, because it expects the order count to be 0 initially, and 1 after the order is created. If another test created an order, and you were using a singleton `SqliteScmContext`, this test would fail. Because xUnit randomizes the test order, this might not happen all the time.

USING THE MICROSOFT DI LIBRARY WITHOUT ADDING A DEPENDENCY ON IT

Your business-logic code depends on some implementation of `IScmContext`, but it doesn't take a dependency on any particular implementation because it's using DI. This is nice, because you don't need to add a project or package reference to the SQLite or SQL Server libraries. Instead, you added a reference to the Microsoft.Extensions.DependencyInjection.Abstractions package. But it turns out you don't have to do that either.

You only add the dependency to the Abstractions library because you're using the `GetRequiredService` extension method. If you rewrite the code as follows, you can remove the reference to the Abstractions library.

> **Listing 6.17   Changing the `GetRequiredService` extension method call to an equivalent**

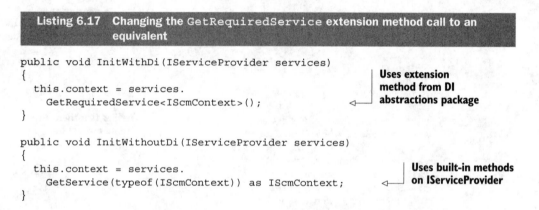

```
public void InitWithDi(IServiceProvider services)
{
  this.context = services.
    GetRequiredService<IScmContext>();          Uses extension
}                                                method from DI
                                                 abstractions package

public void InitWithoutDi(IServiceProvider services)
{
  this.context = services.
    GetService(typeof(IScmContext)) as IScmContext;   Uses built-in methods
}                                                      on IServiceProvider
```

`IServiceProvider` is used in .NET for all kinds of things, not just DI, and it's included in .NET Core. You only want to use one DI library in your application's code, so if you're publishing a NuGet package, other developers will appreciate that your library doesn't depend on any particular DI implementation.

Note that there are some advanced features of the Microsoft Extensions DI library that may not work with `IServiceProvider`. But for this simple example, it will work for both singleton and transient.

6.1.6   *Configuring the application*

Until now, you've only used in-memory databases with SQLite. That has allowed you to get away with hard-coding the connection string to `Data Source=:memory:`. But real applications have different connection strings based on the environment in which they're deployed, so hard-coding isn't an option. You'll need a way to configure the connection string.

XML CONFIGURATION IN .NET .NET Framework developers are familiar with XML configuration via the app.config file. When built, it has the same name as the executable, but appended with .config. App.config has a special section for connection strings, which are retrieved in code using the System.Configuration library. .NET Core doesn't have XML configuration built in, as of the writing of this book (but it may be added in later versions). This means .NET Core applications need to provide their own configuration.

To handle configuration in .NET Core, you'll again turn to the `Microsoft.Extensions` libraries. Modify the SqliteScmTest.csproj file as shown in the following listing to add references to the `Microsoft.Extensions.Configuration` packages.

> **Listing 6.18   Add `Microsoft.Extensions.Configuration` reference to test project**

```
<Project Sdk="Microsoft.NET.Sdk">

  <PropertyGroup>
    <TargetFramework>netcoreapp2.0</TargetFramework>
  </PropertyGroup>

  <ItemGroup>
    <PackageReference Include="Microsoft.NET.Test.Sdk" Version="15.3.0" />
    <PackageReference Include="xunit" Version="2.2.0" />
    <PackageReference Include="xunit.runner.visualstudio" Version="2.2.0" />
    <PackageReference Include="Microsoft.Data.Sqlite" Version="2.0.0" />
    <PackageReference
      Include="Microsoft.Extensions.DependencyInjection.Abstractions"
      Version="2.0.0" />
    <PackageReference Include="Microsoft.Extensions.DependencyInjection"
                      Version="2.0.0" />
    <PackageReference Include="Microsoft.Extensions.Configuration"
                      Version="2.0.0" />
    <PackageReference Include="Microsoft.Extensions.Configuration.Json"
                      Version="2.0.0" />
    <ProjectReference Include="../SqliteDal/SqliteDal.csproj" />
    <None Include="config.json">
      <CopyToOutputDirectory>PreserveNewest</CopyToOutputDirectory>
    </None>
  </ItemGroup>

</Project>
```

Configuration package →

There are lots of ways to configure; use JSON.

The `SampleScmDataFixture` class will read the configuration, because it needs the connection string in order to create the `IScmContext` object. To do this, modify the test class fixture, as follows.

> **Listing 6.19   `SampleScmDataFixture` using configuration to get the connection string**

```
using System;
using System.Collections.Generic;
using ScmDataAccess;
```

```
using Microsoft.Data.Sqlite;
using Microsoft.Extensions.Configuration;
using Microsoft.Extensions.DependencyInjection;
using Microsoft.Extensions.DependencyInjection.Abstractions;
using SqliteDal;

namespace SqliteScmTest
{
  public class SampleScmDataFixture
  {
    const string PostsTable = ...;                          ◁── Copy from the previous
                                                                chapter or from companion
                                                                code on GitHub

    const string ConnStrKey = "ConnectionString";
    const string DefConnStr = "Data Source=:memory:";       ◁── This will be your
                                                                fallback in case the
                                                                config file isn't there.

    static Dictionary<string, string> Config {get;} =       ◁── Dictionary serves as a
      new Dictionary<string, string>()                          key/value pair collection
      {
        [ConnStrKey] = DefConnStr                           ◁── Adds a key with the
      };                                                        name ConnectionString

    public IServiceProvider Services { get; private set; }

    public SampleScmDataFixture()
    {
      var configBuilder = new ConfigurationBuilder();       ─┐  This coding style is
      configBuilder                                          │  called method chaining
        .AddInMemoryCollection(Config)                      ◁┘  or fluent interface.
        .AddJsonFile("config.json", true);                  ◁── Serves as the default;
      var configRoot = configBuilder.Build();                   last one with a value wins
      var connStr = configRoot[ConnStrKey];
      var serviceCollection = new ServiceCollection();      ─┐  Retrieves the
      serviceCollection.AddTransient<IScmContext>(provider => {   connection string,
        var conn = new SqliteConnection(connStr);            │  given the key
        conn.Open();
        (new SqliteCommand(PartTypeTable, conn)).ExecuteNonQuery();

        return new SqliteScmContext(conn);                  ─┐  The rest of the code
      });                                                    │  is available online.
      Services = serviceCollection.BuildServiceProvider();
    }
  }
}
```

true indicates the file is optional.

To get the configuration, you start with the `ConfigurationBuilder`. The order in which you add configuration sources to the builder matters. The first source added is the last source tapped for configuration data. In this case, if a configuration value doesn't exist in the config.json file, it'll check the in-memory collection. If you have default values for configuration, it makes sense to put them in an in-memory collection and add it to the builder as the first source.

The `AddInMemoryCollection` method is built into the regular configuration package, but the `AddJsonFile` method is an extension method from the JSON package. There are several configuration packages, such as XML, INI, command line, and

Azure Key Vault. They all implement an extension method with the method-chaining pattern. Method chaining is a nice way to make code cleaner. Each `Add` method returns the `ConfigurationBuilder` object so another `Add` method can be applied. It prevents you from having to write the `configBuilder.` on each line.

Once all the configuration sources are applied to the builder, you call the `Build` method to get an object that implements the `IConfigurationRoot` interface. `IConfigurationRoot` inherits from `IConfiguration`, which has an indexer for getting configuration values. In this case, the indexer takes the name of the configuration property and returns the first value it finds when searching through the configuration sources in the reverse order of how they were added.

You put a value for the connection string in the in-memory collection, which serves as your default value. If the configuration library can't find the config.json file, or if the file doesn't contain a definition for `ConnectionString`, you'll still have the default value. That means you can execute this code without creating the config.json file.

To test how the JSON configuration works, create a config.json file with a connection string, as shown in the next listing.

Listing 6.20 config.json file with the SQLite connection string

```
{
  "ConnectionString": "Data Source=scm.db"          ⟵—— File-based data source
}
```

SQLite can use a file-based database instead of an in-memory database. You wouldn't commonly use file-based databases with unit tests because the tests modify the database, which would make testing results inconsistent from run to run. But it's a great way to detect whether the configuration system is finding the config.json file instead of using the default connection string.

You'll need to copy this file to the build output so that the configuration library can find it. Modify the SqliteScmTest.csproj file by adding the item group shown in the following listing.

Listing 6.21 Copy the configuration file to the output folder

```
<ItemGroup>
  <None Include="config.json">
    <CopyToOutputDirectory>PreserveNewest</CopyToOutputDirectory>
  </None>
</ItemGroup>
```

Execute the tests and check the bin/Debug/netcoreapp2.0 folder to make sure that a file called scm.db was created. The presence of this file proves that the connection string from the config.json file was used.

Configuring the connection string through a separate file is necessary for deploying to different environments. You could also use configuration to specify which implementation of `IScmContext` to use in your DI library. Some DI libraries allow you to configure them through configuration files, but because there isn't a standard way of doing that in .NET Core, there's no built-in support for configuration in the Microsoft DI extensions library.

Where to learn more about configuration

The `Microsoft.Extensions.Configuration` library has lots of options and makes it easy to chain in implementations. In this chapter, we only looked at JSON and in-memory objects. If you search on nuget.org, you'll find an array of other options, such as XML, INI files, Docker secrets, Azure Key Vault, and various key/value stores. I'm also a big fan of the command-line arguments and environment-variable implementations, because instead of giving special attention to these methods, you can treat them like any other configuration.

This book doesn't delve deeply into all the possibilities for using the `Microsoft .Extensions.Configuration` library. It's an important enough subject that I considered writing an appendix for it, but there's already a really comprehensive article on configuration online, titled "Configure an ASP.NET Core App," at http://mng.bz/3G45. It's geared toward ASP.NET Core, but it still applies universally and it covers many of the configuration providers.

6.1.7   *When to build your own data-access layer*

We've looked at two approaches for building a custom data-access layer.

The first was to use the barebones approach of executing queries by supplying parameters and reading the results into objects manually. This may be a useful technique in certain circumstances, such as for object-mapping rules that are too complicated for an ORM library, or for high-performance applications.

The second approach was to use a micro-ORM to do the tedious work. This allows you to be more productive while not sacrificing much performance. You still need to know SQL, though, and the potential for SQL injection attacks is still there, because you're writing SQL statements to a string. But you spend less time writing boilerplate code to transfer data between objects and database entities.

Both of these methods require significant design work. Different databases use different flavors of SQL, so it helps to have DI. You also need to be able to unit test your code. The code should also support configuration so that it can be easily and securely configured in all environments.

Many of the applications I've worked on haven't needed custom data-access layers. The SQL queries themselves always took more time than the ORM code. In those cases, it was more important to make developers more productive than to squeeze performance out of the code. But the more code you write, the more you need to maintain. This is why I often turn to full ORM libraries like Entity Framework.

6.2   *Entity Framework Core*

Alongside ASP.NET Core, Microsoft is building Entity Framework (EF) Core. EF Core is a .NET Core version of Entity Framework, which is a full ORM built by Microsoft for the .NET Framework. Instead of porting EF from the .NET Framework, the team decided to rewrite most of EF—much like how ASP.NET Core is a rewrite of ASP.NET. You'll explore EF briefly by using it to rewrite your supply-chain management data-access layer.

You can start by creating the projects using the following commands. You'll create the ScmDataAccess project as before, but you won't need a project for implementing each type of database. You'll include an xUnit test project called ScmDalTest to make sure everything's working:

```
cd ..
mkdir EfTest
cd EfTest
dotnet new classlib -o EfScmDataAccess
dotnet new xunit -o EfScmDalTest
```

The `PartType` class remains the same, but the `InventoryItem` and `Supplier` classes will be slightly different for EF. The changes are shown in listings 6.22 and 6.23.

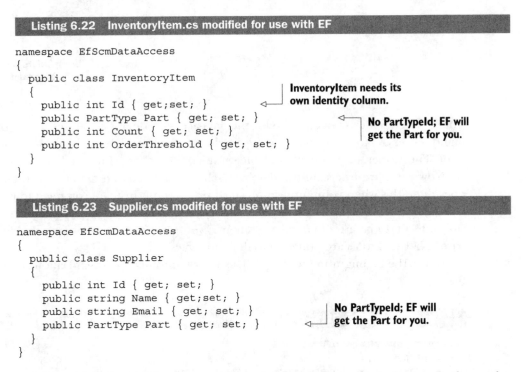

Listing 6.22   InventoryItem.cs modified for use with EF

```
namespace EfScmDataAccess
{
  public class InventoryItem
  {
    public int Id { get;set; }          ◁── InventoryItem needs its
    public PartType Part { get; set; }        own identity column.
    public int Count { get; set; }      ◁── No PartTypeId; EF will
    public int OrderThreshold { get; set; }    get the Part for you.
  }
}
```

Listing 6.23   Supplier.cs modified for use with EF

```
namespace EfScmDataAccess
{
  public class Supplier
  {
    public int Id { get; set; }
    public string Name { get;set; }
    public string Email { get; set; }
    public PartType Part { get; set; }  ◁── No PartTypeId; EF will
  }                                          get the Part for you.
}
```

Just like with Dapper, EF uses conventions so your code can look cleaner. Both can also work with custom attributes if you need to specify certain behaviors. As a micro-ORM,

Dapper doesn't know about the relationships between objects. This is where a full ORM, like EF, differentiates itself.

In listings 6.22 and 6.23, you add a `PartType` object. EF interprets this as a one-to-one relationship between an `InventoryItem` or `Supplier` object and a `PartType` object. It also understands that there are foreign keys between the associated tables. Two of the conventions EF uses are `<otherclassname><idproperty>`, indicating a relationship, and the `Id` or `<classname>Id` property, indicating an identity.

Now, let's take a look at the `EfScmContext` class in the next listing.

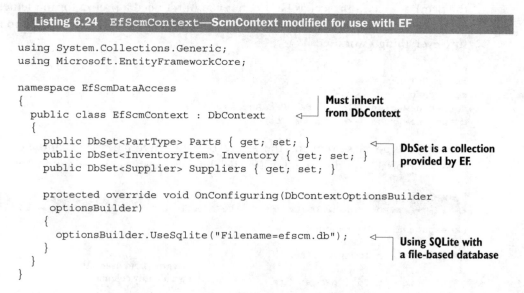

Listing 6.24   `EfScmContext`—ScmContext modified for use with EF

```
using System.Collections.Generic;
using Microsoft.EntityFrameworkCore;

namespace EfScmDataAccess
{
  public class EfScmContext : DbContext                    ⟵ Must inherit from DbContext
  {
    public DbSet<PartType> Parts { get; set; }
    public DbSet<InventoryItem> Inventory { get; set; }    ⟵ DbSet is a collection provided by EF.
    public DbSet<Supplier> Suppliers { get; set; }

    protected override void OnConfiguring(DbContextOptionsBuilder
      optionsBuilder)
    {
      optionsBuilder.UseSqlite("Filename=efscm.db");       ⟵ Using SQLite with a file-based database
    }
  }
}
```

That's basically all you need to do for the data-access code. EF generates the SQL commands necessary to perform the create, retrieve, update, and delete operations that you want. These operations are all available on the `DbSet` class, which we'll look into later.

Now you have to create the database schema, and EF can generate it for you. It doesn't do this when your application starts up, though. Instead, you need to use EF's .NET CLI migration tool to apply the schema to the database. This also means that if you want EF to create the database schema, you can't use an in-memory Sqlite database. .NET CLI tools are pulled in as dependencies.

To use the EF migration tool, the first step is to modify the EfScmDataAccess.csproj file.

Listing 6.25   EfScmDataAccess.csproj modified for EF and EF migration tool

```
<Project Sdk="Microsoft.NET.Sdk">
  <PropertyGroup>
    <TargetFramework>netcoreapp2.0</TargetFramework>       ⟵ Custom tools require netcoreapp instead of netstandard.
  </PropertyGroup>
```

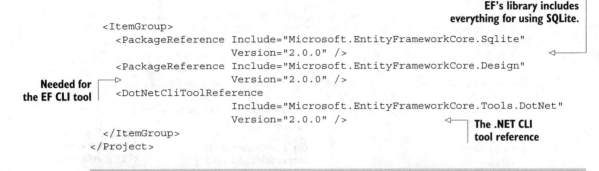

EF's library includes everything for using SQLite.

Needed for the EF CLI tool

```
    <ItemGroup>
      <PackageReference Include="Microsoft.EntityFrameworkCore.Sqlite"
                        Version="2.0.0" />
      <PackageReference Include="Microsoft.EntityFrameworkCore.Design"
                        Version="2.0.0" />
      <DotNetCliToolReference
                        Include="Microsoft.EntityFrameworkCore.Tools.DotNet"
                        Version="2.0.0" />
    </ItemGroup>
  </Project>
```

The .NET CLI tool reference

> **Custom tools in the .NET CLI**
>
> The .NET CLI is designed for extensibility. Partly that's to allow custom tools. These tools aren't accessible from the code in the project; instead, they're intended for use during the build. For example, you may wish to obfuscate your JavaScript code as part of the build process for your ASP.NET web application. That can be done with a custom tool.

6.2.1 Using EF migrations to create the database

EF has a custom tool to generate something called a *migration*, which is essentially a means of migrating your database from one version to the next. In our example, the database has no tables to start out with. The EF migration will create tables to match your model. If you were to build a new version of the code where you made changes to the model, another migration step would be added to migrate an existing database to the new schema. EF keeps track of all the migrations, so it can migrate a database from any previous version (or from scratch) to the latest version. In some cases, there are data changes as well as schema changes. EF cleverly keeps track of all that.

UPDATE MIGRATIONS DON'T WORK ON SQLITE Migrations for SQLite only work to create the database. They won't update an existing database to a new version.

CLI TOOLS ONLY WORK ON CONSOLE APPLICATIONS One of the issues with custom tools in the .NET CLI is that they can only be used on console applications. You don't want your data-access layer to be a console application, so you're using a workaround where EfScmDalTest stands in as the console application.

In order to get your migration tool to work, you'll need to modify the EfScmDalTest unit test project. The following listing shows the modified project file.

Listing 6.26 EfScmDalTest.csproj file modified to support the EF migration tool

```
<Project Sdk="Microsoft.NET.Sdk">
  <PropertyGroup>
    <TargetFramework>netcoreapp2.0</TargetFramework>
  </PropertyGroup>
```

```
<ItemGroup>
  <PackageReference Include="Microsoft.NET.Test.Sdk" Version="15.0.0" />
  <PackageReference Include="xunit" Version="2.2.0" />
  <PackageReference Include="xunit.runner.visualstudio" Version="2.2.0" />
  <PackageReference Include="Microsoft.EntityFrameworkCore.Design"
                   Version="2.0.0" />
  <PackageReference Include="System.Runtime.Serialization.Primitives"
                   Version="4.3.0" />
  <ProjectReference Include="../EfScmDataAccess/EfScmDataAccess.csproj" />
</ItemGroup>

<ItemGroup>
  <None Include="efscm.db"
        Condition="Exists('efscm.db')">
    <CopyToOutputDirectory>Always</CopyToOutputDirectory>
  </None>
</ItemGroup>
</Project>
```

Copies database file to output folder for testing

Needed to ensure the correct version of EF is referenced

Only copies if the file exists

After you've run the `dotnet build` command on both projects, you can use the EF migration tool. Change to the EfScmDataAccess folder and execute the following command:

```
dotnet ef --startup-project ../EfScmDalTest migrations add EfScmMigration
```

This creates a Migrations folder in the project with a set of C# files in it. This is the code generated by EF to perform the migration.

Now all you need to do is test this code out.

6.2.2   *Running the tests using EF*

Before you can execute the tests, you'll need to create the database. This is done using the same EF migration tool you used earlier. From the EfScmDataAccess folder, execute the following command to create the SQLite file-based database:

```
dotnet ef --startup-project ../EfScmDalTest database update
```

The tool creates the efscm.db file in the EfScmDalTest folder with the schema generated from the classes in the EfScmDataAccess project. When you build the EfScmDalTest project, this database file is copied to the build output.

Now test out this database by going back to the EfScmDalTest project and editing UnitTest1.cs as follows.

Listing 6.27   Test exercising some EF functionality

```
using System;
using System.Linq;
using Xunit;
using EfScmDataAccess;

namespace EfScmDalTest
{
```

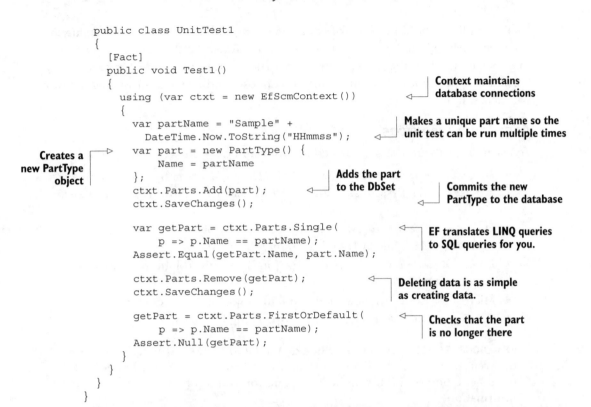

```
public class UnitTest1
{
  [Fact]
  public void Test1()
  {
    using (var ctxt = new EfScmContext())        Context maintains
    {                                            database connections
      var partName = "Sample" +
        DateTime.Now.ToString("HHmmss");         Makes a unique part name so the
      var part = new PartType() {                unit test can be run multiple times
          Name = partName
      };                              Adds the part
      ctxt.Parts.Add(part);          to the DbSet        Commits the new
      ctxt.SaveChanges();                                PartType to the database

      var getPart = ctxt.Parts.Single(                 EF translates LINQ queries
          p => p.Name == partName);                    to SQL queries for you.
      Assert.Equal(getPart.Name, part.Name);

      ctxt.Parts.Remove(getPart);              Deleting data is as simple
      ctxt.SaveChanges();                      as creating data.

      getPart = ctxt.Parts.FirstOrDefault(       Checks that the part
          p => p.Name == partName);              is no longer there
      Assert.Null(getPart);
    }
  }
}
```

Labels (left): **Creates a new PartType object**

Understanding the LINQ queries

There are two LINQ queries used in listing 6.27, and they both use the same anonymous delegate: `p => p.Name == partName`. Translated to English, this means "for a given PartType object, `p`, return `true` if the `Name` property is equal to the `partName` variable; otherwise return `false`." The `Single` extension method enumerates through all the parts in `DbSet` and makes sure that exactly one of them gets the `true` return value. If that's the case, it returns that one `PartType` object. Otherwise, it throws an exception. `FirstOrDefault` just returns the first part that matches the part name, or `null` if it doesn't find anything.

In our example, the `EfScmContext` object has the connection to the SQLite database written in its constructor, but EF has plenty of other ways to construct the context and connect it to a database. When using EF, you don't have to build a custom data-access layer with DI. The configuration extension library may be helpful, though.

`DbSet` operates much like a collection. When getting values from `DbSet`, your LINQ queries will be interpreted into SQL statements by EF. So just because you have thousands of parts in your inventory, doesn't mean thousands of `PartType` objects will be held in memory. EF keeps track of the objects you retrieve in the context. If you make a change to an object and save it to `DbSet`, EF detects the change you made and generates the SQL `UPDATE` statement.

EF handles a lot of the work of communicating with a database—it has many providers to work with all kinds of databases. But regardless of the database you connect to, the code remains the same. Developers write queries using LINQ instead of SQL. For many applications, this can significantly boost productivity over writing a custom data-access layer.

Additional resources

To learn more about what we covered in this chapter, try the following resources:

- *Design Patterns: Elements of Reusable Object-Oriented Software* by Erich Gamma, Richard Helm, Ralph Johnson, and John Vlissides (Addison-Wesley Professional, 1994)
- *Dependency Injection in .NET*, second edition, by Steven van Deursen and Mark Seemann (Manning, 2018)—http://mng.bz/xSnW
- *Entity Framework Core in Action* by Jon P Smith (Manning, 2018)—http://mng.bz/cOH4
- Microsoft's Entity Framework documentation—http://docs.efproject.net
- Configuration in ASP.NET Core—http://mng.bz/30T8

> **EF RESOURCES FOR .NET FRAMEWORK APPLY IN MOST CASES**   Although there are differences between the Framework and Core versions of Entity Framework, documentation on EF for the .NET Framework should have plenty of useful information.

Summary

In this chapter you learned about the Dapper and Entity Framework object-relational mapping libraries available in .NET Core. We covered these key concepts:

- Eliminating most boilerplate object-table mapping code with an ORM
- Using dependency injection to separate different data-access implementations
- Applying many kinds of configuration to .NET Core applications with extensions libraries for .NET Standard
- Executing custom tools with the .NET CLI

Here are some important techniques to remember from this chapter:

- The Microsoft.Extensions family has lots of useful libraries built on the .NET Standard.
- Micro-ORMs like Dapper can increase productivity without sacrificing performance.
- There are many options for configuration in .NET Core applications, including fallbacks.
- Some libraries, like Entity Framework, come with custom tools that can be used from the .NET CLI.

- In order to use custom tools on a library, specify another project with an entry point (like an xUnit test project) when running the tool.

ORM libraries increase developer productivity in many cases. Choosing an ORM depends on many factors, and we covered two different types in this chapter. There are a lot of data-access libraries out there, and many of them should make their way to .NET Standard in the future. You also learned about some useful stuff in the Microsoft.Extensions family of libraries, such as configuration and dependency injection. Other extensions libraries will be used later in the book.

Although relational data is important for many applications, not all data is in relational stores. In the next chapter we'll cover how to get data from other services over a network.

Creating a microservice

7

This chapter covers

- Writing web services with ASP.NET Core
- Making HTTP requests to web services
- Introduction to creating microservices

My personal blog is written in .NET Core (http://mode19.net). Originally I wrote each post in its own page. Those pages were all part of the source code of the blog and had corresponding metadata in a database. But as the number of posts increased, the site became hard to manage, especially since the older pages were written using older libraries and techniques. The contents of the blog posts didn't change—only the formatting changed.

That's when I decided to convert my blog posts to Markdown. Markdown allows me to write just the content of the blog post without having to worry about the formatting. That way, I could store my blog posts in a database or BLOB storage and not have to rebuild the web application every time I posted a new entry. I could also convert every page on the blog to use the latest libraries I wanted to try out, without touching the posts' content.

To handle the storing of posts and conversion from Markdown to HTML, I created a microservice. To describe what a microservice is, I'll borrow some of the characteristics listed in Christian Horsdal Gammelgaard's book *Microservices in .NET Core* (Manning, 2017). A microservice is

- Responsible for a single piece of functionality (blog posts)
- Individually deployable (separate from a blog web app)
- Singularly responsible for its datastore (creates, updates, and deletes posts in Azure Blob Storage)
- Replaceable (another service can replace it as long as it implements the same interface)

In this chapter, you'll create a blog post microservice. The data store will be Azure Blob Storage. I picked Azure Blob Storage because it presents a challenge in that HTTP requests made to it need special headers and security information. There's support for Azure Blob Storage in the Azure SDK, which is available for .NET Standard. But as an exercise, you'll make the HTTP requests directly.

7.1 Writing an ASP.NET web service

In chapter 2 you used the `dotnet new web` template. That template is tuned more for websites than web services. You'll start with that template and make the necessary adjustments to turn it into a web service-only project.

But before you begin, let's find something interesting for your service to do.

7.1.1 Converting Markdown to HTML

There are many implementations of Markdown, and several are available in .NET Core or .NET Standard. The library you'll be using is called Markdown Lite.

You can see how it works by creating an empty web application. Create a new folder called MarkdownLiteTest and run the `dotnet new console` command in it. Add a reference to `Microsoft.DocAsCode.MarkdownLite` in the project file, as follows.

Listing 7.1 Adding Markdown Lite as a package reference

```
<Project Sdk="Microsoft.NET.Sdk">
  <PropertyGroup>
    <OutputType>Exe</OutputType>
    <TargetFramework>netcoreapp2.0</TargetFramework>
  </PropertyGroup>

  <ItemGroup>
    <PackageReference Include="Microsoft.DocAsCode.MarkdownLite"
                      Version="2.13.1" />         ⟵┐ Or pick a later version
  </ItemGroup>                                      └ from nuget.org
</Project>
```

Now try out some sample code. The following listing shows a test to convert simple Markdown text into HTML and write the HTML to the console.

Listing 7.2   Test console application using Markdown Lite

```
using System;
using Microsoft.DocAsCode.MarkdownLite;

namespace MarkdownLiteTest
{
  public class Program
  {
    public static void Main()
    {
      string source = @"
Building Your First .NET Core Applications
=======

In this chapter, we will learn how to setup our development environment,
create an application, and
";

      var builder = new GfmEngineBuilder(new Options());
      var engine = builder.CreateEngine(              ⟵ Renders
        new HtmlRenderer());                                to HTML
      var result = engine.Markup(source);   ⟵┐ Outputs to
      Console.WriteLine(result);              ┘ a string
    }
  }
}
```

The output should look like this:

```
<h1 id="building-your-first-net-core-applications">
Building Your First .NET Core Applications</h1>
<p>In this chapter, we will learn how to setup our development environment,
create an application, and</p>
```

Markdown Lite doesn't add <html> or <body> tags, which is nice for inserting the generated HTML into a template.

Now that you know how to use Markdown Lite, you can put it into a web service.

7.1.2   *Creating an ASP.NET web service*

In chapter 2 you created an ASP.NET Core service using Kestrel and some simple request-handling code that returned a "Hello World" response for all incoming requests. In this chapter's example, you'll need to process the input that comes in. ASP.NET has some built-in mechanisms to route requests based on URI and HTTP verb that you'll take advantage of.

Start by creating a new folder called MarkdownService and running `dotnet new web`. Modify the project file as shown in the following listing.

Listing 7.3 Modifying the default web template project file

```
<Project Sdk="Microsoft.NET.Sdk.Web">

  <PropertyGroup>
    <TargetFramework>netcoreapp2.0</TargetFramework>
  </PropertyGroup>

  <ItemGroup>
    <PackageReference Include="Microsoft.AspNetCore.All"
                      Version="2.0.0" />
    <PackageReference Include="Microsoft.DocAsCode.MarkdownLite"
                      Version="2.13.1" />
  </ItemGroup>

</Project>
```

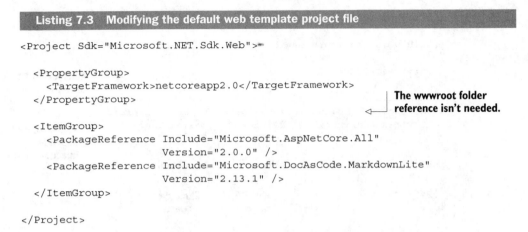
The wwwroot folder reference isn't needed.

The Program.cs file is responsible for starting the web server. Its code can be simplified to what's shown in the next listing.

Listing 7.4 Program.cs for the Markdown Lite service starts the web server

```
using Microsoft.AspNetCore;
using Microsoft.AspNetCore.Hosting;

namespace MarkdownService
{
  public class Program
  {
    public static void Main(string[] args)
    {
      BuildWebHost(args).Run();
    }

    public static IWebHost BuildWebHost(string[] args) =>
      WebHost.CreateDefaultBuilder(args)
        .UseStartup<Startup>()
        .Build();
  }
}
```

The Startup class is where you'll configure ASP.NET MVC. MVC handles the incoming requests and routes them depending on configuration and convention. Modify the Startup.cs file to look like the code in the next listing.

Listing 7.5 A Startup.cs file for the Markdown Lite service that sets up MVC

```
using Microsoft.AspNetCore.Builder;
using Microsoft.Extensions.DependencyInjection;
using Microsoft.DocAsCode.MarkdownLite;

namespace MarkdownService
{
```

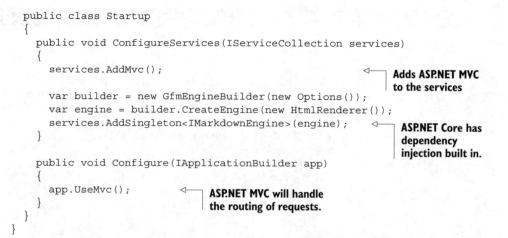

```
public class Startup
{
  public void ConfigureServices(IServiceCollection services)
  {
    services.AddMvc();                                          ◁── Adds ASP.NET MVC
                                                                    to the services
    var builder = new GfmEngineBuilder(new Options());
    var engine = builder.CreateEngine(new HtmlRenderer());
    services.AddSingleton<IMarkdownEngine>(engine);             ◁── ASP.NET Core has
  }                                                                 dependency
                                                                    injection built in.
  public void Configure(IApplicationBuilder app)
  {
    app.UseMvc();          ◁── ASP.NET MVC will handle
  }                            the routing of requests.
}
}
```

> **MVC and Web API**
>
> MVC stands for "model, view, controller," which is a pattern for building web applications. ASP.NET MVC was introduced as an alternative to the old WebForms approach for building web applications. Neither was intended for REST services, so another product called Web API was introduced for that purpose. In ASP.NET Core, Web API and MVC have been merged into one, and WebForms no longer exists.

The IMarkdownEngine object is created at startup and added as a singleton to the dependency injection. ASP.NET Core uses the same Microsoft.Extensions.DependencyInjection library you used in chapter 6.

The next thing you need to do is create a controller. MVC uses reflection to find your controllers, and it routes incoming requests to them. You just need to follow the conventions. Create a new file called MdlController.cs and add the following code.

Listing 7.6   MdlController accepts Markdown text and returns HTML

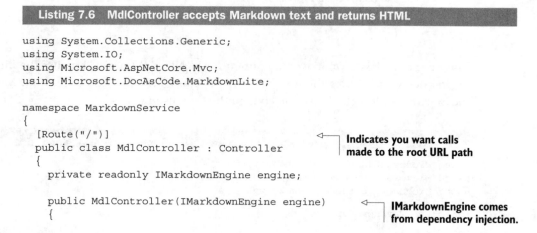

```
using System.Collections.Generic;
using System.IO;
using Microsoft.AspNetCore.Mvc;
using Microsoft.DocAsCode.MarkdownLite;

namespace MarkdownService
{
  [Route("/")]                                          ◁── Indicates you want calls
  public class MdlController : Controller                   made to the root URL path
  {
    private readonly IMarkdownEngine engine;

    public MdlController(IMarkdownEngine engine)         ◁── IMarkdownEngine comes
    {                                                        from dependency injection.
```

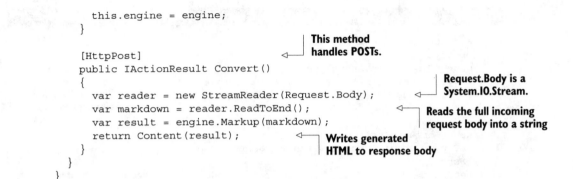

```
        this.engine = engine;
    }

    [HttpPost]                                          This method
    public IActionResult Convert()                      handles POSTs.
    {
        var reader = new StreamReader(Request.Body);    Request.Body is a
        var markdown = reader.ReadToEnd();              System.IO.Stream.
        var result = engine.Markup(markdown);           Reads the full incoming
        return Content(result);         Writes generated request body into a string
    }                                   HTML to response body
  }
}
```

7.1.3 Testing the web service with Curl

After executing `dotnet run`, you should have a web server running on http://local-host:5000. But if you navigate to this URL with a browser, you'll get a 404. That's because in listing 7.6 you only created an `HttpPost` method. There's no `HttpGet` method. In order to test the service, you need to be able to send a `POST` with some Markdown text in it.

The quickest way to do this with Curl. Curl is a command-line tool that you'll find very useful when developing web services and applications. It handles many more protocols than HTTP and HTTPS.

> **HOW TO GET CURL** Curl is available on all platforms. Visit https://curl.haxx.se/download.html to download the version for your OS.

For our purposes, you'll create an HTTP `POST` with the body contents taken from a file. First, create a file, such as test.md, with some Markdown text in it. Then execute a curl command like this one:

```
curl -X POST --data-binary @test.md http://localhost:5000
this was styled as tip
```

> **PRESERVE NEWLINES IN THE MARKDOWN FILE** Use `--data-binary` instead of `-d` to preserve newlines.

If all goes correctly, the generated HTML should be printed on the command line. Curl made it possible to test your web service before writing the client code.

Now that you have a working service, let's look at how a client can make requests to web services in .NET Core.

7.2 Making HTTP calls

You'll use the Markdown Lite service created in the previous section to test with, so leave it running and open another terminal. Go to the MarkdownLiteTest folder created earlier. Add a test.md file to this folder with some sample Markdown (or copy the file you used in the previous section). To make this file available while running the MarkdownLiteTest application, you'll need to copy it to the output folder, as follows.

Listing 7.7   Copy test.md to project output, remove Markdown Lite reference

```
<Project Sdk="Microsoft.NET.Sdk">
  <PropertyGroup>
    <OutputType>Exe</OutputType>
    <TargetFramework>netcoreapp2.0</TargetFramework>
  </PropertyGroup>

  <ItemGroup>
    <None Include="test.md">
      <CopyToOutputDirectory>PreserveNewest</CopyToOutputDirectory>
    </None>
  </ItemGroup>
</Project>
```

Remove Markdown
Lite dependency

Recall from chapter 3 how to
copy files to project output.

Next, write the code that will POST data to an HTTP endpoint. The best option for
this in .NET Core is HttpClient. Modify the Program.cs file to add the code from
listing 7.8.

> **WEBCLIENT VS. HTTPCLIENT**   .NET Framework veterans may remember Web-
> Client, which was originally not included in .NET Core because Http-
> Client is a better option. Developers asked for WebClient to be included
> because not all old WebClient code can be ported to HttpClient easily.
> But when writing new code, stick with HttpClient.

Listing 7.8   Using HttpClient to call a web service, POST a file, and read the response

```
using System;
using System.IO;
using System.Net.Http;

namespace MarkdownLiteTest
{
  public class Program
  {
    public static void Main(string[] args)
    {
      var client = new HttpClient();
      var response = client.PostAsync(
        "http://localhost:5000",
        new StreamContent(
          new FileStream("test.md", FileMode.Open))
        ).Result;
      string markdown = response.Content.
        ReadAsStringAsync().Result;
      Console.WriteLine(markdown);
    }
  }
}
```

Can optionally set a base address
in the HttpClient constructor

Reads the test.md markdown
file into an HttpContent object

Result blocks until
the PostAsync
operation is finished

ReadAsStringAsync returns a Task
object; call Result to get the string.

The StreamContent object inherits from HttpContent. You can provide any stream
to StreamContent, which means you don't have to keep the full content of the POST

in memory. The `PostAsync` method is also nice if you don't want to block the thread while waiting for the `POST` to complete.

In this example, you didn't take advantage of the async features of .NET, but to build high-performance microservice applications, you need to understand how to use those features.

7.3 *Making the service asynchronous*

In listing 7.8 you explicitly call `.Result` on the returned values of two async methods: `PostAsync` and `ReadAsStringAsync`. These methods return `Task` objects. Your client doesn't need to be asynchronous because it's only doing one thing. It doesn't matter if you block the main thread, because there's nothing else that needs to happen.

Services, in contrast, can't afford to tie up threads waiting for something. Let's take a closer look at the service code that converts the posted Markdown to HTML in the next listing.

> **Listing 7.9 Synchronous `Convert` method blocks a thread waiting for request content**

```
[HttpPost]
public IActionResult Convert()
{
  var reader = new StreamReader(Request.Body);
  var markdown = reader.ReadToEnd();          ◁─┐ This is the call that
  var result = engine.Markup(markdown);         │ blocks the thread.
  return Content(result);
}
```

The problem with blocking the thread to read the incoming HTTP request is that the client may not be executing as quickly as you think. If the client has a slow upload speed or is malicious, it could take minutes to upload all the data. Meanwhile, the service has a whole thread stuck on this client. Add enough of these clients, and soon you'll run out of available threads or memory.

The solution to this problem is to rely on two powerful C# constructs called `async` and `await`. The following listing shows how you could rewrite the `Convert` method to be asynchronous.

> **Listing 7.10 Asynchronous `Convert` method that doesn't block the thread**

```
[HttpPost]
public async Task<IActionResult> Convert()      ◁─┐ Marks the method as async and
{                                                  │ returns a Task or Task<T>
  using (var reader = new StreamReader(Request.Body))  ◁─┐
  {                                                       │ This using block is just to
    var markdown = await reader.ReadToEndAsync();  ◁─┐   │ clean up the reader; it's
    var result = engine.Markup(markdown);            │   │ not necessary for Async.
    return Content(result);                          │
  }                         Awaits on the result ────┘
}                           of ReadToEndAsync()
```

HOW DOES ASYNC/AWAIT WORK? The `async/await` constructs are a bit of compiler magic that make asynchronous code much easier to write. The `await` signals a point in the method where the code will need to wait for something. The C# compiler will split the `Convert` method into two methods, with the second being invoked when the awaited item is finished. This all happens behind the scenes, but if you're curious about how it works, try viewing the IL (the .NET Intermediate Language—the stuff inside a .NET DLL) generated for `async` methods in the ILDASM tool that comes with Visual Studio.

Now if the client uploads its request content slowly, the only impact is that it will hold a socket open. The layers beneath your service code will gather the network I/O and buffer it until the request content length is reached. This means your service can handle more requests with fewer threads.

Writing asynchronous code becomes more important when your service depends on other services, which limit operations to the speed of the network. You'll see an example of this in the next section.

7.4 *Getting data from Azure Blob Storage*

Now that you've figured out how to convert Markdown to HTML, you can incorporate Azure Blob Storage for storing posts. Instead of posting data to the Markdown service, you'll send it a BLOB name and have it return the converted HTML. You can do this by adding a GET method to your service.

Before going into that, though, you need to pull some values from configuration.

7.4.1 *Getting values from configuration*

Your code uses the Microsoft.Extensions.Configuration library, which you learned about in chapter 6. You learned how to add a config.json file to your project, copy it to the build output, and add the dependency on the Configuration library. Do that now for this project, and consult chapter 6 if you need any tips.

In order to read the config, you'll need to create an `IConfigurationRoot` object, as follows.

Listing 7.11   Creating `IConfigurationRoot` object to get the configuration on startup

```
using Microsoft.AspNetCore.Builder;
using Microsoft.Extensions.Configuration;                  ◁──┐  Add reference to
using Microsoft.Extensions.DependencyInjection;               │  configuration library
using Microsoft.DocAsCode.MarkdownLite;

namespace MarkdownService
{
  public class Startup
  {
    public void ConfigureServices(IServiceCollection services)
    {
      services.AddMvc();
```

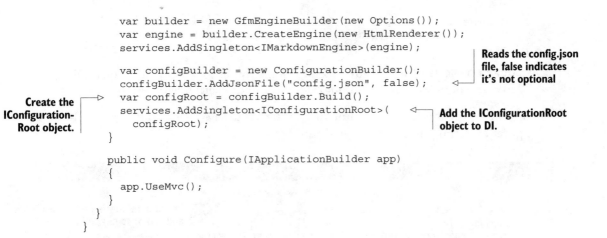

```
            var builder = new GfmEngineBuilder(new Options());
            var engine = builder.CreateEngine(new HtmlRenderer());
            services.AddSingleton<IMarkdownEngine>(engine);

            var configBuilder = new ConfigurationBuilder();
            configBuilder.AddJsonFile("config.json", false);
            var configRoot = configBuilder.Build();
            services.AddSingleton<IConfigurationRoot>(
                configRoot);
        }

        public void Configure(IApplicationBuilder app)
        {
            app.UseMvc();
        }
    }
}
```

Reads the config.json file, false indicates it's not optional

Create the IConfiguration-Root object.

Add the IConfigurationRoot object to DI.

In listing 7.11 you didn't introduce a fallback for the configuration. That's why the config.json file isn't optional.

You'll need to read the config values in the `MdlController` class. The code for doing this is shown next.

Listing 7.12 Code to read the Azure storage account information from configuration

```
using Microsoft.Extensions.Configuration;

public class MdlController : Controller
{
    private static readonly HttpClient client = new HttpClient();
    private readonly IMarkdownEngine engine;
    private readonly string AccountName;
    private readonly string AccountKey;
    private readonly string BlobEndpoint;
    private readonly string ServiceVersion;

    public MdlController(IMarkdownEngine engine,
        IConfigurationRoot configRoot)
    {
        this.engine = engine;
        AccountName = configRoot["AccountName"];
        AccountKey = configRoot["AccountKey"];
        BlobEndpoint = configRoot["BlobEndpoint"];
        ServiceVersion = configRoot["ServiceVersion"];
    }
```

Add the using for the config library.

The configRoot object will come from DI.

Extract the config values.

The config.json file will have the four properties read in listing 7.12. The next listing shows an example config file.

Listing 7.13 Example config.json file for the Markdown service

```
{
    "AccountName": "myaccount",
    "AccountKey": "<accountkey>",
```

```
    "BlobEndpoint": "https://myaccount.blob.core.windows.net/",
    "ServiceVersion": "2009-09-19"
}
```

COPY CONFIG.JSON TO OUTPUT FOLDER   Don't forget to modify the project file to copy config.json to the output folder as you did earlier with test.md.

If you're using the Azure emulator, often referred to as *development storage,* use the configuration settings in the following listing.

Listing 7.14   config.json for connecting to the Azure emulator

```
{
  "AccountName": "devstoreaccount1",                         The account key is well known
  "AccountKey":                                       ◁──    and can be found online.
    "Eby8vdM02xNOcqFlqUwJPLlmEtlCDXJ1OUzFT50uSRZ6IFsuFq2UVErCz4I6tq/
    K1SZFPTOtr/KBHBeksoGMGw==",
  "BlobEndpoint": "http://127.0.0.1:10000/devstoreaccount1/",
  "ServiceVersion": "2009-09-19"
}
```

7.4.2   Creating the GetBlob method

In the following listing, you expect the caller to pass in the container and BLOB names in the query string. The method makes a request to Azure Blob Storage to retrieve the Markdown content. Your code uses Markdown Lite to convert the result to HTML and sends the response to the caller. Add this code to the `MdlController` class.

Listing 7.15   `GetBlob` converts Markdown content from Azure Blob Storage to HTML

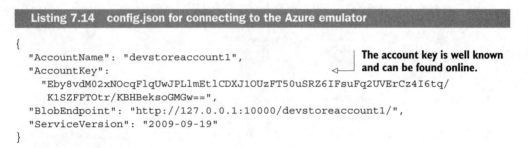

```
using System;
using System.Net.Http;
using System.Security.Cryptography;          ◁──    Add these usings to
using System.Text;                                  the top of the file.
using System.Threading.Tasks;
using Microsoft.Extensions.Configuration;
                                                    HttpGet indicates this method
[HttpGet]                                     ◁──    is hit when using a GET verb.
public async Task<IActionResult> GetBlob(
  string container, string blob)              ◁──    Parameters can be specified in the
{                                                   query string or request body.
  var path = $"{container}/{blob}";
  var rfcDate = DateTime.UtcNow.ToString("R");
  var devStorage = BlobEndpoint.StartsWith("http://127.0.0.1:10000") ?
                     $"/{AccountName}" : "";
  var signme =  "GET\n\n\n\n\n\n\n\n\n\n\n" +   ◁──   The empty lines are header
                "x-ms-blob-type:BlockBlob\n" +       properties you don't want to specify.
                $"x-ms-date:{rfcDate}\n" +
                $"x-ms-version:{ServiceVersion}\n" +  ◁──   ServiceVersion comes
                $"/{AccountName}/{path}";                  from config.json.
  var uri = new Uri(BlobEndpoint + path);      ◁──
                                                   BlobEndpoint comes
                                                   from config.json.
```

Storage emulator computes URI slightly differently

```
var request = new HttpRequestMessage(HttpMethod.Get, uri);
request.Headers.Add("x-ms-blob-type", "BlockBlob");          Notice the same
request.Headers.Add("x-ms-date", rfcDate);                    properties
request.Headers.Add("x-ms-version", ServiceVersion);    ⟵    in signme string.

string signature = "";                              AccountKey comes from config.json,
using (var sha = new HMACSHA256(                        used to created signature
  System.Convert.FromBase64String(AccountKey)))                ⟵
{                                                   Use SHA to create the signature
  var data = Encoding.UTF8.GetBytes(signme);  ⟵    in the authorization property.
  signature = System.Convert.ToBase64String(sha.ComputeHash(data));
}

var authHeader = $"SharedKey {AccountName}:{signature}";   AccountName comes
request.Headers.Add("Authorization", authHeader);    ⟵    from config.json.

var response = await client.SendAsync(request);      ⟵    Sending the request
var markdown = await response.Content.ReadAsStringAsync();   and receiving the
var result = engine.Markup(markdown);                        response are both
return Content(result);                                      async methods.
}
```

The code in listing 7.15 can seem overwhelming, so let's break it down into manageable pieces. The first part is the method signature, shown in the next listing.

Listing 7.16 Signature for the `GetBlob` method

```
[HttpGet]
public async Task<IActionResult> GetBlob(
  string container, string blob)
```

The `HttpGet` attribute tells ASP.NET MVC that `GetBlob` receives client HTTP requests using the GET verb. The parameters of the method, `container` and `blob`, are expected to be passed from the client in the query string. For example, the client could make a GET request to http://localhost:5000?container=somecontainer&blob =test.md. MVC will extract the name/value pairs from the query string and match them to the method parameters.

Most of the code in `GetBlob` creates an HTTP request to send to Azure Blob Storage. You'll need an Azure storage account to test this (Azure has a 30-day free trial if you don't already have a subscription). There's also an Azure storage emulator available as part of the Azure SDK, but it only works on Windows. Finally, there's an open source, cross-platform Azure storage emulator called Azurite, which you can find at https://github.com/arafato/azurite.

The GET blob request is encapsulated in an `HttpRequestMessage` object. Put the code that creates that object into its own method, as shown in the next listing.

Listing 7.17 Create an `HttpRequestMessage` GET BLOB request to Azure storage

```
private HttpRequestMessage CreateRequest(
  HttpMethod verb, string container, string blob)
```

```
{
    var path = $"{container}/{blob}";
    var rfcDate = DateTime.UtcNow.ToString("R");
    var uri = new Uri(BlobEndpoint + path);
    var request = new HttpRequestMessage(verb, uri);
    request.Headers.Add("x-ms-blob-type", "BlockBlob");
    request.Headers.Add("x-ms-date", rfcDate);
    request.Headers.Add("x-ms-version", ServiceVersion);

    var authHeader = GetAuthHeader(
      verb.ToString().ToUpper(), path, rfcDate);
    request.Headers.Add("Authorization", authHeader);

    return request;
}
```

Constructs the URI → (points to `var uri = new Uri(BlobEndpoint + path);`)

The date and time of the request in RFCII23 format ← (points to `var rfcDate` line)

Indicates BLOB type— blocks are a good default ← (points to `x-ms-blob-type` line)

Azure storage version ← (points to `x-ms-version` line)

Covered later in this section ← (points to `var authHeader = GetAuthHeader(` line)

Although this chapter focuses on making requests to Azure Blob Storage, the same techniques apply to other HTTP services. You'll be writing several operations against Azure Blob Storage in this chapter, so you'll be able to reuse CreateRequest in other operations.

Azure BLOB containers have different levels of exposure. It's possible to expose the contents publicly so that a request doesn't need authentication. In this case, the container is private. The only way to access it is to use a shared key to create an authentication header in the request. In listing 7.17, the code for creating the authentication header is split into a separate method called GetAuthHeader. The code for GetAuthHeader is shown in the following listing.

Listing 7.18 Create authentication header for Azure storage using shared account key

```
private string GetAuthHeader(string verb, string path, string rfcDate)
{
    var devStorage = BlobEndpoint.StartsWith("http://127.0.0.1:10000") ?
                    $"/{AccountName}" : "";
    var signme = $"{verb}\n\n\n\n\n\n\n\n\n\n\n\n" +
                "x-ms-blob-type:BlockBlob\n" +
                $"x-ms-date:{rfcDate}\n" +
                $"x-ms-version:{ServiceVersion}\n" +
                $"/{AccountName}{devStorage}/{path}";

    string signature;
    using (var sha = new HMACSHA256(
      System.Convert.FromBase64String(AccountKey)))
    {
      var data = Encoding.UTF8.GetBytes(signme);
      signature = System.Convert.ToBase64String(
        sha.ComputeHash(data));
    }

    return $"SharedKey {AccountName}:{signature}";
}
```

The newlines are fields you don't need to specify. ← (points to `var signme` block)

The account key is available in the Azure portal. ← (points to `FromBase64String(AccountKey)` line)

Hashes the bytes from the signme string with the account key ← (points to `sha.ComputeHash(data)` line)

There's also SharedKeyLite, which has fewer newlines. ← (points to `return $"SharedKey` line)

The aim of this method is to produce a hashed version of the request header. The server will perform the same hash and compare it against the value you sent. If they don't match, it will report an error and tell you what content it hashed. This helps in case you've mistyped something.

LEARN MORE ABOUT AUTHENTICATING WITH AZURE Authentication for Azure storage is covered in depth in "Authentication for the Azure Storage Services" at http://mng.bz/7j0B.

The previous helper methods have made the `GetBlob` method much shorter. The updated version is shown in the next listing.

Listing 7.19 `GetBlob` **using helper methods to create HTTP request**

```
[HttpGet]
public async Task<IActionResult> GetBlob(string container, string blob)
{
  var request = CreateRequest(HttpMethod.Get, container, blob);

  var response = await client.SendAsync(request);
  var markdown = await response.Content.ReadAsStringAsync();
  var result = engine.Markup(markdown);
  return Content(result);
}
```

7.4.3 *Testing the new Azure storage operation*

The Markdown service now has a GET operation. The first step in testing it is to put a Markdown file in an Azure BLOB container. There are many tools for doing this, including the Azure portal. You'll also need to get the account name and key from the Azure portal to populate the values in the config.json file.

Once the Markdown files are in place, you can make a request to the Markdown service with a console application. The following listing shows the contents of the Program.cs file in a console application that tests the new Azure storage operation.

Listing 7.20 **Console application that calls Markdown service's Azure storage operation**

```
using System;
using System.IO;
using System.Net.Http;

namespace ConsoleApplication
{
  public class Program
  {
    public static void Main(string[] args)
    {
      var client = new HttpClient();
      var response = client.GetAsync(
        "http://localhost:5000?container=somecontainer&blob=test.md")
        .Result;
```

```
        string markdown = response.Content.
          ReadAsStringAsync().Result;
        Console.WriteLine(markdown);
      }
    }
}
```

Conversely, you can use the following curl command:

```
curl http://localhost:5000?container=somecontainer&blob=test.md
```

> **USE QUOTES ON WINDOWS** The quotations around the URL in listing 7.20 are
> necessary for Windows. The & symbol has a special meaning in Windows com-
> mand-line scripting.

7.5   *Uploading and receiving uploaded data*

Your Markdown service isn't technically a microservice. One of the key principles of a
microservice is that it has its own isolated data source. In the previous section, you
added BLOBs to the Azure storage account either through the Azure portal or an
external tool.

In order to isolate the data source for the Markdown service, you'll need to add
methods to upload new BLOBs and change existing BLOBs. To achieve this, you'll
add a PUT operation, as in the following listing.

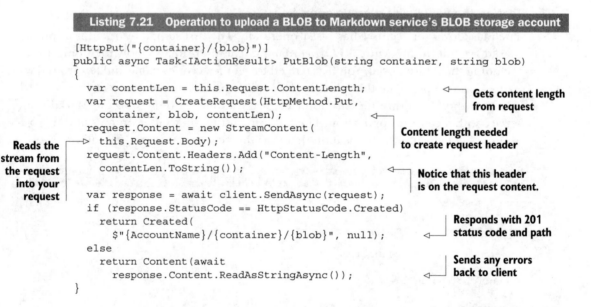

Listing 7.21   Operation to upload a BLOB to Markdown service's BLOB storage account

```
[HttpPut("{container}/{blob}")]
public async Task<IActionResult> PutBlob(string container, string blob)
{
  var contentLen = this.Request.ContentLength;                    ← Gets content length
  var request = CreateRequest(HttpMethod.Put,                        from request
    container, blob, contentLen);                      ←
  request.Content = new StreamContent(           Content length needed
    this.Request.Body);                          to create request header
  request.Content.Headers.Add("Content-Length",
    contentLen.ToString());                          ←  Notice that this header
                                                         is on the request content.
  var response = await client.SendAsync(request);
  if (response.StatusCode == HttpStatusCode.Created)
    return Created(                                  Responds with 201
      $"{AccountName}/{container}/{blob}", null);  ←  status code and path
  else
    return Content(await                             Sends any errors
      response.Content.ReadAsStringAsync());      ←  back to client
}
```

(margin note at left of StreamContent lines:) **Reads the stream from the request into your request**

In the PutBlob method, you're essentially taking a PUT request and creating your
own request with the right authorization header for Azure Blob Storage. In a production service, you wouldn't expose a secure resource through an insecure one—secur-
ing services with ASP.NET Core is a deep subject that you can read about in *ASP.NET*

Core in Action by Andrew Lock (Manning, 2018). The purpose of this example is to explore how PUT operations work.

An HTTP PUT operation is considered *idempotent*, which means that no matter how many times you call it, it will result in the same outcome. If you PUT the same BLOB multiple times, each call will return a 201—a duplicate call won't result in adverse effects. Contrast this with POST, which isn't idempotent. If you perform a POST and it times out, the state of the resource is unknown, and you'd need to make a GET call to verify the state of the resource before retrying the POST. In the Markdown service, you use POST only for an operation that doesn't save data.

The content of the Markdown file that the client is requesting to store in your service is in the body of the request. You can get a Stream with the content data directly from this.Request.Body. Rather than measure the length of the content yourself, you get it from the incoming request using this.Request.ContentLength. The content length is a required header for PUT operations to Azure Blob Storage, but you'll notice that it's added to Request.Content.Headers instead of Request.Headers. Content headers include things like length, type, and encoding. This is probably because these headers are special and are indicated by position rather than name. To see what I mean by that, look at how the authentication header is created in the next listing.

Listing 7.22 GetAuthHeader method modified to allow content-length specification

```
private string GetAuthHeader(string verb, string path,
   string rfcDate, long? contentLen)            ←── Optional value for content length
{
   var devStorage = BlobEndpoint.StartsWith("http://127.0.0.1:10000") ?
                    $"/{AccountName}" : "";
   var signme = $"{verb}\n\n\n" +               ←┐ Content length is three
                $"{contentLen}\n" +              │ lines after the verb
                "\n\n\n\n\n\n\n\n" +
                "x-ms-blob-type:BlockBlob\n" +
                $"x-ms-date:{rfcDate}\n" +
                $"x-ms-version:{ServiceVersion}\n" +
                $"/{AccountName}{devStorage}/{path}";

   string signature;
   using (var sha = new
      HMACSHA256(System.Convert.FromBase64String(AccountKey)))
   {
     var data = Encoding.UTF8.GetBytes(signme);
     signature = System.Convert.ToBase64String(sha.ComputeHash(data));
   }

   return $"SharedKey {AccountName}:{signature}";
}
```

Only the number is written, not "Content-Length:".

For a PUT operation against Azure Blob Storage, only the content length is required. It goes three lines after the verb.

Because contentLen is a nullable long, nothing will be written if it's null. If you used a regular long value type contentLen would have some default value (like 0), and that would get written to the `signme` string. Using the nullable long means you don't have to do anything special for GET vs. PUT requests. The `CreateRequest` helper method needs to provide a default null value, as shown in the following listing.

Listing 7.23   `CreateRequest` method changed to allow content-length specification

```
private HttpRequestMessage CreateRequest(HttpMethod verb,
  string container, string blob,
  long? contentLen = default(long?))          ◁──┐ Default parameter, in
{                                                  │ case it's not specified
  ...

  var authHeader = GetAuthHeader(verb.ToString().ToUpper(),
    path, rfcDate, contentLen);               ◁──┐ Default contentLen
  request.Headers.Add("Authorization", authHeader);  │ is null

  return request;
}
```

> **DEFAULT PARAMETERS** Default parameters are a handy C# feature. They must go at the end of the parameter list and they're specified by assigning a default value with =. The `default()` keyword creates a constant value. In the case of nullable types, like `long?`, the default is `null`.

To test this new method in the Markdown service, you can use the same code and curl commands as in the code snippet in section 7.1.3, earlier in the chapter. Simply change POST to PUT and modify the URL to include the container and BLOB name. Listings 7.24 and 7.25 show how to do this.

Listing 7.24   Curl command to test the `PutBlob` operation

```
curl -X PUT --data-binary @test.md
http://localhost:5000/somecontainer/foo.md
```

Listing 7.25   C# client code to test the `PutBlob` operation

```
var response = client.PutAsync(
  "http://localhost:5000/somecontainer/foo.md",
  new StreamContent(
    new FileStream("test.md", FileMode.Open))
  ).Result;
```

7.6   *Listing containers and BLOBs*

Now that you have the ability to upload BLOBs to containers, you should expose a way for clients to get the list of containers and of BLOBs in the containers. The most straightforward way is to modify the `HttpGet` operation to allow `null` values for BLOB or container. A `null` BLOB parameter would indicate that the client wants a list of all BLOBs in the container. A `null` container parameter would indicate that they want a list of all containers.

Azure Blob Storage supports list requests, returning the lists in XML documents. Up until now, you haven't specified a content type for the response. The default content type from ASP.NET is "text/html", which is perfect for a response that's Markdown converted to HTML. In this example, you'll return the result of the Azure storage call. The following listing shows the modifications to support returning XML.

Listing 7.26 `HttpGet` operation can also list containers and BLOBs

```
[HttpGet]
public async Task<IActionResult> GetBlob(string container, string blob)
{
  var request = CreateRequest(HttpMethod.Get, container, blob);
  var contentType = blob == null ? "text/xml" :        ◁── Assumes that if container
    "text/html";                                              is null, so is BLOB

  var response = await client.SendAsync(request);
  var responseContent = await response.Content.ReadAsStringAsync();
  if (blob != null)                                    ◁── Only converts if
    responseContent = engine.Markup(responseContent);        it's Markdown
  return Content(responseContent, contentType);    ◁──
}
                                                    Overrides default
                                                    content type of text/html
```

Making a GET request to the service with the BLOB or container parameter not specified will result in `null` values being passed into the `GetBlob` method. To request a list of BLOBs in the "somecontainer" container, you'd use the URL http://localhost:5000?container=somecontainer. To get a list of all the containers, you'd use http://localhost:5000.

A list request to Azure Blob Storage is slightly different than the GET requests you've made so far. The following listing shows the updates to the helper methods for listing BLOBs and containers.

Listing 7.27 Modifying helper methods to support listing BLOBs and containers

```
private HttpRequestMessage CreateRequest(HttpMethod verb,
  string container, string blob, long? contentLen = default(long?))
{
  string path;
  Uri uri;
  if (blob != null)                          ◁── Gets BLOB
  {                                               content
    path = $"{container}/{blob}";
    uri = new Uri(BlobEndpoint + path);
  }                                                           Lists BLOBs
  else if (container != null)                      ◁───────  in a container
  {
    path = container;
    uri = new Uri($"{BlobEndpoint}{path}?restype=container&comp=list");
  }
  else                                    ◁──── Lists containers
```

```
{
  path = "";
  uri = new Uri($"{BlobEndpoint}?comp=list");
}

var rfcDate = DateTime.UtcNow.ToString("R");
var request = new HttpRequestMessage(verb, uri);     ◁─── Doesn't write this
if (blob != null)                                         header for list requests
  request.Headers.Add("x-ms-blob-type", "BlockBlob");
request.Headers.Add("x-ms-date", rfcDate);
request.Headers.Add("x-ms-version", ServiceVersion);

var authHeader = GetAuthHeader(verb.ToString().ToUpper(), path, rfcDate,
  contentLen, blob == null, container == null);
request.Headers.Add("Authorization", authHeader);

return request;
}

private string GetAuthHeader(string verb, string path, string rfcDate,
  long? contentLen, bool listBlob, bool listContainer)
{
  var devStorage = BlobEndpoint.StartsWith("http://127.0.0.1:10000") ?
               $"/{AccountName}" : "";
  var signme = $"{verb}\n\n\n" +
               $"{contentLen}\n" +
               "\n\n\n\n\n\n\n\n" +                       ◁─── Leaves BLOB type
               (listBlob ? "" : "x-ms-blob-type:BlockBlob\n") +   out of auth header
               $"x-ms-date:{rfcDate}\n" +
               $"x-ms-version:{ServiceVersion}\n" +
               $"/{AccountName}{devStorage}/{path}";
  if (listContainer)                              ◁─── Adds query string parameters
    signme +=   "\ncomp:list";                         to auth header when listing
  else if (listBlob)
    signme +=   "\ncomp:list\nrestype:container";

  string signature;
  using (var sha = new
    HMACSHA256(System.Convert.FromBase64String(AccountKey)))
  {
    var data = Encoding.UTF8.GetBytes(signme);
    signature = System.Convert.ToBase64String(sha.ComputeHash(data));
  }

  return $"SharedKey {AccountName}:{signature}";
}
```

7.7   *Deleting a BLOB*

To round out the functionality of the Markdown service, you'll add the ability to delete a BLOB from a container. A request with a DELETE verb has a similar structure as a GET request. The only real consideration is what status code to return.

Azure Blob Storage will return a 202 (Accepted) status code when issuing a delete BLOB command. This is because the BLOB immediately becomes unavailable but isn't deleted until a garbage collection happens. This is in line with RFC 2616 of the HTTP specification:

> *A successful response SHOULD be 200 (OK) if the response includes an entity describing the status, 202 (Accepted) if the action has not yet been enacted, or 204 (No Content) if the action has been enacted but the response does not include an entity.*
>
> — RFC 2616 (https://tools.ietf.org/html/rfc2616#section-9.7)

For the Markdown service, the BLOB is essentially deleted. You won't return the value of the BLOB in the response, so a 204 (No Content) seems more appropriate. The following listing shows how to write the delete operation.

Listing 7.28 `DeleteBlob` operation to delete a BLOB from a container

```
[HttpDelete]
public async Task<IActionResult> DeleteBlob(string container, string blob)
{
  var request = CreateRequest(HttpMethod.Delete,          ◄─┐ Don't forget to use
    container, blob);                                        │ the right verb here.

  var response = await client.SendAsync(request);
  if (response.StatusCode==HttpStatusCode.Accepted)        ◄─┐ Successfully deleted
    return NoContent();                                      │ blob, return 204
  else
    return Content(await response.Content.ReadAsStringAsync());
}
```

With the `HttpDelete` operation added, your service now handles the GET, PUT, POST, and DELETE HTTP verbs. The only verb we won't cover is PATCH (`[HttpPatch]`), which is used for partial modification of a record. Azure Blob Storage doesn't support PATCH, so it doesn't apply to this example.

Additional resources

To learn more about what we covered in this chapter, try the following resources:

- *Microservices in .NET Core* by Christian Horsdal Gammelgaard (Manning, 2017)—http://mng.bz/qREF
- *ASP.NET Core in Action* by Andrew Lock (Manning, 2018)—http://mng.bz/DI1O
- Azurite Azure storage emulator for Mac/Linux—https://github.com/arafato/azurite
- "Authentication for the Azure Storage Services"—http://mng.bz/7j0B
- Curl—https://curl.haxx.se/

Summary

In this chapter you learned how to write a microservice and communicate with other HTTP services as a client. These key concepts were covered:

- Use `HttpClient` to make requests.

- ASP.NET Core routes messages based on the `HttpGet`, `HttpPost`, and other attributes.
- ASP.NET Core automatically populates method parameters and also allows access to the raw stream from the request.
- Microservices control their own data stores.

Here are some important techniques to remember from this chapter:

- A library called Markdown Lite is available for quick and easy conversion of Markdown to HTML.
- Async programming leaves threads unblocked, which improves the performance of your application.
- Curl is a powerful and simple tool for quickly testing your services.

Much of modern programming involves writing and communicating with HTTP services. ASP.NET Core makes writing HTTP REST services quick and intuitive by using a convention-based approach. Methods like `Content`, `Created`, `Accepted`, and the like match the HTTP specifications. Routing requests to the right methods is handled via the `Http*` attributes, and accessing parameters from the URI or query string doesn't require manual parsing.

Making HTTP requests from .NET Core code is also straightforward. The `Http-Client` class offers useful helper methods. In this chapter, you used `HttpClient` to communicate with Azure storage. For .NET Framework developers used to having the Azure SDK, contacting the HTTP services directly can seem daunting. But once you understand how to authenticate, it's easy.

Debugging 8

This chapter covers

- Debuggers in the Visual Studio line of products
- WinDBG/CDB—an advanced debugger that works from the command line
- LLDB for debugging on Linux and macOS
- SOS—the extension that makes CDB and LLDB work with .NET Core

Debuggers are valuable tools when developing any kind of software. Most of them are fairly intuitive to use, which may make you wonder why I would dedicate a chapter to this subject.

Many developers, especially if they're used to Visual Studio and the .NET Framework, don't realize what options are available for debugging in other editors or on other operating systems. Also, command-line debuggers still have a place in the modern developer's toolbox because they can do powerful things that GUI debuggers can't. By the end of this chapter, you'll be armed with the information you need to debug .NET Core applications almost anywhere.

8.1   *Debugging applications with Visual Studio Code*

I introduced Visual Studio Code (VS Code) in chapter 2. It's Microsoft's lightweight, cross-platform, extensible text editor (similar to the Atom text editor). If you installed the C# extension from Microsoft, then you've likely seen the debug capabilities show up on both the menu and the left-side bar. VS Code may have also nagged you to add "required assets to build and debug." If not, try creating a new project and opening VS Code with the following commands:

```
mkdir Test1
cd Test1
dotnet new console
code .
```

Open the Program.cs file and click somewhere on the text in the file. You'll see a couple of things happen: a bin folder will be created because VS Code is building the code immediately, and a warning message will be displayed at the top asking you to add assets to Test1. Clicking Yes will create a new folder under Test1 called .vscode with two files: launch.json and tasks.json (shown in listings 8.1 and 8.2).

> **GENERATING VS CODE BUILDING ASSETS**   If you missed the prompt to add building assets, you can open the command palette and select .NET: Generate Assets for Build and Debug.

Listing 8.1   launch.json allows you to configure the debugger for your application

```
{
  "version": "0.2.0",
  "configurations": [
    {
      "name": ".NET Core Launch (console)",
      "type": "coreclr",
      "request": "launch",
      "preLaunchTask": "build",                    ⟵  If you change to netstandard,
      "program":                                       change this value.
        "${workspaceRoot}/bin/Debug/netcoreapp2.0/Test1.dll",
      "args": [],                                  ⟵  Command-line
      "cwd": "${workspaceRoot}",                      arguments for Test1
      "console": "internalConsole",
      "stopAtEntry": false,
      "internalConsoleOptions": "openOnSessionStart",  ⟵  Turning this off lets you
      "justMyCode": true,                                 step into other libraries.
      "requireExactSource": true,                    ⟵  Turning this off lets
      "enableStepFiltering": true              ⟵        you use a different
    },                                                  version of the source.
    {                             Turning this off
      "name": ".NET Core Attach", lets you debug
      "type": "coreclr",          into properties.
      "request": "attach",
      "processId": "${command:pickProcess}"
```

Where console output goes ⟶ (points to `"console": "internalConsole",`)

```
        }
    ]
}
```

USING AN EXTERNAL TERMINAL If you're used to Visual Studio's external command prompt, you can change the `"console"` setting to `"external-Terminal"` to get the same behavior.

DEBUGGING THROUGH REFERENCED CODE When using a library developed by another team, you can step into their code by setting `"justMyCode"` to `false`. But you may have trouble if your local copy of their source doesn't match the version of the package you're using. By turning off the `"require-ExactSource"` flag, the debugger will make a best guess as to what line you're on. This can sometimes be good enough to figure out the cause of an issue.

Listing 8.2   tasks.json defines how to perform tasks such as build and test

```
{
  "version": "0.1.0",
  "command": "dotnet",                              ◁—— Calls the dotnet
  "isShellCommand": true,                               CLI command
  "args": [],
  "tasks": [
    {
      "taskName": "build",                          ◁—— "build" is added to the dotnet command
      "args": [                                          (for example, "dotnet build").
        "${workspaceRoot}/mytests.csproj"
      ],
      "isBuildCommand": true,
      "problemMatcher": "$msCompile"
    },
    {
      "taskName": "test",                           ◁—— "test" is not included by default,
      "args": [                                          but you can add it as shown.
        "${workspaceRoot}/mytests.csproj"
      ],
      "isTestCommand": true,                        ◁—— Currently unused
      "problemMatcher": "$msCompile"                     by VS Code
    }
  ]
}
```

The Tasks menu in VS Code has a Run Build Task option with a shortcut defined as Ctrl-Shift-B (the same shortcut used in Visual Studio 2017). This will execute the `build` task defined in tasks.json. You can also use the Run Task option item and pick the task you want to run.

   If you defined `test` like in listing 8.2, the list of available tasks will include `test`.

YOU CAN ADD CUSTOM TASKS You may find it useful to add other tasks, such as for packaging, publishing, or running tools like the Entity Framework tools.

8.1.1   *Using the .NET Core debugger*

Let's look at an example application and see how the VS Code debugger works in action. Back in chapter 6 you created a data access library using Dapper and dependency injection (you can get the code from GitHub at http://mng.bz/F146 if you don't have it handy). The data-access library has a method that creates an order in a database based on an `Order` object. If a field isn't specified in this object, `CreateOrder` may fail, and you can use the debugger to determine where the failure occurs.

All the chapter 6 Dapper projects are contained in a folder called DapperDi. From a terminal or command prompt, change to the DapperDi folder and run `code  .\` to start VS Code with the current folder open. Add the build and debug resources as prompted. Then find the unit test file and modify the test as follows.

Listing 8.3   An example of a test that you'll need to debug

```
[Fact]
public void Test1()
{
  var orders = context.GetOrders();
  Assert.Equal(0, orders.Count());
  var supplier = context.Suppliers.First();
  var part = context.Parts.First();
  var order = new Order() {
    SupplierId = supplier.Id,
    Supplier = supplier,
    PartTypeId = part.Id,
    //Part = part,                        ←┐  This is the change
    PartCount = 10,                         │  from the existing test.
    PlacedDate = DateTime.Now
  };
  context.CreateOrder(order);
  Assert.NotEqual(0, order.Id);
  orders = context.GetOrders();
  Assert.Equal(1, orders.Count());
}
```

> **USE AN IN-MEMORY DATABASE FOR THIS EXAMPLE** You may also want to change the config.json file to use the in-memory database, because you'll likely run this test many times.

It's easy to forget to set all the properties on an Order with the data-access layer you created in chapter 6. Let's see how you could debug this issue with VS Code.

As you learned in chapter 4, VS Code will put links above the test method that allow you to run or debug an individual test. Click the Debug Test link. The debugger will stop when it gets a `NullReferenceException`. You should see something like figure 8.1.

The stack trace for the `NullReferenceException` shows the line `throw;` as being the line where the exception occurred. Normally, the `throw;` would preserve the stack trace from the original exception. But in this case you performed some work,

The debug pane has familiar debugging sections: Locals, Watch, Call Stack, and Breakpoints.

Lists profiles for debugging that are controlled by launch.json.

Toolbar contains debugger commands like resume, step into, and stop.

This exception is reported on line 77.

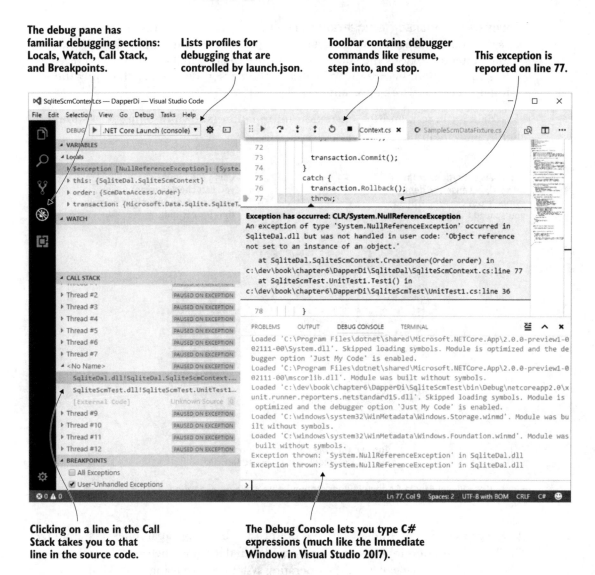

Clicking on a line in the Call Stack takes you to that line in the source code.

The Debug Console lets you type C# expressions (much like the Immediate Window in Visual Studio 2017).

Figure 8.1   Visual Studio Code debugger stopped on an exception

(transaction.Rollback();), and that resulted in the stack trace being lost. You can fix this by changing the code in this catch statement, as shown in the following listing.

Listing 8.4   Modifying catch to wrap the original exception

```
catch (Exception exc) {
  transaction.Rollback();
  throw new AggregateException(exc);
}
```

AggregateException can hold many inner exceptions.

WHY USE AN AGGREGATEEXCEPTION? The `AggregateException` is common to asynchronous programming because it's possible that multiple threads can encounter exceptions and you want to capture all of them. I use an `Aggregate-Exception` here because it indicates to the person debugging that only the inner exceptions are important.

Now debug the test, and the exception information (shown in figure 8.2) should be slightly more helpful.

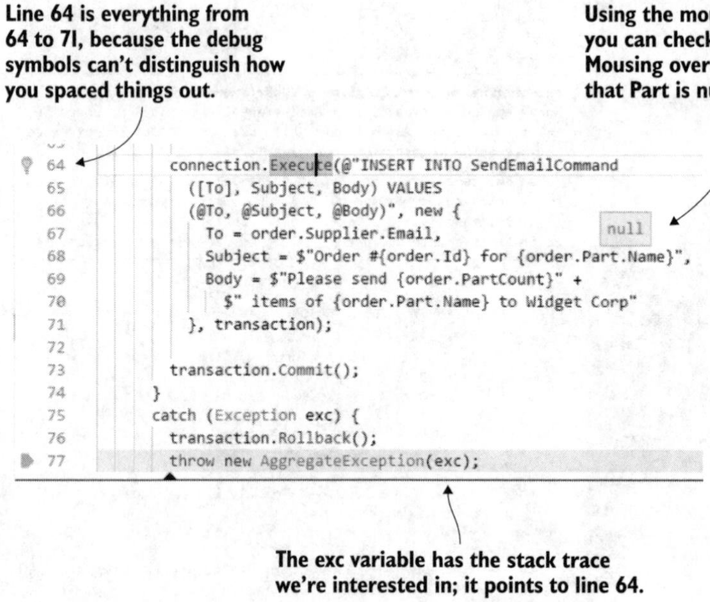

Line 64 is everything from 64 to 71, because the debug symbols can't distinguish how you spaced things out.

Using the mouse cursor, you can check current values. Mousing over order.Part reveals that Part is null.

```
64      connection.Execute(@"INSERT INTO SendEmailCommand
65        ([To], Subject, Body) VALUES
66        (@To, @Subject, @Body)", new {
67          To = order.Supplier.Email,                        null
68          Subject = $"Order #{order.Id} for {order.Part.Name}",
69          Body = $"Please send {order.PartCount}" +
70            $" items of {order.Part.Name} to Widget Corp"
71        }, transaction);
72
73      transaction.Commit();
74    }
75    catch (Exception exc) {
76      transaction.Rollback();
77      throw new AggregateException(exc);
```

The exc variable has the stack trace we're interested in; it points to line 64.

Figure 8.2 Visual Studio Code debugger stopped on a wrapped exception

As you can see, Visual Studio Code has powerful debugging capabilities. It should feel familiar to most developers who have worked with debuggers before. Also, all of these features will work regardless of the operating system you're using.

8.2 *Debugging with Visual Studio 2017*

Visual Studio 2017 is the latest version of the flagship integrated development environment from Microsoft, and it has a rich set of debugging capabilities. To see the differences between VS 2017 and VS Code, try debugging the same unit test as before. Figure 8.3 shows what this might look like.

VISUAL STUDIO NEEDS A PROJECT TO DISCOVER TESTS In VS Code, you open a folder. In Visual Studio there's an option to open a folder, but even though it may build the projects, it doesn't see the tests. The Test Explorer will be empty. Instead, you need to create a new solution and add the projects.

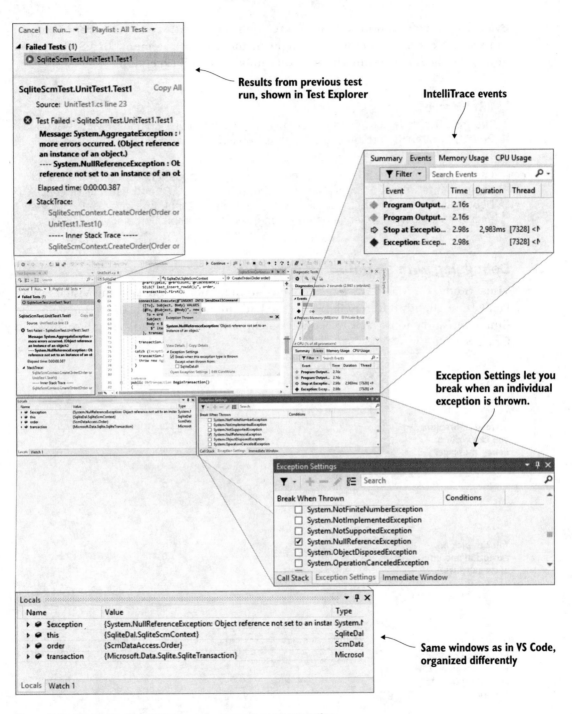

Figure 8.3 Visual Studio 2017 debugger stopped on an exception

By altering the exception settings to break on the `NullReferenceException`, you can see the exception before it's caught in the `catch` statement. In VS Code, you don't have the same granularity, but you can break on all exceptions.

IntelliTrace

The IntelliTrace feature doesn't come with the Community edition of Visual Studio 2017. If you happen to have an Enterprise edition, this is definitely a feature worth checking out.

IntelliTrace will capture events during the debugging session. You can then select these events from the Events window (shown in figure 8.3) and use the Historical Debugging feature to see the state of your application at that time with local variables and call stack. This comes in handy when unwinding complex problems.

8.3   *Debugging with Visual Studio for Mac*

Visual Studio for Mac bears a resemblance to the other products in the Visual Studio family. One slightly different feature is the Exception Catchpoint. To try this, go to the Run menu and choose New Exception Catchpoint. You'll see the dialog box shown in figure 8.4.

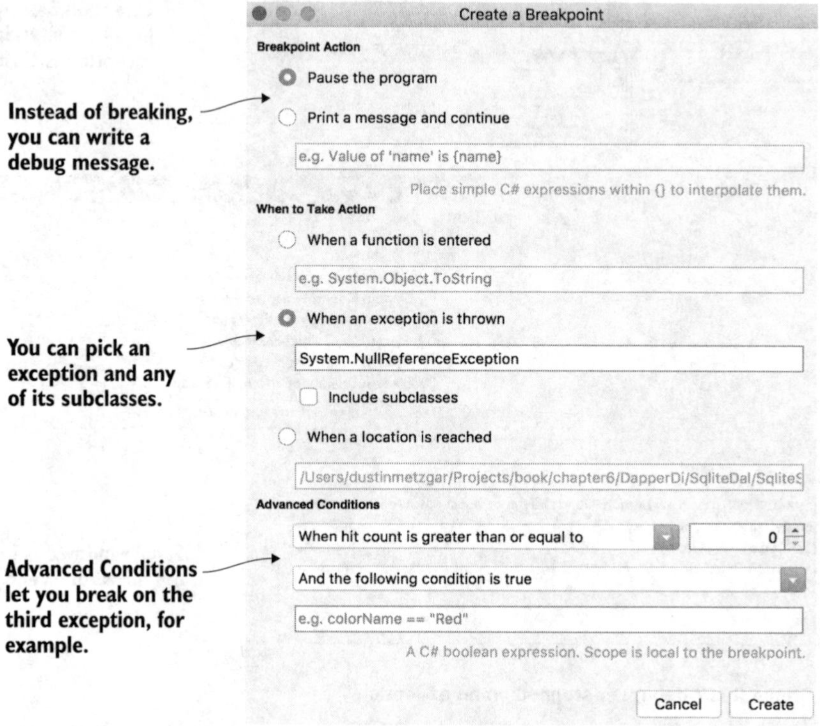

Figure 8.4   Visual Studio for Mac New Exception Catchpoint dialog box

The same Advanced Conditions functionality is available in other debuggers, including Visual Studio 2017 and Visual Studio Code, with the name "conditional breakpoints." The slight differences in terminology stem from VS for Mac actually being a rebranded Xamarin Studio.

Visual Studio for Mac doesn't look that different from Visual Studio 2017, at least when it comes to debugging. Figure 8.5 shows what VS for Mac looks like in action.

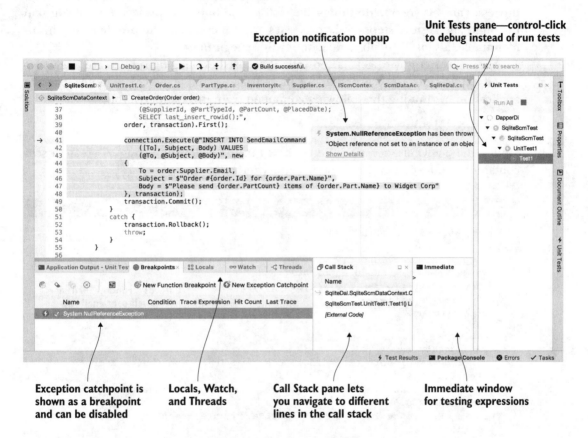

Exception notification popup

Unit Tests pane—control-click to debug instead of run tests

Exception catchpoint is shown as a breakpoint and can be disabled

Locals, Watch, and Threads

Call Stack pane lets you navigate to different lines in the call stack

Immediate window for testing expressions

Figure 8.5 Visual Studio for Mac debugging a `NullReferenceException`

8.4 SOS

So far, we've only explored graphical debuggers. But some things can't easily be expressed in a GUI. That's why every developer should have a command-line debugger in their toolbox.

The .NET Framework comes with an extension for the Windows Debugger (WinDBG) that contains powerful commands for interpreting .NET's managed memory, types, functions, and so on. This extension is called SOS. It works for .NET Core and on the cross-platform LLDB debugger.

WHAT DOES SOS MEAN?   SOS isn't a distress signal—it stands for Son Of Strike. If you're interested in trivia, you can do a search to find out the history of the name.

8.4.1   *Easier to get started with a self-contained app*

One of the nice things about the Visual Studio debuggers is that they hide some of the more confusing parts of the .NET SDK. When you run `dotnet test`, several child processes are spawned to do things like restore and build the project. Even if you skip the build and restore steps, child processes are still created. The problem isn't insurmountable; it's just difficult to take on if you're beginning.

A much easier way to get started with SOS-based debugging is to create a self-contained application. You learned about these back in chapter 2. Create a new console application by running the following command from the DapperDi folder:

```
dotnet new console -o ScmConsole
```

Modify the ScmConsole.csproj file as shown in the following listing to create a self-contained application and add the necessary references.

Listing 8.5   Contents of ScmConsole.csproj

```
<Project Sdk="Microsoft.NET.Sdk">
  <PropertyGroup>
    <OutputType>Exe</OutputType>
    <TargetFramework>netcoreapp2.0</TargetFramework>
    <RuntimeIdentifiers>win10-x64;osx.10.12-x64      ⟵─┐  Needs a runtime identifier
    </RuntimeIdentifiers>                                  for a self-contained app
  </PropertyGroup>                                         (see appendix A)

  <ItemGroup>
    <PackageReference
      Include="Microsoft.Extensions.DependencyInjection.Abstractions"
      Version="2.0.0-*" />
    <PackageReference Include="Microsoft.Extensions.DependencyInjection"
      Version="2.0.0-*" />
    <PackageReference Include="SQLitePCLRaw.bundle_green"
      Version="1.1.8" />                                         ⟵─┐
    <ProjectReference Include="../SqliteScmTest/SqliteScmTest.csproj" />
  </ItemGroup>                                              Needed for running
</Project>                                                  SQLite on Mac and Linux
```

This project takes an indirect dependency on SqliteDal. In order to get the self-contained application building, you need to change SqliteDal to .NET Standard 2.0 and change some of its references. Make the following changes.

Listing 8.6   Making SqliteDal.csproj a self-contained app on Windows

```
<Project Sdk="Microsoft.NET.Sdk">
  <PropertyGroup>
```

```
  <TargetFramework>netstandard2.0</TargetFramework>
</PropertyGroup>

<ItemGroup>
  <PackageReference Include="Microsoft.Data.Sqlite.Core"
                    Version="2.0.0-*" />
  <PackageReference Include="Dapper"
                    Version="1.50.2" />
  <PackageReference Include="System.Data.SqlClient"
                    Version="4.3.1" />
  <ProjectReference Include="../ScmDataAccess/ScmDataAccess.csproj" />
</ItemGroup>
</Project>
```

Dapper references old version of SqlClient

You need a later version to create a self-contained app.

Next, add the following code to the Program.cs file of ScmConsole.

Listing 8.7 Program.cs for the ScmConsole app will create an order, like in the unit test

```csharp
using System;
using System.Linq;
using Microsoft.Extensions.DependencyInjection;
using ScmDataAccess;
using SqliteScmTest;

namespace ScmConsole
{
  class Program
  {
    static void Main(string[] args)
    {
      SQLitePCL.Batteries.Init();
      var fixture = new SampleScmDataFixture();
      var context = fixture.Services.
        GetRequiredService<IScmContext>();
      var supplier = context.Suppliers.First();
      var part = context.Parts.First();
      var order = new Order() {
        SupplierId = supplier.Id,
        Supplier = supplier,
        PartTypeId = part.Id,
        //Part = part,
        PartCount = 10,
        PlacedDate = DateTime.Now
      };
      context.CreateOrder(order);
    }
  }
}
```

Sets up SQLite before you open the connection

Now you can run `dotnet restore` to make sure all the packages are set up correctly. Then run the `publish` command to create the self-contained app:

```
dotnet publish -c Debug -r win10-x64
```

You can use Release, but Debug will be easier for debugging.

The executable will be published to the ScmConsole\bin\Debug\netcoreapp2.0\win10-x64\publish\ folder. You can run ScmConsole.exe from there, and it should crash.

8.4.2   *WinDBG/CDB*

WinDBG and CDB are essentially the same debugger, except CDB is command-line-based, whereas WinDBG is GUI-based. For the purposes of this chapter, it doesn't matter which one you use.

To get these tools, you'll need to install the Debugging Tools for Windows that come with the Windows SDK (http://mng.bz/j0xk). You can choose to install only the Debugging Tools during the installation.

Once they're installed, go back to your console and change to the folder where the self-contained ScmConsole app was published. Launch the app with the debugger attached by using the following command:

```
"C:\Program Files (x86)\Windows Kits\10\Debuggers\x64\cdb.exe" ScmConsole.exe
```

GETTING THE DEBUGGER TO STOP WHEN AN EXCEPTION IS THROWN
The debugger will pause once it's started. That gives you a chance to set up stops and breakpoints.

In this case, you need the process to load the .NET Core CLR before you set any breakpoints. To do that, you can tell the debugger to stop when it loads a certain module or assembly. Use the following commands to tell CDB to stop when the Scm-Console assembly is loaded:

```
sxe ld ScmConsole
g                          Tells the debugger
                           to "go"
```

The program should stop shortly. You'll see some log messages indicating which assemblies have been loaded. Among those should be coreclr.dll from your publish folder.

Now you can load SOS and set a breakpoint for when the `AggregateException` is thrown:

```
.loadby sos coreclr
!soe -create System.AggregateException      "soe" is short for
g                                           "stop on exception."
```

You should see two access violations before hitting the breakpoint. You'll need to resume (g) each time an access violation is hit. The output will look something like the following.

Listing 8.8   Output when hitting access violations and then the `AggregateException`

```
(1ec8.4c34): Access violation - code c0000005 (first chance)
First chance exceptions are reported before any exception handling.
This exception may be expected and handled.
00007ffd`d54e22bf 3909            cmp     dword ptr [rcx],ecx
    ds:00000000`00000000=????????
```

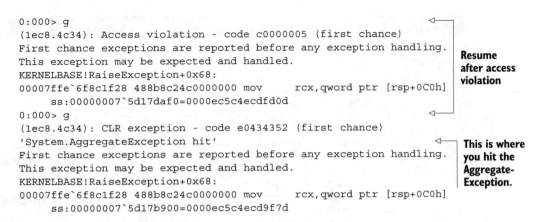

```
0:000> g
(1ec8.4c34): Access violation - code c0000005 (first chance)
First chance exceptions are reported before any exception handling.
This exception may be expected and handled.
KERNELBASE!RaiseException+0x68:
00007ffe`6f8c1f28 488b8c24c0000000 mov    rcx,qword ptr [rsp+0C0h]
    ss:00000007`5d17daf0=0000ec5c4ecdfd0d
0:000> g
(1ec8.4c34): CLR exception - code e0434352 (first chance)
'System.AggregateException hit'
First chance exceptions are reported before any exception handling.
This exception may be expected and handled.
KERNELBASE!RaiseException+0x68:
00007ffe`6f8c1f28 488b8c24c0000000 mov    rcx,qword ptr [rsp+0C0h]
    ss:00000007`5d17b900=0000ec5c4ecd9f7d
```

Resume after access violation

This is where you hit the Aggregate-Exception.

VIEWING THE CONTENTS OF AN EXCEPTION

You can use the Print Exception command (!pe) to see the AggregateException.
The command will output another command so you can see the NullReference-
Exception. The following listing shows what this might look like.

Listing 8.9   Printing an exception and an inner exception

```
0:000> !pe
Exception object: 00000151b0e54230
Exception type:   System.AggregateException
Message:          One or more errors occurred.
InnerException:   System.NullReferenceException,
                  Use !PrintException 00000151b0e51a38 to see more.
StackTrace (generated):
<none>
StackTraceString: <none>
HResult: 80131500
0:000> !PrintException 00000151b0e51a38
Exception object: 00000151b0e51a38
Exception type:   System.NullReferenceException
Message:          Object reference not set to an instance of an object.
InnerException:   <none>
StackTrace (generated):
    SP               IP                  Function
    000000075D17E070 00007FFDD54E22BF
       SqliteDal!SqliteDal.SqliteScmContext.CreateOrder(ScmDataAccess.Order)+0x
       19f

StackTraceString: <none>
HResult: 80004003
```

Gives you the command to see the inner exceptions

Command to see inner exception

Stacks have offsets instead of line numbers.

VIEWING THE STACK AND LOCAL VARIABLES ON THE CURRENT THREAD

Because the debugger is paused at the point when the exception was thrown, you can
view the current stack. This will also show the local variables for each method.

To do this, use the command !clrstack -a. It will produce output like the
following.

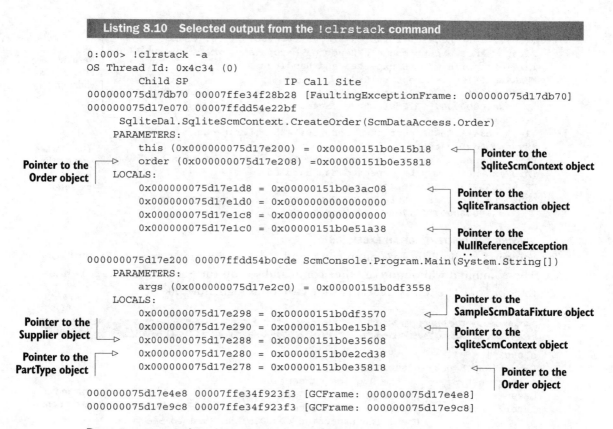

Listing 8.10 Selected output from the `!clrstack` command

```
0:000> !clrstack -a
OS Thread Id: 0x4c34 (0)
        Child SP               IP Call Site
000000075d17db70 00007ffe34f28b28 [FaultingExceptionFrame: 000000075d17db70]
000000075d17e070 00007ffdd54e22bf
    SqliteDal.SqliteScmContext.CreateOrder(ScmDataAccess.Order)
    PARAMETERS:
        this (0x000000075d17e200) = 0x00000151b0e15b18
        order (0x000000075d17e208) =0x00000151b0e35818
    LOCALS:
        0x000000075d17e1d8 = 0x00000151b0e3ac08
        0x000000075d17e1d0 = 0x0000000000000000
        0x000000075d17e1c8 = 0x0000000000000000
        0x000000075d17e1c0 = 0x00000151b0e51a38
000000075d17e200 00007ffdd54b0cde ScmConsole.Program.Main(System.String[])
    PARAMETERS:
        args (0x000000075d17e2c0) = 0x00000151b0df3558
    LOCALS:
        0x000000075d17e298 = 0x00000151b0df3570
        0x000000075d17e290 = 0x00000151b0e15b18
        0x000000075d17e288 = 0x00000151b0e35608
        0x000000075d17e280 = 0x00000151b0e2cd38
        0x000000075d17e278 = 0x00000151b0e35818
000000075d17e4e8 00007ffe34f923f3 [GCFrame: 000000075d17e4e8]
000000075d17e9c8 00007ffe34f923f3 [GCFrame: 000000075d17e9c8]
```

Pointer to the Order object → order (0x000000075d17e208) =0x00000151b0e35818

Pointer to the SqliteScmContext object ← this (0x000000075d17e200) = 0x00000151b0e15b18

Pointer to the SqliteTransaction object ← 0x000000075d17e1d8 = 0x00000151b0e3ac08

Pointer to the NullReferenceException ← 0x000000075d17e1c0 = 0x00000151b0e51a38

Pointer to the SampleScmDataFixture object ← 0x000000075d17e298 = 0x00000151b0df3570

Pointer to the SqliteScmContext object ← 0x000000075d17e290 = 0x00000151b0e15b18

Pointer to the Supplier object → 0x000000075d17e288 = 0x00000151b0e35608

Pointer to the PartType object → 0x000000075d17e280 = 0x00000151b0e2cd38

Pointer to the Order object ← 0x000000075d17e278 = 0x00000151b0e35818

DUMPING AN OBJECT'S CONTENTS

To view a .NET object, run the `!do` command with the object pointer. The following
listing shows the output when viewing theOrder object.

Listing 8.11 Viewing the `Order` object (elided)

```
0:000> !do 0x00000151b0e35818
Name:        ScmDataAccess.Order
MethodTable: 00007ffdd5357c98
EEClass:     00007ffdd54a7ee8
Size:        72(0x48) bytes
File:        ...\netcoreapp2.0\win10-x64\publish\ScmDataAccess.dll
Fields:
              Type             Value Name
        System.Int32               1 <Id>k__BackingField
        System.Int32               1 <SupplierId>k__BackingField
...taAccess.Supplier 00000151b0e35608 <Supplier>
        System.Int32               0 <PartTypeId>k__BackingField
...taAccess.PartType 0000000000000000 <Part>k__BackingField
        System.Int32              10 <PartCount>
    System.DateTime 00000151b0e35840 <PlacedDate>k__BackingField
...Private.CoreLib]] 00000151b0e35848 <FulfilledDate>k__BackingField
```

DumpObject command with pointer to Order object ← 0:000> !do 0x00000151b0e35818

Type name ← Name: ScmDataAccess.Order

Pointer to Supplier object ← ...taAccess.Supplier 00000151b0e35608 <Supplier>

Value of the PartCount property → System.Int32   10 <PartCount>

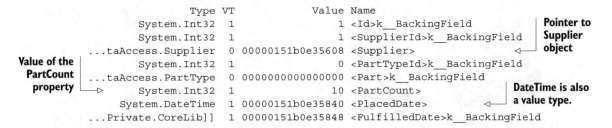

VALUE VS. REFERENCE TYPES PartCount is a value type in C#, which means the value is held in memory directly. Supplier is a reference type, which is why you get a pointer value. A C# struct is also considered a value type, but in memory it's a pointer, as you can see from the PlacedDate property. The VT column indicates 1 for a value type and 0 for a reference type. If you try !do on the PlacedDate pointer, it won't work.

HOW TO VIEW AN ARRAY If you want to view an array, like the arguments passed to Program.Main, use the !da command instead.

EXAMINING THE REST OF THE MANAGED MEMORY HEAP

All of these commands are powerful, but they're not providing much of an advantage over what the Visual Studio debuggers do. There's an area where SOS really shines, though, and it's when you care about what's in memory besides what's on the current thread. To see what I mean, try executing !dumpheap -stat. You'll see every .NET object in memory grouped by type and ordered by how much memory they take up. This includes objects created by the SQLite library, the dependency-injection library, and .NET Core.

To see this in action, try executing the following command.

Listing 8.12 Using the !dumpheap command with a type filter

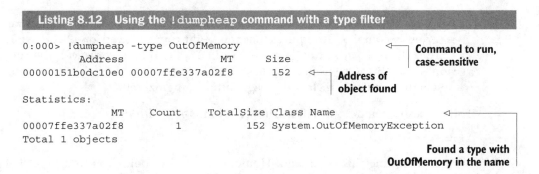

If you're looking at memory to find all the exceptions (!dumpheap -type Exception), you'll always find OutOfMemoryException. .NET creates this exception in memory up front, because in the event that you do run out of memory, it won't be able to allocate the memory to create the OutOfMemoryException. Instead, it will throw the one it created earlier. Creating a stack trace will also take memory, so you won't get a stack trace for the OutOfMemoryException, but that's typically not a problem.

Debugging unit tests with CDB

If you're interested in trying to debug the unit tests, you can use a CDB command like this:

```
cdb.exe -o dotnet test --no-build --no-restore
```

That command starts CDB and launches `dotnet test` without restoring or building and debugging all the child processes.

You'll have to resume a few breaks to get to the `AggregateException`, so you need to pay attention to the output and stack at each break to know where you are.

WHERE TO LEARN MORE ABOUT THE CDB COMMANDS

After you've loaded SOS, you can get a full list of SOS commands by running the `!help` command. You can similarly get more detailed help on a command, like this: `!help dumpheap`.

Commands that don't start with an exclamation mark (`!`) are part of CDB, and they can be a little archaic. There's a good quick reference for managed code debugging called "WinDbg cheat sheet" at http://mng.bz/u7Ag. The reference is a bit old (it still refers to mscorwks, which is pre-.NET Framework 4.0) but still relevant.

8.4.3   *LLDB*

LLDB is a debugger that's part of the larger LLVM project, which is a collection of modular compiler and toolchain technologies. LLVM is used by Xcode, the integrated development environment for developing Mac and iOS applications.

USING LLDB ON A MAC

If you're using a Mac, the easiest way to install LLDB is to install Xcode.

> **SOS ON LLDB IS HARD TO GET WORKING**   Working with SOS and LLDB on a Mac is seriously complex. It requires that you build your own version of the .NET Core CLR so that you can get an SOS LLDB plugin that works with the version of LLDB you're using. To get the .NET Core team to fix this issue, vote on GitHub on the coreclr issues page: http://mng.bz/r50R.

You can also attempt to install LLDB with Homebrew with this command:

```
brew install llvm --with-lldb
```

When attempting this command, Homebrew will first point you to a page that tells you how to install the code-signing certificate for LLDB. As mentioned in the warning, though, the next step is to build the Core CLR code, which will build the SOS plugin for LLDB. Assuming you did all these steps, you'll have a file called libsosplugin.dylib. Use the `plugin load` command in LLDB, followed by the full path of the libsosplugin.dylib file to install the plugin.

Given the complexities of this method, I recommend installing Xcode instead. Xcode is free and installs LLDB without much difficulty.

USING LLDB ON LINUX

On Linux, use the following command to install LLDB:

```
sudo apt install lldb-3.5
```

To test that LLDB is installed, run `./lldb` from the terminal. It should give you a prompt like this: `(lldb)`.

LLDB doesn't have a command that breaks on module load, so you'll need to add a `Console.ReadLine` to the test application. Make it the first line in the `Main` method in Program.cs. Then go to the publish folder for the ScmConsole application, and execute the application. It should wait for you to press Enter before continuing on with the program.

At this point you can start LLDB in another terminal and attach to it. But first, you'll need the process ID. Use the following command to get the process ID:

```
ps -eclx | grep 'ScmConsole' | awk '{print $2}' | head -1
```

Now start LLDB and use the following command to attach to the process:

```
process attach -p [processid]
```

    Replace processid with the process from the previous command.

Now you'll need to locate the libsosplugin.so file. Open a new terminal and run the following command to find it:

```
find /usr -name libsosplugin.so
```

You may see multiple versions of this file. Choose the one that matches the .NET SDK version you're using, which is usually the latest one. Back in LLDB, enter the command `plugin load` followed by the full path of libsosplugin.so.

Now you can try the following sequence of commands, just like you did in section 8.4.2 on WinDBG:

```
!soe -create System.AggregateException
process continue
!pe
!dumpheap -type OutOfMemory
```

Additional resources

SOS is addictive. It's especially useful when you're trying to diagnose an issue on a production server. You won't want to set breakpoints, but you can get a memory dump of the process and copy it to your workstation for analysis. Having access to all of the .NET objects in memory gives you all kinds of power. If you're interested in learning more about debugging .NET, check out some of these resources:

- Run the `help` command in SOS (`!help` in WinDBG or `soshelp` in LLDB).
- CLRMD (https://github.com/microsoft/clrmd)—Allows you to write .NET Code to debug processes.

- SOSEX (http://www.stevestechspot.com/)—A library for WinDBG like SOS, but with even more powerful commands.
- MEX (http://mng.bz/cFP4)—A library for WinDBG like SOS and SOSEX, but with yet more powerful commands.
- Tess Ferrandez's blog (http://mng.bz/D9T1)—A great starting resource for tips and techniques on using SOS.
- WinDBG cheat sheet: http://mng.bz/u7Ag.

Summary

In this chapter you learned about the various tools for debugging .NET Core applications. These are some key concepts from this chapter:

- Many of the debugging tools available for .NET Core are free and powerful.
- The Visual Studio family of debuggers has similar capabilities on Windows, Mac, and Linux.
- .NET Core provides the SOS extension, which can be used in the command-line debuggers LLDB and WinDBG.

You also used a few techniques to debug your application:

- Debugging tests from Visual Studio editors
- Wrapping an exception in an `AggregateException` if the `catch` block does work that will lose the stack trace
- Creating a self-contained application when debugging from the console, because it's easier to debug than `dotnet test` or `dotnet run`
- Using WinDBG's `sxe ld` command to stop when the coreclr module is loaded, so you can load SOS and set a breakpoint

If you're a .NET Framework developer, you're probably used to Visual Studio and its powerful debugging capabilities. In this chapter, you learned that those same capabilities are available in .NET Core. We also explored some other options when developing on Mac and Linux. Command-line debuggers give you the power to work with a memory dump or via terminal or SSH, which comes in handy when a bug only happens in production.

In the next chapter, we'll explore how to test and analyze the performance of your .NET applications.

Performance and profiling

This chapter covers

- Measuring performance with the xUnit.Performance library
- Profiling with PerfView
- Options on Linux for performance profiling

Premature optimization is the root of all evil.

— *Sir C. Antony R. Hoare*

This quote by Sir Tony Hoare, popularized by Donald Knuth, is perhaps the most misunderstood guidance for writing applications that perform well. Optimizations, in this context, refer to CPU cycle counting and tuning low-level operations. Programmers love to do these things, but they can often get lost in the minutiae and miss the big picture. Sir Tony wasn't trying to tell us to forgo considering performance when designing our applications. He was warning us against getting mired down in optimizing the wrong things.

The Bing search engine has an internal plugin system. Teams build services (plugins) that receive the search query sent by the user, and they must provide a

173

response within a certain time limit. If the service responds too slowly, the Bing infrastructure notifies the team of the performance issue and turns off the plugin. In order to provide a new feature in Bing, teams must meet the performance criteria.

> **LEARN MORE ABOUT .NET PERFORMANCE** If you want to learn more about performance from one of the engineers that built the Bing system, seek out Ben Watson's book, *Writing High-Performance .NET Code* (Ben Watson, 2014).

Let's contemplate how you'd build a new feature in this environment. You wouldn't start by writing code and optimizing blindly. You'd start by measuring everything. What data store provides the fastest response while still providing the functionality you need? Where are the bottlenecks as scale increases? What are all the components in your service, and how much time do they take to respond?

> *Good perf does not just happen. You have to plan, and to plan you have to measure.*
> — *Vance Morrison*

In this chapter, we'll explore how you can measure and analyze performance in .NET Core. Every application works differently, so it's up to the developers to determine performance targets. There's no "go faster" button in software development, which is why measurement is paramount. We'll go through some examples of identifying poor-performing code, analyzing why it's slow, and making iterative adjustments.

9.1 *Creating a test application*

Back in chapter 3 you built a small CSV parser. In this chapter you'll build a CSV writer. Writing large amounts of data to files is a fairly common task for C# applications. If you want your CSV-writing library to succeed, you'll need to outperform the other libraries.

First you'll build some simple CSV-writing code. Then we'll look at how you can measure it.

Start by creating a new library called CsvWriter: `dotnet new library -o CsvWriter`. Create a new class called `SimpleWriter`, and add the following code.

> **Listing 9.1   A `SimpleWriter` class that writes comma-separated values to a stream**

```
using System;
using System.Collections.Generic;
using System.IO;

namespace CsvWriter
{
  public class SimpleWriter
  {
    private TextWriter target;
    private string[] columns;

    public SimpleWriter(TextWriter target)
    {
```

```
        this.target = target;
    }

    public void WriteHeader(params string[] columns)        ◁─┐  Specifies name and
    {                                                          │  order of columns
        this.columns = columns;
        this.target.Write(columns[0]);
        for (int i = 1; i < columns.Length; i++)
            this.target.Write("," + columns[i]);
        this.target.WriteLine();
    }

    public void WriteLine(Dictionary<string, string>        ◁─┐  Dictionary has key/value
        values)                                                │  pairs with keys matching
    {                                                          │  column names
        this.target.Write(values[columns[0]]);
        for (int i = 1; i < columns.Length; i++)
            this.target.Write("," + values[columns[i]]);
        this.target.WriteLine();
    }
  }
}
```

FOR THOSE NOT FAMILIAR WITH C# The params keyword allows the caller to specify a variable number of arguments. The caller doesn't need to create the string array themselves—C# will do this automatically. This makes the code easier to read. See the unit test code to find out how this is used.

Next, create an xUnit project to test the functionality of SimpleWriter. Use the command dotnet new xunit -o CsvWriterUnitTests. Copy the Marvel.csv file from chapter 3 to the new project folder (or use the sample code that accompanies this book). Be sure that Marvel.csv has an empty line at the end.

Then modify the project file as follows.

Listing 9.2   Modifying the project file for CsvWriterUnitTests

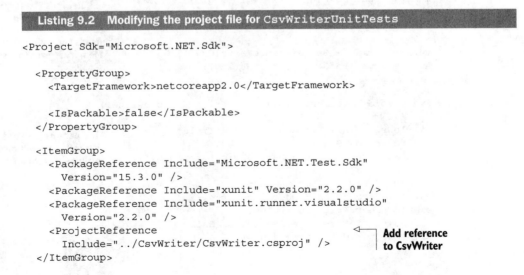

```
<Project Sdk="Microsoft.NET.Sdk">

  <PropertyGroup>
    <TargetFramework>netcoreapp2.0</TargetFramework>

    <IsPackable>false</IsPackable>
  </PropertyGroup>

  <ItemGroup>
    <PackageReference Include="Microsoft.NET.Test.Sdk"
      Version="15.3.0" />
    <PackageReference Include="xunit" Version="2.2.0" />
    <PackageReference Include="xunit.runner.visualstudio"
      Version="2.2.0" />
    <ProjectReference                                       ◁─┐  Add reference
      Include="../CsvWriter/CsvWriter.csproj" />               │  to CsvWriter
  </ItemGroup>
```

```
  <ItemGroup>
    <EmbeddedResource Include="Marvel.csv" />
  </ItemGroup>
```
◁┐ **Embed
   Marvel.csv.**

```
</Project>
```

Finally, you'll build a unit test to make sure `SimpleWriter` is able to produce the same output as your original file. In the UnitTest1.cs file created with the unit test project, add the code from the following listing.

Listing 9.3   Unit test for SimpleWriter

```
using System;
using System.Collections.Generic;
using System.IO;
using System.Reflection;
using Xunit;
using CsvWriter;

namespace CsvWriterUnitTests
{
  public class UnitTest1
  {
    const string Marvel = "Marvel Studios";
    const string Fox = "20th Century Fox";

    [Fact]
    public void TestSimpleWriter()
    {
      var memoryStream = new MemoryStream();
      var streamWriter = new StreamWriter(memoryStream);
      var simpleWriter = new SimpleWriter(streamWriter);
      WriteMarvelCsv(simpleWriter);
      streamWriter.Flush();
      memoryStream.Seek(0, SeekOrigin.Begin);
      var streamReader = new StreamReader(memoryStream);
      var testString = streamReader.ReadToEnd();

      var refString = GetReferenceMarvelCsv();
      Assert.Equal(refString, testString);
    }

    private void WriteMarvelCsv(SimpleWriter simpleWriter)
    {
      simpleWriter.WriteHeader("Year", "Title",
        "Production Studio");
      var values = new Dictionary<string, string>();
      values["Year"] = "2008";
      values["Title"] = "Iron Man";
      values["Production Studio"] = Marvel;
      simpleWriter.WriteLine(values);
      values["Title"] = "The Incredible Hulk";
      simpleWriter.WriteLine(values);
```

◁┘ **Make these constants,
   because they're reused.**

◁── **MemoryStream manages an
   in-memory buffer for you.**

┌ **Guarantees StreamWriter
│ has written everything to
│ the MemoryStream**

◁─┘

◁┐ **Rewinds MemoryStream
   to the beginning**

◁── **Reads the contents of the
   MemoryStream to a string**

◁── **The params keyword on
   WriteHeader will turn the
   arguments into an array.**

```
        values["Title"] = "Punisher: War Zone";
        simpleWriter.WriteLine(values);
        values["Year"] = "2009";
        values["Title"] = "X-Men Origins: Wolverine";
        values["Production Studio"] = Fox;
        simpleWriter.WriteLine(values);
        values["Year"] = "2010";
        values["Title"] = "Iron Man 2";
        values["Production Studio"] = Marvel;
        simpleWriter.WriteLine(values);
        values["Year"] = "2011";
        values["Title"] = "Thor";
        simpleWriter.WriteLine(values);
        values["Title"] = "X-Men: First Class";
        values["Production Studio"] = Fox;
        simpleWriter.WriteLine(values);
    }

    private string GetReferenceMarvelCsv()
    {
        var stream = typeof(UnitTest1).GetTypeInfo().Assembly.
          GetManifestResourceStream(
            "CsvWriterUnitTests.Marvel.csv");          ◁─┐ Reads the embedded
        var reader = new StreamReader(stream);             │ Marvel.csv file
        return reader.ReadToEnd();
    }
  }
}
```

Run the test to make sure everything works correctly.

Once you've verified that this works properly, how well does it perform? You could put timers into the unit test, but that doesn't provide much information, and it may yield inconsistent results. Luckily, there's a .NET Standard library for performance testing called xUnit.Performance.

9.2   *xUnit.Performance makes it easy to run performance tests*

In test-driven development (TDD), test cases are written from requirements, and developers iterate on the software until it passes all the tests. TDD tends to focus on small units of code, and unit-testing frameworks (like xUnit) help developers get quick feedback. The xUnit.Performance library offers a similar feedback loop on performance. It allows you to try new things and share your performance tests and results with others in a standardized way.

xUnit.Performance is still in the beta stage, so it's not as polished as xUnit. If you find it useful, I encourage you to participate in the project (https://github.com/Microsoft/xunit-performance). Because of the early stage of development, you'll need to create your own harness and get the NuGet packages from a different NuGet feed (chapter 12 has more on NuGet feeds).

Start by creating a file called nuget.config in the parent folder of your projects with the following contents.

Listing 9.4 nuget.config file with local feed

```
<?xml version="1.0" encoding="utf-8"?>
<configuration>
  <packageSources>                              The dotnet-core myget
    <add key="dotnet-core" value=               feed has beta projects.
      "https://dotnet.myget.org/F/dotnet-core/api/v3/index.json" />
  </packageSources>
</configuration>
```

Then, create a new console project called CsvWriterPerfTests with the command dot-net new console -o CsvWriterPerfTests. Modify the project file to include a reference to xUnit.Performance, as follows.

Listing 9.5 Add reference to xUnit.Performance in the CsvWriterPerfTests project file

```
<Project Sdk="Microsoft.NET.Sdk">

  <PropertyGroup>
    <OutputType>Exe</OutputType>
    <TargetFramework>netcoreapp2.0</TargetFramework>
  </PropertyGroup>

  <ItemGroup>
    <PackageReference Include="xunit.performance.api" Version="1.0.0-*" />
  </ItemGroup>
</Project>
```

The Program.cs file will serve as the harness for running the performance tests. With regular xUnit, you don't have to do this because an entry point is provided via the xunit.runner.visualstudio package. Fortunately, as the following listing shows, creating the harness is simple.

Listing 9.6 Program.cs modified to start the xUnit.Performance test harness

```
using System.Reflection;
using Microsoft.Xunit.Performance.Api;

namespace CsvWriterPerfTests
{
  class Program
  {
    static void Main(string[] args)
    {
      using (var harness = new XunitPerformanceHarness(args))
      {
```

```
            var entryAssemblyPath = Assembly.GetEntryAssembly().Location;
            harness.RunBenchmarks(entryAssemblyPath);    ◀──┐
        }                                                    │
    }                                                        │
}                                                            │
}
```

Tells the harness to search for tests in the current assembly

Now, create a performance test. Writing a performance test is a bit different than writing a unit test. The performance test will run many iterations and compute averages, because factors beyond your control can affect the measurements from one execution to the next. Also, you need to consider that the memory use of the test code can affect the measurement of the product code, because the garbage collector will pause threads regardless of where they are.

You know that your code is functionally correct, so you don't need to verify the output during a performance test. But keep in mind that code, especially multithreaded code, can produce inconsistent results under stress. To detect this, you can write stress tests. Stress tests usually run for long periods of time (hours to days) and try to simulate heavy user load. For performance testing, we generally only care about speed.

Add a class called `PerfTests` with the following code.

Listing 9.7 `PerfTests` class with a test of the `SimpleWriter` class

```
using System.Collections.Generic;
using System.IO;
using System.Text;
using Microsoft.Xunit.Performance;
using CsvWriter;

namespace CsvWriterPerfTests
{
  public class PerfTests
  {
    [Benchmark(InnerIterationCount=10000)]     ◀──┘  Number of lines you'll
    public void BenchmarkSimpleWriter()                write to the CSV
    {
      var buffer = new byte[500000];          ◀──  Creates a static memory
      var memoryStream = new MemoryStream(buffer);      buffer ahead of time
      var values = new Dictionary<string, string>();   ◀──┐ Preps the dictionary
      values["Year"] = "2008";                            │ ahead of time
      values["Title"] = "Iron Man";
      values["Production Studio"] = "Marvel Studios";

      foreach (var iteration in Benchmark.Iterations)    Creates StreamWriter
      {                                                   outside of measurement
        using (var streamWriter = new StreamWriter(  ◀──┘
          memoryStream, Encoding.Default, 512, true))  ◀──┐ 512 is the buffer size for
        {                                                 │ the StreamWriter; "true"
          using (iteration.StartMeasurement())           │ leaves the stream open.
          {
            var simpleWriter = new SimpleWriter(streamWriter);
```

```
    simpleWriter.WriteHeader("Year", "Title", "Production Studio");
    for (int innerIteration = 0;
      innerIteration < Benchmark.InnerIterationCount;
      innerIteration++)                              ◁─┐ Writes many
    {                                                  │ lines to the CSV
      simpleWriter.WriteLine(values);
    }
    streamWriter.Flush();
  }
}
memoryStream.Seek(0, SeekOrigin.Begin);              ◁─┐ Rewinds the stream
}                                                      │ before the next iteration
}
}
}
```

Use the following command to execute the performance test:

```
dotnet run --perf:collect stopwatch                  ◁─┐ Does only stopwatch
                                                       │ timing of the iterations
```

> ## What is StopWatch?
> In the System.Diagnostics namespace, there's a `StopWatch` class. It has `Start` and `Stop` methods and a set of properties for getting the elapsed time. The stopwatch is implemented on all operating systems. When running performance tests on non-Windows platforms, only timing operations via `StopWatch` are supported, so you only get the times for the tests. If you're running on Windows, other facilities are available, such as kernel ETW events and CPU performance counters that can give you in-depth data, such as CPU branch mispredictions or how often you're hitting the L2 cache. That kind of performance data is beyond the scope of this book.

As part of the test, xUnit.Performance will write the test results table to the console. It will also put the results into a CSV, a Markdown file, and an XML file. The results should look similar to those in table 9.1.

Table 9.1 Test results from performance benchmark of `SimpleWriter` with 10k lines written to memory

Test Name	Metric	Iterations	AVERAGE	STDEV.S	MIN	MAX
BenchmarkSimpleWriter	Duration	100	2.229	0.380	1.949	5.077

In table 9.1, the measurements are in milliseconds. On average, `SimpleWriter` only takes 2.229 milliseconds to write 10,000 lines.

Let's see what happens when you write to a file instead of memory. Add another method to PerfTests.cs, as follows.

Listing 9.8 Measures the performance of writing to a file instead of memory

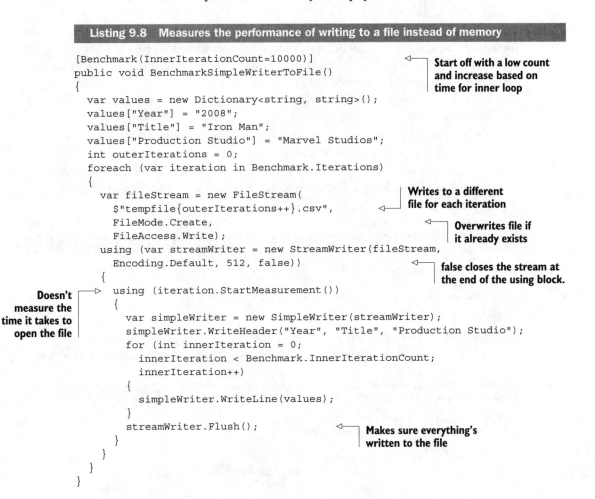

```
[Benchmark(InnerIterationCount=10000)]            Start off with a low count
public void BenchmarkSimpleWriterToFile()         and increase based on
{                                                 time for inner loop
  var values = new Dictionary<string, string>();
  values["Year"] = "2008";
  values["Title"] = "Iron Man";
  values["Production Studio"] = "Marvel Studios";
  int outerIterations = 0;
  foreach (var iteration in Benchmark.Iterations)
  {
    var fileStream = new FileStream(              Writes to a different
      $"tempfile{outerIterations++}.csv",        file for each iteration
      FileMode.Create,                           Overwrites file if
      FileAccess.Write);                         it already exists
    using (var streamWriter = new StreamWriter(fileStream,
      Encoding.Default, 512, false))             false closes the stream at
    {                                            the end of the using block.
      using (iteration.StartMeasurement())
      {
        var simpleWriter = new SimpleWriter(streamWriter);
        simpleWriter.WriteHeader("Year", "Title", "Production Studio");
        for (int innerIteration = 0;
          innerIteration < Benchmark.InnerIterationCount;
          innerIteration++)
        {
          simpleWriter.WriteLine(values);
        }
        streamWriter.Flush();                    Makes sure everything's
      }                                          written to the file
    }
  }
}
```

Doesn't measure the time it takes to open the file

START LOW WITH INNERITERATIONCOUNT When first trying this, set the Inner-IterationCount low and increase it based on the test results. If your disk is slow, you may wait a long time for the performance test to finish.

Running this test with a couple of different solid state disks (SSDs), I got results like those shown in table 9.2.

Table 9.2 Test results from performance benchmark of SimpleWriter with 10k lines written to memory and files

Test Name	Metric	Iterations	AVERAGE	STDEV.S	MIN	MAX
BenchmarkSimpleWriter	Duration	100	2.469	0.709	1.954	4.922
BenchmarkSimpleWriterToFile	Duration	100	3.780	0.985	2.760	9.812

Compare these results with table 9.1. It's common for there to be fluctuations in performance measurements. Some techniques for handling this include removing all unnecessary processes from the machine running the tests, running the tests multiple times, and increasing the number of iterations.

One pattern I noticed is that writing to files does have an impact, but not as big an impact as I originally thought. Try the test again with the files already created, and you'll see that the impact is even less. This tells me that if I need to improve the performance of this library, optimizing the CSV-writing code rather than the file-writing code will have the most impact, because it uses the biggest percentage of the overall time.

Test this out by making a slight tweak to the `SimpleWriter` class. Add the following method.

Listing 9.9   Adding method to `SimpleWriter`

```
public void WriteLine(params string[] values)
{
    this.target.WriteLine(string.Join(",", values));
}
```

This method assumes the user will provide the strings in the correct order.

You'll also need to add a couple new benchmarks to the `PerfTests` class, as follows.

Listing 9.10   Adding benchmark tests to the `PerfTests` class

```
[Benchmark(InnerIterationCount=10000)]
public void BenchmarkSimpleWriterJoin()
{
  var buffer = new byte[500000];
  var memoryStream = new MemoryStream(buffer);          ◁── Writes to
                                                             memory buffer
  foreach (var iteration in Benchmark.Iterations)
  {
    using (var streamWriter = new StreamWriter(memoryStream,
      Encoding.Default, 512, true))
    {
      using (iteration.StartMeasurement())
      {
        var simpleWriter = new SimpleWriter(streamWriter);
        simpleWriter.WriteHeader("Year", "Title", "Production Studio");
        for (int innerIteration = 0;
          innerIteration < Benchmark.InnerIterationCount;
          innerIteration++)
        {
          simpleWriter.WriteLine(
            "2008", "Iron Man", "Marvel Studios");        ◁── Writes the strings using
        }                                                      the join method
        streamWriter.Flush();
      }
    }
    memoryStream.Seek(0, SeekOrigin.Begin);
```

```
    }
}
[Benchmark(InnerIterationCount=10000)]                          Tests for writing
public void BenchmarkSimpleWriterToFileJoin()    ◁──┐ to file.
{
    int outerIterations = 0;
    foreach (var iteration in Benchmark.Iterations)
    {                                                          Writes to
        var fileStream = new FileStream(         ◁──┐ file stream
            $"tempfile{outerIterations++}.csv", FileMode.Create, FileAccess.Write);
        using (var streamWriter = new StreamWriter(fileStream,
            Encoding.Default, 512, false))
        {
            using (iteration.StartMeasurement())
            {
                var simpleWriter = new SimpleWriter(streamWriter);
                simpleWriter.WriteHeader("Year", "Title", "Production Studio");
                for (int innerIteration = 0;
                    innerIteration < Benchmark.InnerIterationCount;
                    innerIteration++)
                {
                    simpleWriter.WriteLine(
                        "2008", "Iron Man", "Marvel Studios");    ◁──┐ Writes the strings
                }                                                      using the join method
                streamWriter.Flush();
            }
        }
    }
}
```

With these new tests, I got the results shown in table 9.3.

Table 9.3 Test results from performance benchmark of `SimpleWriter`

Test Name	Metric	Iterations	AVERAGE	STDEV.S	MIN	MAX
BenchmarkSimpleWriter	Duration	100	2.529	1.646	1.706	13.312
BenchmarkSimpleWriterJoin	Duration	100	1.259	0.315	0.918	2.250
BenchmarkSimpleWriterToFile	Duration	100	3.780	0.985	2.760	9.812
BenchmarkSimpleWriter-ToFileJoin	Duration	100	2.122	0.689	1.429	6.985

PERFORMANCE TESTS ARE IMPACTED BY EXTERNAL FACTORS The Max measurement for `BenchmarkSimpleWriter` is 13.312 milliseconds, which is much higher than any other measurement. If you look at the order in which the tests were run, you'll notice this test came last. The likely explanation for the high maximum latency is that the garbage collector kicked in. Some ways to handle this would be randomizing the order of the tests, which would require a change to xUnit.Performance, or increasing the number of iterations to absorb the GC cost.

As you can see from the test results, using the new `WriteLine` method in `Simple-Writer` has a dramatic impact on performance. There are two changes in the method. One is that it doesn't use a dictionary, and the other is that it uses `string.Join` instead of a custom loop to write the fields. Which change had the most impact? You can try to determine this by using a profiler like PerfView.

9.3   *Using PerfView on .NET Core applications*

PerfView is a Windows application invented by Vance Morrison, a performance legend at Microsoft. He actively maintains the project on GitHub (https://github.com/Microsoft/perfview) and has all kinds of tutorials on how to use it and how to understand performance in general.

PerfView works by recording Event Tracing for Windows (ETW) events. ETW is a powerful feature built into the Windows operating system that gives you all kinds of information on the operation of your computer. In chapter 10 you'll learn how to emit your own ETW events. But for now, there are plenty of ETW events in .NET Core and the Windows kernel to help you diagnose your performance issues.

9.3.1   *Getting a CPU profile*

A profile gives you a window into what exactly your application is doing when it's running. You could get a memory profile to see how memory is being allocated and freed, or you could get a disk profile to see disk reads and writes.

CPU profiles tell you how your application uses the processor. In most cases, this means recording what code is executing to see what methods take the most CPU or appear most often in the stack. PerfView is a free tool for CPU profiles and much more.

> **What's a stack?**
>
> Suppose you have a program with a `Main` method. It calls the `WriteLog` method, which calls a `ToString` method. The stack in this scenario is `Main`→`Write-Log`→`ToString` with `ToString` on the top and `Main` at the bottom of the stack.
>
> Your high-level, object-oriented language is doing some work under the covers to make each method call. Part of that work is to push the contents of the CPU registers to the stack before making the jump to the method (flash back to your assembly class in college). This is why the term *stack* is used to refer to the chain of method calls.
>
> Each level of the stack (called a *frame*) needs some uniquely identifying information. Programs are divided into assemblies, assemblies into classes (and other types), and classes into methods. Most profilers will write each level of the stack with assembly, class name, and method name. Line-number information usually isn't available in CPU profiles.

You can download PerfView from the GitHub site (https://github.com/Microsoft/perfview). PerfView is a single exe file that has no install. Just copy it to a machine and run it as administrator. You can run your application using the Collect > Run menu option, as shown in figure 9.1.

Opens the Run dialog box, which is used to profile a specific command.

Memory allows you to view memory heaps.

Collect is similar to Run, except it collects all process on the machine.

Lots of help is available.

The command to run for profiling—the profile collection is still machine-wide, but it stops when the command finishes.

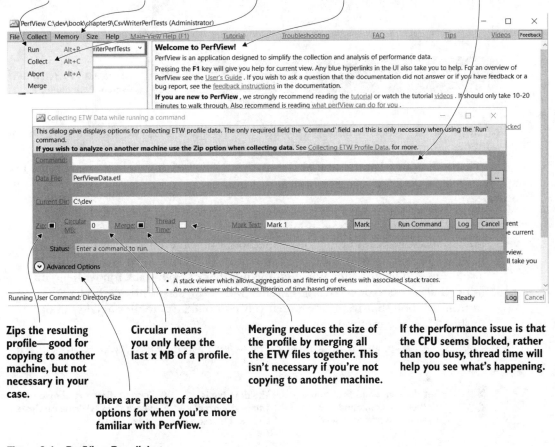

Zips the resulting profile—good for copying to another machine, but not necessary in your case.

Circular means you only keep the last x MB of a profile.

Merging reduces the size of the profile by merging all the ETW files together. This isn't necessary if you're not copying to another machine.

If the performance issue is that the CPU seems blocked, rather than too busy, thread time will help you see what's happening.

There are plenty of advanced options for when you're more familiar with PerfView.

Figure 9.1   PerfView Run dialog

CIRCULAR PROFILING Profiles can create big files on disk very quickly. This is OK, as long as the thing you're trying to profile happens quickly. But if it takes some time to reproduce the issue, you could end up with a really large profile that takes a long time to analyze. This is where circular profiling comes in handy. If you specify that you only want 500 MB in your profile, only the latest 500 MB will be kept on disk. That allows you to start the profiler, wait until the performance issues reproduce, and then stop the profiler with the resulting profile being no larger than 500 MB.

Try to run your performance tests in PerfView. Close the Run dialog box, and find the text box directly below the File menu. Enter the full path to the CsvWriterPerfTests folder in this text box. It should update the tree below the text box to show the contents of that folder (without files).

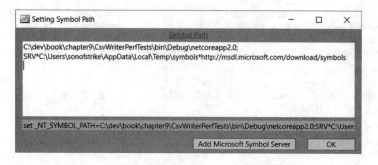

Figure 9.2   PerfView Set Symbol Path dialog

Next, go to File > Set Symbol Path. As shown in figure 9.2, add the full path to the .pdb files built under the CsvWriterPerfTests folder.

The other symbol path is the Microsoft Symbol Server. If you don't see it in the text box, click the Add Microsoft Symbol Server button.

> **WHAT ARE SYMBOLS FOR?**   When debugging or profiling, you'll use stacks to determine what code is executing. Each level (frame) of the stack indicates the assembly, class, and function or method. But sometimes this isn't enough information to determine the exact line of code. By matching symbols, you'll also be able to see the filename and line number of each stack frame. Keep in mind that stacks from .NET assemblies will show class and method names without symbols, but frames from natively compiled assemblies need symbols to show class and method names.

Next, open the Collect > Run menu option and fill out the dialog box as shown in figure 9.3.

Set the command field to the dotnet run command you used in the previous section.

The data file is where the profile data will be stored.

Current directory should be where the CsvWriterPerfTests code is located.

```
Collecting ETW Data while running a command                                        —  □  ×

This dialog give displays options for collecting ETW profile data. The only required field the 'Command' field and this is only necessary when using the 'Run'
command.
If you wish to analyze on another machine use the Zip option when collecting data. See Collecting ETW Profile Data for more.

Command:   dotnet run --perf:collect stopwatch

Data File:  C:\dev\book\chapter9\CsvWriterPerfTests\PerfViewData.etl                              [...]

Current Dir: C:\dev\book\chapter9\CsvWriterPerfTests

Zip:☐  Circular MB: 0   Merge:☐  Thread Time:☐       Mark Text: Mark 1        [Mark]   [Run Command]  [Log] [Cancel]

Status:  Enter a command to run.

⊙ Advanced Options
```

Turn off zip.   Turn off merge.   Click the Run Command button.

Figure 9.3   PerfView Run dialog box with commands to run your xUnit.Performance tests

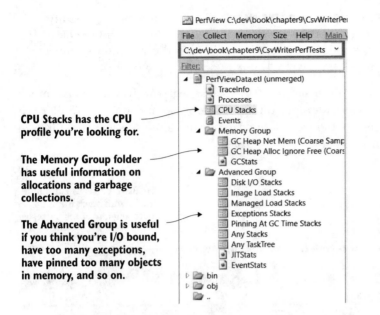

Once the profiling is complete, the Run dialog box will close, and the tree view on the left side of the main window will update to include your profile (see figure 9.4).

CPU Stacks has the CPU profile you're looking for.

The Memory Group folder has useful information on allocations and garbage collections.

The Advanced Group is useful if you think you're I/O bound, have too many exceptions, have pinned too many objects in memory, and so on.

Figure 9.4
PerfView profile tree

9.3.2 Analyzing a CPU profile

Double-click the CPU Stacks item in the tree. PerfView will then let you pick the process you want to analyze—remember that a PerfView profile is machine-wide, so all CPU stacks from all processes active on the machine during the profile are recorded. The dotnet run command executes several child processes, which can make it tricky to find the right one. The CommandLine portion will help greatly. Figure 9.5 shows what the Select Process window looks like.

There are multiple dotnet processes—notice the parent process ID is 12624, which is the dotnet run command you executed.

Notice also that MSBuild is executed to restore and build the project.

Select Process Window

The data that was collect was machine wide, but typically you are interested in only one process. This dialog box allows you to choose a particular process to focus on by eith or by selecting a process and hitting OK. The 'All Procs' button can be used if you wish to look at all data. See Selecting A Process Help for more.

Name	ID	Parent	CPU MSec	Start	Duration	CommandLine
dotnet	8700	12624	4,656	17-08-14 08:45:30	4.17 sec	"dotnet.exe" exec "C:\Program Files\dotnet\sdk\2.0.0-preview2-006497\MSBuild.dll" /m /v:m C:\dev\b
dotnet	12028	12624	1,905	17-08-14 08:45:34	2.27 sec	"dotnet" exec "C:\dev\book\chapter9\CsvWriterPerfTests\bin\Debug\netcoreapp2.0\CsvWriterPerfTest
dotnet	2052	12624	1,741	17-08-14 08:45:28	1.72 sec	"dotnet.exe" exec "C:\Program Files\dotnet\sdk\2.0.0-preview2-006497\MSBuild.dll" /m /v:m /NoLogo
explorer	6096	3416	1,015	17-08-14 08:45:28	12.33 sec	C:\windows\Explorer.EXE
MsMpEng	2568	692	949	17-08-14 08:45:28	12.33 sec	"C:\Program Files\Windows Defender\MsMpEng.exe"
dotnet	12624	15024	672	17-08-14 08:45:28	8.76 sec	"dotnet" run --perf:collect stopwatch
System	4	0	652	17-08-14 08:45:28	12.33 sec	
Code	4904	7648	536	17-08-14 08:45:28	12.33 sec	"C:\Program Files (x86)\Microsoft VS Code\Code.exe" --type=renderer --js-flags=--nolazy --no-sandb

OK		All Procs		Cancel

The dotnet exec command of CsvWriterPerfTests.dll is the one that actually runs our perf tests.

Figure 9.5 PerfView Select Process dialog box

IDENTIFYING YOUR APPLICATION'S PROCESS NAME To make it easier to identify the process, you can create a self-contained application, like you did in chapter 8. A self-contained application's process will have the assembly's name instead of dotnet, such as CsvWriterPerfTests.exe.

Once you pick the process, you'll see the CPU Stacks window. It won't make much sense at first because PerfView attempts to filter it to only what you need. You'll need to change the filters to get a better view of the data. Figure 9.6 shows what the filters at the top of the stack window are for.

Start and End define the time period to display from the profile, measured in milliseconds.

Exclusive patterns cut out stacks with stack frames matching any of the patterns.

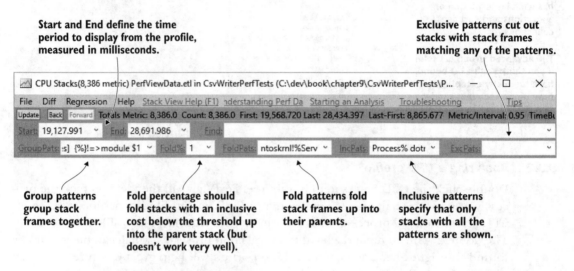

Group patterns group stack frames together.

Fold percentage should fold stacks with an inclusive cost below the threshold up into the parent stack (but doesn't work very well).

Fold patterns fold stack frames up into their parents.

Inclusive patterns specify that only stacks with all the patterns are shown.

Figure 9.6   PerfView CPU Stacks filters

Inclusive vs. exclusive costs

Every method contains some instructions that run on the CPU. The amount of time spent executing the instructions within a particular method is considered the *exclusive cost* of that method. Because that method is likely called multiple times, profiles sum up the total time and show that as the exclusive cost of the method. Costs are usually presented as percentages of the total CPU cost for the whole profile.

The *inclusive cost* of a method is its exclusive cost plus the cost of any methods it calls. Suppose you have a method, A, that calls methods B and C. The exclusive costs for A, B, and C are 1%, 5%, and 6% respectively. Let's assume that B and C don't call anything else, so their inclusive costs are equivalent to their exclusive costs. That makes method A's inclusive cost 12%—1% exclusive for itself, plus 5% and 6% for the inclusive costs of B and C.

It may take some time to understand the difference between group, fold, include, and exclude patterns. You'll use them to filter down to a couple of tests so you can get a better feel for how they work.

The first step is the group pattern. The default group pattern is very restrictive, as it will try to look for only your code. It does this by looking for the name of the application that you ran (`dotnet`), which isn't helpful in this case. Setting the group pattern takes a bit of trial and error.

Start by clearing the field and pressing Enter— that will show all stacks. Switch over to the CallTree tab, and you'll see a deep set of stacks. I start by looking for assemblies I'm not interested in and adding them to the group pattern.

In this case, I found that using `xunit%->xunit;clr%=>coreclr` worked best. I wanted to hide the xUnit library because I'm not interested in its internals, and it has pretty deep stacks. The `->` groups everything together as `xunit`. For CLR (common language runtime) libraries, I cared about the entry point, but nothing inside. To see the entry point but nothing else inside the group, you use the `=>` command instead of the `->`. You can add as many of these as you like, separated by semicolons. Keep in mind that they run in order from left to right.

The next filter is the fold patterns. The default fold pattern, `ntoskrnl!%Service-CopyEnd`, can remain. I add to that a pattern that folds the threads: `^Thread`. For this profile, I'm not interested which thread a particular test was run on. Folding gets it out of the stack and simplifies the stack tree.

For .NET Core profiles, I found that two other stacks were uninteresting and added these entries to the fold patterns: `system.private.corelib%;system.runtime.extensions%`. I folded these because I don't have the symbols for them, and it helped to declutter the stack.

PerfView has already set the inclusive pattern filter to the process ID that you picked. If you were to clear this filter, it would show all stacks from all processes. For this example, we'll focus on the two tests that wrote to files. To do this, add this pattern to the inclusive patterns: `csvwriterperftests!CsvWriterPerfTests.PerfTests.BenchmarkSimpleWriterToFile`.

Right-click somewhere on the stack and choose Lookup Warm Symbols from the menu. At this point, you should have a good view of the stack involved in running the two file tests. Figure 9.7 shows how this could look.

WHAT ARE CPU STACKS, AND HOW ARE THEY MEASURED? The CPU Stacks window measures percentages based on the number of samples that appeared in a particular stack versus the total number of samples included by the filters. It's not a percentage of the whole profile. A *sample* in this context comes from a periodic sampling of all stacks. The default for PerfView is to take a sample every millisecond, but this is adjustable.

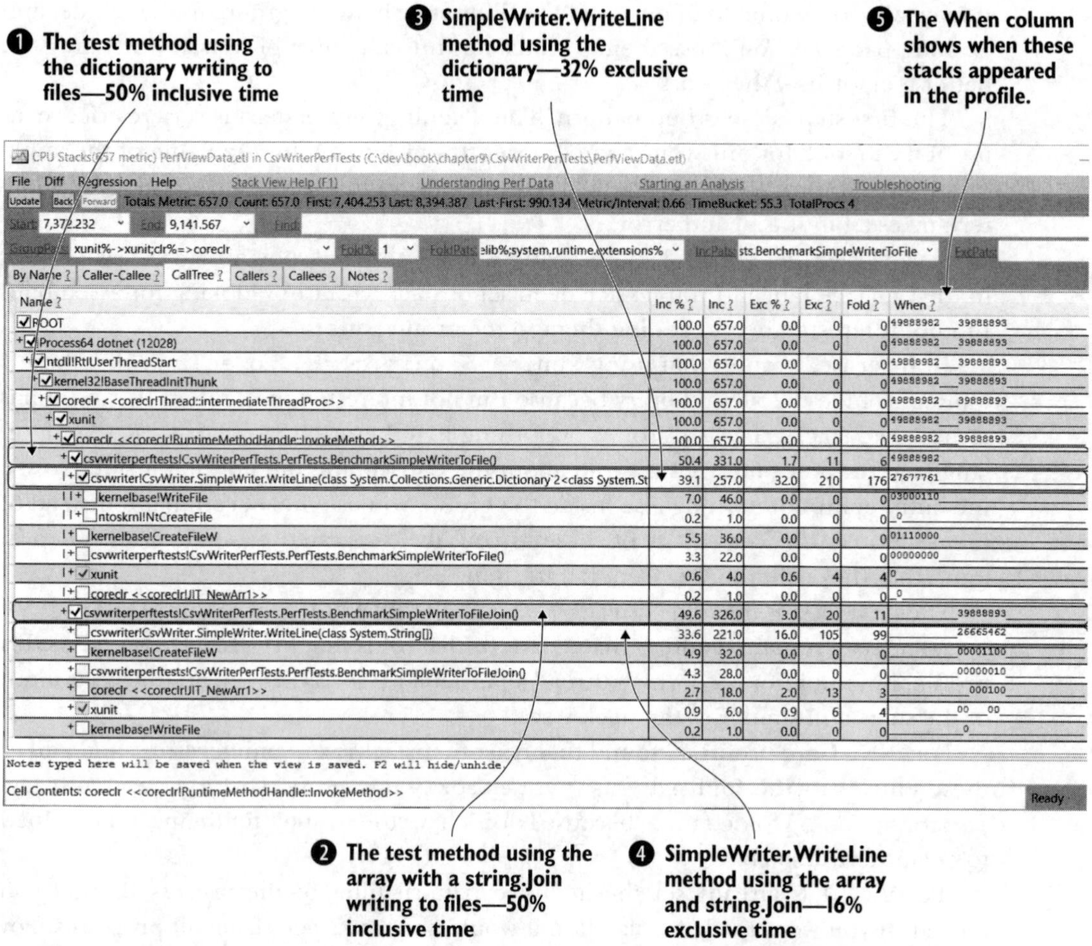

❶ **The test method using the dictionary writing to files—50% inclusive time**

❸ **SimpleWriter.WriteLine method using the dictionary—32% exclusive time**

❺ **The When column shows when these stacks appeared in the profile.**

Figure 9.7   PerfView CPU Stacks window showing the xUnit.Performance tests that write to files

❷ **The test method using the array with a string.Join writing to files—50% inclusive time**

❹ **SimpleWriter.WriteLine method using the array and string.Join—16% exclusive time**

Notice that the two tests took the same amount of CPU time (compare the Inc column from figure 9.7 for lines ❶ and ❷), but the time spent in SimpleWriter varies greatly (compare the Inc column for lines ❸ and ❹). If you expand the stacks, you'll see that the file manipulation is the source of the fluctuation. By viewing the profile, you can cancel these things out and compare the two WriteLine methods directly against each other. The performance difference is most notable in the exclusive percentage.

The calls to TextWriter.WriteLine and string.Join are still not visible in the stack. This can happen if the compiler "inlines" the methods, which is an optimization to avoid calling methods by sticking the code from one method directly into its caller. Another reason could be the lack of symbols. Usually PerfView will show a stack frame with a question mark (?) for any symbol it doesn't have. The missing symbols likely come from system.private.corelib or system.runtime.extensions.

Unfortunately, .NET Core symbols aren't published to the public Microsoft symbol store or included in their NuGet packages.

9.3.3 Looking at GC information

Back in the main PerfView window, expand the Memory Group folder in the tree and double-click GCStats. This opens an HTML page with links at the top for each process. Find the one with the process ID you analyzed in the CPU Stacks window. It should look like `dotnetc CsvWriterPerfTests.dll --perf:collect stop-watch`. I think the `c` suffixed to `dotnet` means *child process*, but that's just a guess.

The page includes a table of information about the garbage collections by generation, which should look similar to table 9.4.

Table 9.4 PerfView GC rollup by generation

GC Rollup By Generation										
All times are in msec.										
Gen	Count	Max Pause	Max Peak MB	Max Alloc MB/sec	Total Pause	Total Alloc MB	Alloc MB/ MSec GC	Survived MB/MSec GC	Mean Pause	Induced
ALL	134	3.1	6.2	1,490.404	57.1	317.3	5.6	0.077	0.4	4
0	130	3.1	6.2	1,490.404	52.6	311.9	0.2	0.024	0.4	0
1	0	0.0	0.0	0.000	0.0	0.0	0.0	NaN	NaN	0
2	4	1.3	3.0	455.380	4.5	5.4	0.0	0.526	1.1	4

The .NET garbage collector has three generations: 0, 1, and 2. When an object is first allocated, it has never been through a garbage collection before, so its GC count is 0. When the .NET GC kicks in, it will first try to collect everything that has a count of 0, hence generation 0. Any object that still has references that are rooted, meaning it's being used or needs to be accessible in some way, survives the garbage collection. The table shows the rate of survival. Survival also means an increment in GC count to 1.

Gen 1 garbage collections are done less often and have more impact. The same process happens for gen 2, which is the most impactful. Notice that table 9.4 has four gen 2 collections but no gen 1 collections. This may seem a bit odd until you look at the Induced column. *Induced* means that the gen 2 collection was triggered manually. In this case, xUnit.Performance induces a gen 2 collection before each test to prevent memory usage from one test causing a gen 2 during another test, which would skew the results. It's not perfect, but it does help.

PerfView also includes some useful summary information for GC usage in the process:

- Total CPU Time: 1,905 msec
- Total GC CPU Time: 47 msec

- Total Allocs : 317.349 MB
- GC CPU MSec/MB Alloc : 0.148 MSec/MB
- Total GC Pause: 57.1 msec
- % Time paused for Garbage Collection: 3.5%
- % CPU Time spent Garbage Collecting: 2.5%
- Max GC Heap Size: 6.204 MB
- Peak Process Working Set: 36.209 MB

Out of the 1,905 milliseconds of CPU time used for the performance tests, only 47 milliseconds were spent in garbage collection. This is also shown in percentages and includes the time paused for GC. Your test only had a max heap size of 6 MB, so it's normal to not see a lot of impact from garbage collection.

> **PERFVIEW CAN ALSO BE USED FOR MEMORY INVESTIGATIONS** If you suspect a memory issue with your application, the GC Stats window is a good place to start. PerfView also has an advanced option during collection to either sample .NET memory allocations or record all of them. These have an impact on the performance of the application, but they can give you all kinds of useful data for digging into who's allocating objects and who's holding them.

9.3.4   *Exposing exceptions*

One of the nice things about taking a PerfView profile is how much it reveals about your application that you didn't know was going on. Take the multiple child processes spawned by the `dotnet` command, or how many stack frames go to xUnit if you don't use a grouping. I also find it interesting to see how many exceptions are thrown and caught without my knowing.

Exceptions are generally bad for performance, so you don't want them in your performance-critical areas. They may be OK in other areas, although most programmers would argue that exceptions should only be used in exceptional cases. In some cases, an exception thrown and handled by one of your dependent libraries can reveal optimizations or issues.

PerfView has two ways to view exceptions. A PerfView profile, by default, listens to the CLR ETW events fired when exceptions are thrown. You can view these events by opening the Events item in the profile tree. Figure 9.8 shows the exceptions for your xUnit.Performance test.

The Rest column in the event grid will have the exception type and message. Notice also that there's a field called `HasStack="true"`. The Events window doesn't show the stack, but you can see it in the Exceptions Stacks item under the Advanced Group in the profile tree. Figure 9.9 shows the exceptions in this view.

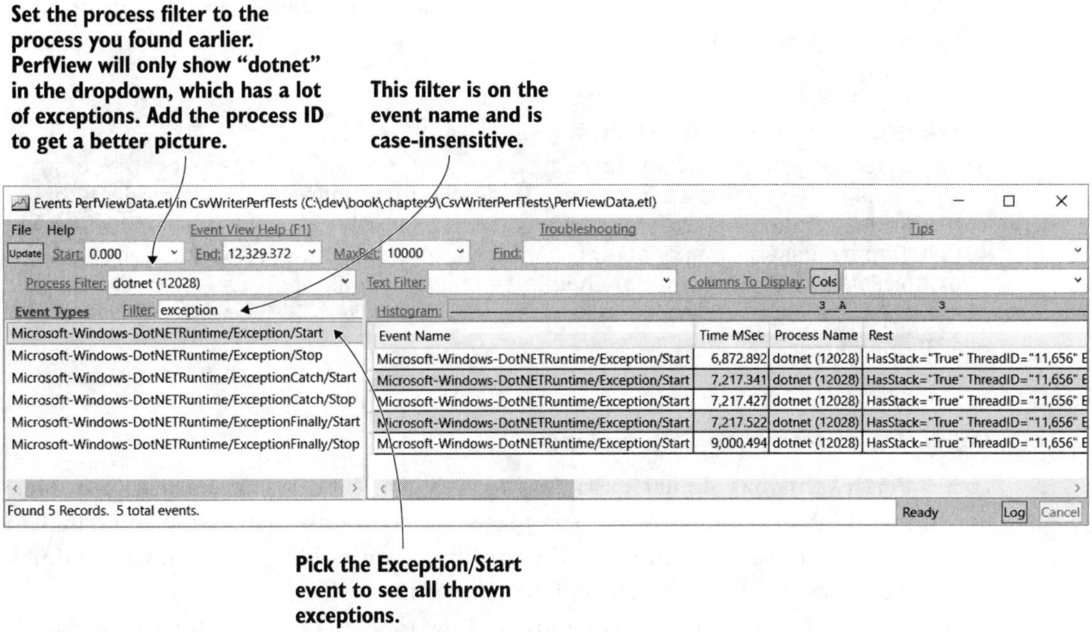

Set the process filter to the
process you found earlier.
PerfView will only show "dotnet"
in the dropdown, which has a lot
of exceptions. Add the process ID
to get a better picture.

This filter is on the
event name and is
case-insensitive.

Pick the Exception/Start
event to see all thrown
exceptions.

Figure 9.8   PerfView Events window filtered to show exceptions

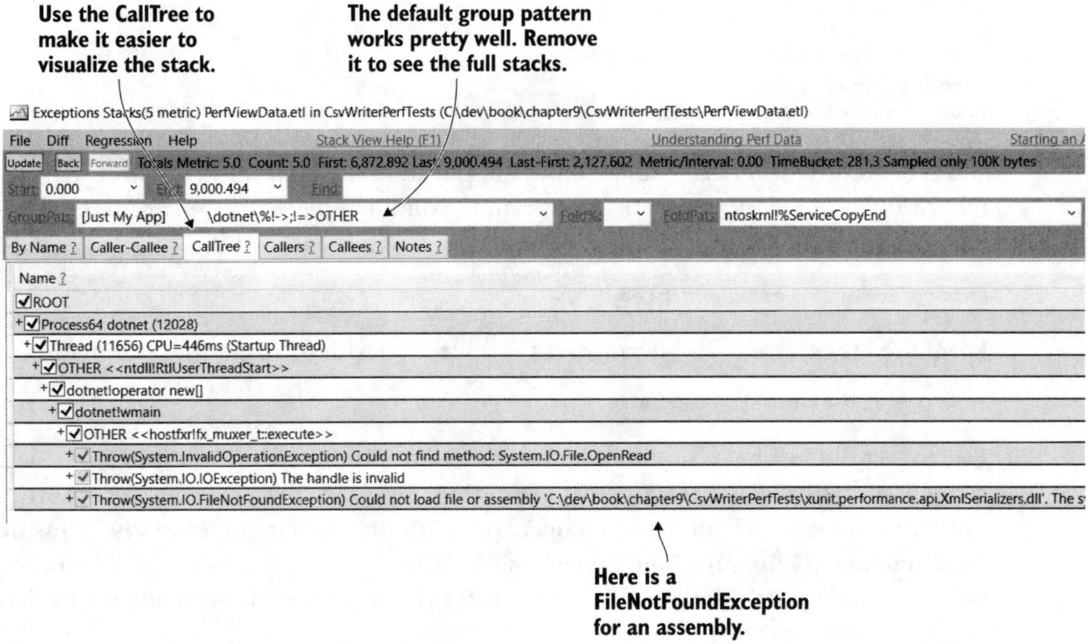

Use the CallTree to
make it easier to
visualize the stack.

The default group pattern
works pretty well. Remove
it to see the full stacks.

Here is a
FileNotFoundException
for an assembly.

Figure 9.9   PerfView Exceptions Stacks window

These exceptions don't affect the performance tests, but they give some insight into the xUnit.Performance library.

> **What is the XmlSerializers.dll for?**
>
> After executing the performance tests, xUnit.Performance produces several output files. One of the files is an XML file with detailed test information. To produce that file, xUnit.Performance uses the `System.Xml.XmlSerializer` class, which can build the necessary components to serialize a given object graph to XML on the fly, or the library's developers can choose to build a serialization assembly ahead of time. Generating the serialization assembly only works in .NET Framework at the time of this writing.

9.3.5   *Collecting performance data on Linux*

Linux Perf Events has similar capability to ETW in Windows. It can capture stacks machine-wide. Some Linux developers prefer flame graphs for viewing the data captured by Perf Events, but I find PerfView grouping and folding more powerful. Luckily, PerfView has a facility for viewing Perf Events data.

For the most up-to-date instructions on how to view Linux performance data in PerfView, consult the help topic "Viewing Linux Data," which is available in the Help menu. The instructions are straightforward. Start by downloading and installing the `perfcollect` script using Curl, which you learned about in chapter 7, with the following commands:

```
curl -OL http://aka.ms/perfcollect
chmod +x perfcollect
sudo ./perfcollect install
```

You'll need two terminals: one to run the application, and another to collect the profile. In the terminal that runs the application, you'll need to set an environment variable that tells .NET to emit symbol information. Use this command:

```
export COMPlus_PerfMapEnabled=1
```

From the other terminal, you can start the collection with the following command:

```
sudo ./perfcollect collect mytrace
```

Perfcollect doesn't have an equivalent to PerfView's Run option. You'll need to start collection manually and use Ctrl-C to stop the collection. Because you have to write the entry point for xUnit.Performance, you can put a `Console.ReadKey()` in the `Main` method before the benchmark starts. Perfcollect will produce a file called mytrace.trace.zip with the profile in it. Transfer this to your Windows machine to view the profile in PerfView.

Additional resources

To learn more about what we covered in this chapter, see the following resources:

- PerfView—https://github.com/Microsoft/perfview
- *Writing High-Performance .NET Code* by Ben Watson (Ben Watson, 2014)—http://www.writinghighperf.net/
- Vance Morrison's blog—https://blogs.msdn.microsoft.com/vancem/

Summary

In this chapter, you learned how to write performance benchmarks and collect profiles. These were the key concepts we covered:

- xUnit.Performance provides a way to write performance tests similar to unit tests.
- Measuring is the best way to understand where to focus energy on optimization.
- External factors such as the garbage collector can impact performance.
- Profiling provides greater insight into the performance of an application.
- A powerful profile viewer like PerfView helps to visualize a profile in useful ways.

These are some important techniques to remember from this chapter:

- Be careful about memory use in performance benchmark tests, as you don't want the tests to impact the results.
- Use group and fold patterns in PerfView to condense stacks to display only the portions you find important.
- The `perfcollect` script allows you to gather profile data from Linux and analyze it in PerfView.

There are many performance tools available, including the performance tools built into the more expensive versions of Visual Studio. Out of all the tools I've used, PerfView stands out as the most powerful—and it's free. PerfView also doesn't hide how it captures the performance data, so there's no magic. That's why I chose to focus on it in this chapter.

When it comes to performance benchmarks, Visual Studio provides a way to run performance tests using unit tests, and it's definitely worth a try. With xUnit.Performance, you can run the tests from the command line. xUnit.Performance also has more interesting data-collection options using ETW on Windows, but the stopwatch method should work on all platforms. One other advantage of using xUnit.Performance is that it's clear what the benchmarks are for. Unit tests are typically not written to be careful about memory and could introduce unwanted side effects when they're repurposed as performance tests.

10
Building world-ready applications

You've built a library that is cross-platform, fast, and well-tested. Before you can publish to NuGet and obsess over download numbers, however, you need to internationalize your application. Anything that can be exposed to the user should be in a form the user can understand. Dates, time zones, languages, measurements, and even sorting order depend on region and culture.

.NET Standard includes powerful capabilities for internationalizing applications. In this chapter, you'll learn about the recommended process for internationalization (and I'll attempt to disambiguate the terms *localization*, *globalization*, and *internationalization*). We'll also explore the techniques and APIs for localization in .NET. Let's begin with an example application.

10.1 *Going international*

One of the companies I had the privilege of consulting for built a unique type of commercial air conditioner. The idea was simple: run the air conditioner at night, when electricity is cheap, to create a block of ice, and then use the block of ice to create cool air during the day. Whereas a company might be interested in replacing their existing air conditioners for one of these for the cost savings, power companies took a greater interest because they could help flatten the power curve by moving energy use from daytime to nighttime. But power companies also want control over the air conditioners so they can handle power surges, avoid brownouts, and the like. Essentially, each block of ice is stored energy, and each air conditioner is connected to the internet so it's manageable by the customer and power company.

Let's say you're on the development team behind the air conditioner controller. Your company has just scored an international deal and is lining up more deals in countries all over the world. But you realize that your application was developed with the assumption that all your customers would be English-speaking and located in California. You need to go through the process of internationalization.

10.1.1 *Setting up the sample application*

To try out the code in this chapter, the simplest way to set everything up is to create a console application called ACController. To do this, create a new folder called ACController, and run `dotnet new console` within that folder.

Add a new file called TempControl.cs, as shown in the following listing. This class will hold some temperature data measured by the air conditioner.

Listing 10.1 `TempControl` class holds temperature information

```
namespace ACController
{
  public class TempControl
  {
    public static double ExhaustAirTemp { get; internal set; }
    public static double CoolantTemp { get; internal set; }
    public static double OutsideAirTemp { get; internal set; }
  }
}
```

Periodically, the application will write the temperatures to the log. This is easy to simulate by building a Program.cs file. You'll use `Console.WriteLine` to write the log messages, as shown in the following listing.

Listing 10.2 Program file to simulate writing a log message

```
using System;

namespace ACController
{
```

```
class Program
{
  static void Main(string[] args)
  {
    Console.WriteLine("Exhaust Air Temp: " +
      TempControl.ExhaustAirTemp);
  }
}
}
```

All this program does is write a string to the console. Pretend the console is your log.

This works fine if your application only has to write the logs in English. But if your customers don't read English, you'll need to give them logs in their own language. The way this code is written, there's no way to change the log based on the customer's region or culture. The code isn't "world-ready."

10.1.2 *Making the sample application world-ready*

The string Exhaust Air Temp: needs to be translated into different languages. You'll need to write some code that can give you the correct string to write to the log. In .NET, the ResourceManager fills this role. The string is considered a *resource*, and the ResourceManager can retrieve the right version of the string based on the region and culture of the current user.

The string resources need to be separated from the code. To do this, create a file named strings.restext with the following code. It should be put in the same folder as the project code.

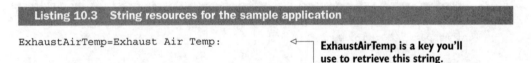

Listing 10.3   String resources for the sample application

```
ExhaustAirTemp=Exhaust Air Temp:          ◁──┐ ExhaustAirTemp is a key you'll
                                               use to retrieve this string.
```

Next, you'll need to modify ACController.csproj to generate a resource file from the strings.restext file and embed it into the ACController assembly. Modify the csproj file as follows.

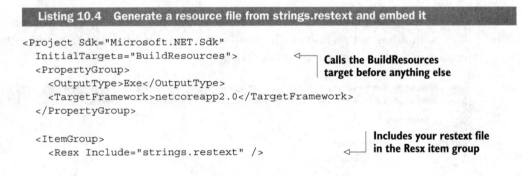

Listing 10.4   Generate a resource file from strings.restext and embed it

```
<Project Sdk="Microsoft.NET.Sdk"
  InitialTargets="BuildResources">          ◁──┐ Calls the BuildResources
  <PropertyGroup>                                target before anything else
    <OutputType>Exe</OutputType>
    <TargetFramework>netcoreapp2.0</TargetFramework>
  </PropertyGroup>

  <ItemGroup>                                      ┌─ Includes your restext file
    <Resx Include="strings.restext" />        ◁──┘   in the Resx item group
```

```
    <EmbeddedResource Include="strings.resources" />          Embeds generated resource
  </ItemGroup>                                                file in the assembly

  <Target Name="BuildResources">
    <GenerateResource ExecuteAsTool="false"                   Custom MSBuild
      Sources="@(Resx)">                                      target
    </GenerateResource>                      ExecuteAsTool set to
  </Target>                                  "false" for .NET Core
</Project>
```

The `ResourceManager` class isn't able to read the restext file directly. It only reads files in the binary .resources format. To convert the restext file into a resources file, a MSBuild task called GenerateResource is built into .NET Core. This task will read the set of files you give it and write out a resources file with the same name as the input file.

The resources file then needs to be embedded into the assembly so `Resource-Manager` can find it. That's why you add the `EmbeddedResource ItemGroup`. Note that the strings.resources file has to exist on disk during build. The easiest way to guarantee this is to create a custom target and add it to the `InitialTargets` list. This will cause the resource to be generated before the build begins (also before restore begins).

> **MSBUILD DOESN'T DETECT RESOURCE FILE CHANGES** Although MSBuild is good at detecting a lack of changes in code files so it can skip building an assembly, modified resources will typically not be noticed by MSBuild. You can add the `--no-incremental` argument when building to get around this and ensure the assembly is rebuilt.

Now that you have an embedded resource file, use `ResourceManager` to get the string resource out of it. Modify Program.cs as follows.

Listing 10.5 File to simulate writing a log message modified to use `ResourceManager`

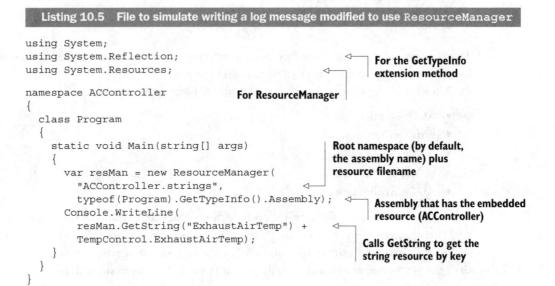

```
using System;
using System.Reflection;
using System.Resources;                                For the GetTypeInfo
                                                       extension method
namespace ACController              For ResourceManager
{
  class Program
  {
    static void Main(string[] args)
    {                                                  Root namespace (by default,
      var resMan = new ResourceManager(                the assembly name) plus
        "ACController.strings",                         resource filename
        typeof(Program).GetTypeInfo().Assembly);       Assembly that has the embedded
      Console.WriteLine(                               resource (ACController)
        resMan.GetString("ExhaustAirTemp") +
        TempControl.ExhaustAirTemp);                   Calls GetString to get the
    }                                                  string resource by key
  }
}
```

SETTING THE ROOT NAMESPACE   You can change the root namespace for your assembly by adding a tag to the csproj file inside a `PropertyGroup`:`<Root-Namespace>ACController.Root</RootNamespace>`.

At this point, you're ready to execute `dotnet run` from the command prompt. After all this work, you've only managed to move the string out of the C# code. But how does this make the application world-ready? To answer that, you'll attempt to make a Spanish language version of your resource file.

Let's say a power company in Mexico has just purchased some of your air conditioners. The culture code for Spanish language in Mexico is "es-MX" (for reference, the culture code for English in the US is "en-US"). You need to create a resource file for this culture code.

Add a new file named strings.es-MX.restext to the project folder with the following contents.

Listing 10.6   String resources for the sample application for the Spanish-Mexico culture

```
ExhaustAirTemp=Temp del aire del extractor:    ◁──┐ You're abbreviating
                                                   temperature in Spanish also.
```

In order for the resources file to be generated and embedded into the assembly, modify the `ResX` and `EmbeddedResource` item groups in ACController.csproj as follows.

Listing 10.7   Modify `ResX` and `EmbeddedResource` groups to support multiple files

```
<ItemGroup>
  <Resx Include="*.restext" />
  <EmbeddedResource Include="*.resources" />
</ItemGroup>
```

The wildcards let you include any .restext or .resources file in the folder, so you don't have to explicitly add an entry in the project file for each culture.

After building, take a look at the files and folders generated:

- ACController/
- bin/Debug/netcoreapp2.0/
- ACController.dll
- es-MX/
- ACController.resources.dll

A subfolder named for the culture code of the embedded resource has been created, and it contains a resources.dll file. As you may guess, this assembly only contains the embedded string resources for the es-MX culture code. The assembly is called a *satellite assembly*. `ResourceManager` will search for satellite assemblies depending on the culture code.

Setting a culture as default (neutral)

By not adding a culture code to the strings.restext filename, you've essentially made this the default, or neutral, culture. Notice that there's no ACController.resources.dll satellite assembly in the same folder as ACController.dll. Instead, the neutral resources are embedded into the ACController.dll.

You don't need to embed a neutral resource, though. As an alternative, you can set a particular culture code as the neutral culture with a custom attribute in Program.cs:

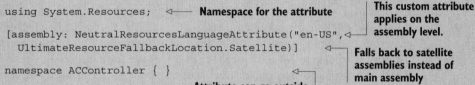

```
using System.Resources;        ◁── Namespace for the attribute

[assembly: NeutralResourcesLanguageAttribute("en-US",◁─┘  This custom attribute
    UltimateResourceFallbackLocation.Satellite)]           applies on the
                                             ◁─            assembly level.
namespace ACController { }                ◁─┐  Falls back to satellite
                                             assemblies instead of
                     Attribute can go outside  main assembly
                       the rest of the code
```

This attribute tells the `ResourceManager` to look for an "en-US" satellite assembly whenever it can't find a satellite assembly that matches the user's current culture. Note that if it can't find the designated neutral satellite assembly, it will throw an exception.

To test this out, you could rename strings.restext to strings.en-US.restext and delete the strings.resources file.

If you run the ACController application on a computer that's set for the es-MX culture, you'll see the log output in Spanish (but see the sidebar). If the computer is using any other culture code, you'll get English. In order to simulate being in the es-MX culture, you can add the following code to Program.cs.

Listing 10.8 Applying es-MX culture code with `ResourceManager`

```
using System.Globalization;          ◁─┐  Add for
using System.Threading;          ◁─      CultureInfo class

class Program                  Add for
{                          Thread class
  static void Main(string[] args)
  {
    var culture = CultureInfo                 Creates a culture using
      .CreateSpecificCulture("es-MX");    ◁─┘  the culture code
    Thread.CurrentThread.CurrentCulture = culture;
    Thread.CurrentThread.CurrentUICulture = culture;   ◁── Also sets the UI culture
    var resMan = new ResourceManager(
      "ACController.strings",
      typeof(Program).GetTypeInfo().Assembly);    You can also pass a culture
    Console.WriteLine(                            to GetString if you don't
      resMan.GetString("ExhaustAirTemp") +    ◁─  want the default.
      TempControl.ExhaustAirTemp);
  }
}
```

Sets the
current
culture

WHAT'S THE DIFFERENCE BETWEEN CURRENTCULTURE AND CURRENTUICULTURE?
You'll generally want the current culture and current UI culture to be the same for testing, but what do these properties mean? `CurrentCulture` is used for formatting, such as for dates, times, and sort order. `CurrentUI-Culture` is used by `ResourceManager` to determine which resources to search for. For this chapter, `CurrentUICulture` will be your means of getting a resource string in the right language.

SETTING CULTURE IN MULTITHREADED APPLICATIONS   The culture is set only on the current thread, rather than on the whole process. If you want the culture applied to all threads, you can use the `CultureInfo.DefaultThread-CurrentCulture` and `CultureInfo.DefaultThreadCurrentUI-Culture` properties. Note, though, that if you set the culture on the current thread and perform asynchronous operations via `async/await` or through tasks, the culture is maintained across threads.

> ### ResourceManager can't find satellite assemblies
> As of .NET Core 2.0, when you run or debug this code using `dotnet run` or your IDE, you won't see the Spanish output. You'll need to create a self-contained version of this application first. Hopefully this will be fixed this in later versions.
>
> To create a self-contained application, add a `<RuntimeIdentifiers>` property in the property group in the ACController.csproj file with the runtime identifier you need. Then run the command `dotnet publish -c Release -r <runtimeid>` to generate the self-contained application. If you then run the executable from the command line, the Spanish text should appear.
>
> Self-contained applications are covered in chapter 2, and a table of runtime identifiers is available in appendix A.

10.2 *Using a logging framework instead of writing to the console*

Your air conditioner controller program may be world-ready, but it writes all logs to the console. It turns out that the air conditioner doesn't have a console. You'll need to write logs to different places, like files and external web services. Rather than write each log several times in the code depending on where it's supposed to go, you can use a logging framework and write the log once. Then multiple subscribers can each work with the log messages independently. But you must maintain your code's world-readiness while using logging frameworks.

There are many logging frameworks for .NET Core. To keep things simple, you'll use another Microsoft.Extensions library called Microsoft.Extensions.Logging. Start by restructuring the classes. Figure 10.1 shows a class diagram for the restructured code using the Microsoft.Extensions.Logging library.

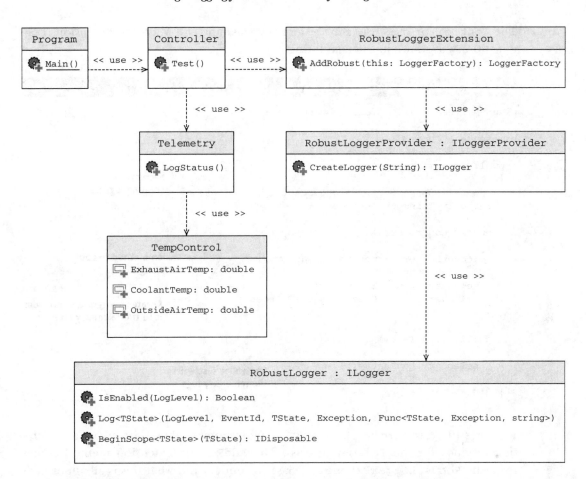

Figure 10.1 Class diagram for the air conditioner controller

The controller has a `Test` method to test the status of the air conditioner. Invoke it using the following code.

Listing 10.9 Program.cs tests the `Controller`

```
namespace ACController
{
  class Program
  {
    static void Main()
    {
      var controller = new Controller();
      controller.Test();
    }
  }
}
```

The `Controller` class uses the `Telemetry` class and the Microsoft.Extensions.Logging library, as shown in the next listing.

Listing 10.10   `Controller` class

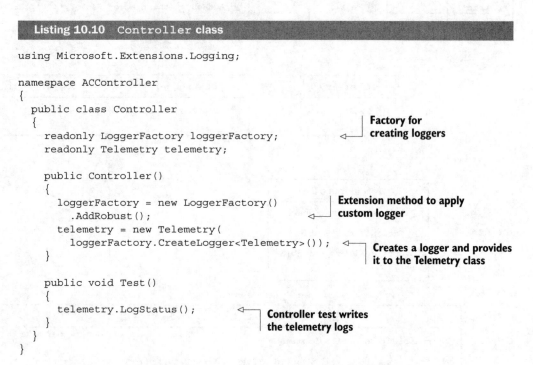

```
using Microsoft.Extensions.Logging;

namespace ACController
{
  public class Controller
  {
    readonly LoggerFactory loggerFactory;           Factory for
    readonly Telemetry telemetry;                   creating loggers

    public Controller()
    {
      loggerFactory = new LoggerFactory()           Extension method to apply
        .AddRobust();                               custom logger
      telemetry = new Telemetry(
        loggerFactory.CreateLogger<Telemetry>());   Creates a logger and provides
    }                                               it to the Telemetry class

    public void Test()
    {
      telemetry.LogStatus();                         Controller test writes
    }                                                the telemetry logs
  }
}
```

In listing 10.10, you create a `LoggerFactory` instance and use it to create an `ILogger` instance for the `Telemetry` class. The `AddRobust` extension method comes from the `RobustLoggerExtension` class. To understand what this is all about, let's explore the Microsoft.Extensions.Logging library.

10.2.1   *Using the Microsoft .Extensions.Logging library*

To use the Microsoft.Extensions.Logging library, you'll need to add a reference to the project file, as follows.

Listing 10.11   Add a reference to Microsoft logging extensions

```
<Project Sdk="Microsoft.NET.Sdk">
  <PropertyGroup>
    <OutputType>Exe</OutputType>
    <TargetFramework>netcoreapp2.0</TargetFramework>
  </PropertyGroup>

  <ItemGroup>
    <PackageReference Include="Microsoft.Extensions.Logging"
                      Version="2.0.0" />
  </ItemGroup>
</Project>
```

The `AddRobust()` extension method in listing 10.10 adds what's called a logging provider to the factory. If you wanted to write logs to the console, you'd use the console logging provider through the `AddConsole()` extension method defined in Microsoft.Extensions.Logging.Console, which is part of a separate package. But as mentioned before, your air conditioner controller doesn't have a console. You need a way to send logs back to the manufacturer that's robust enough to handle connectivity issues, power failures, and so on. You need to create your own logger implementation.

An example implementation is shown in the following listing.

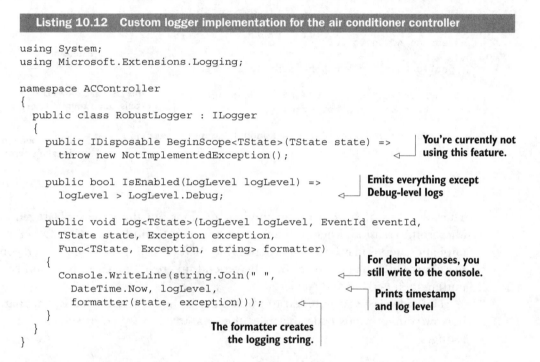

Listing 10.12 Custom logger implementation for the air conditioner controller

```
using System;
using Microsoft.Extensions.Logging;

namespace ACController
{
  public class RobustLogger : ILogger
  {
    public IDisposable BeginScope<TState>(TState state) =>        You're currently not
      throw new NotImplementedException();                        using this feature.

    public bool IsEnabled(LogLevel logLevel) =>        Emits everything except
      logLevel > LogLevel.Debug;                       Debug-level logs

    public void Log<TState>(LogLevel logLevel, EventId eventId,
      TState state, Exception exception,
      Func<TState, Exception, string> formatter)
    {                                                          For demo purposes, you
      Console.WriteLine(string.Join(" ",                       still write to the console.
        DateTime.Now, logLevel,                               Prints timestamp
        formatter(state, exception)));                        and log level
    }
  }                           The formatter creates
}                             the logging string.
```

> **ROBUST ONLY IN NAME** Although I call this a `RobustLogger`, an actual robust logger wouldn't write to the console.

In order to add the `RobustLogger` to the factory, you need a provider. The simplest version of a provider is shown in the following listing.

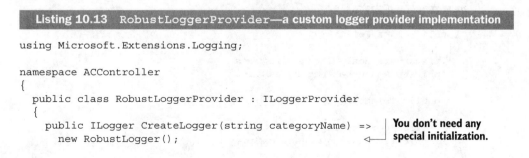

Listing 10.13 `RobustLoggerProvider`—a custom logger provider implementation

```
using Microsoft.Extensions.Logging;

namespace ACController
{
  public class RobustLoggerProvider : ILoggerProvider
  {
    public ILogger CreateLogger(string categoryName) =>        You don't need any
      new RobustLogger();                                       special initialization.
```

```
    public void Dispose() { }          ◁──┐  ILoggerProvider
  }                                        │  inherits IDisposable.
}
```

Most providers include extension methods so they can be used in the method-chaining pattern you learned about in chapter 6. The following listing shows how to implement this extension method.

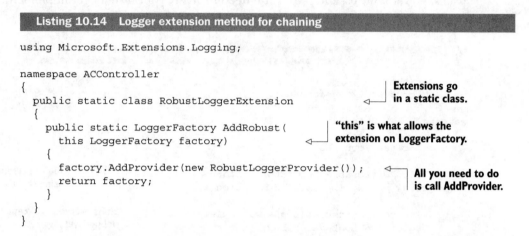

Listing 10.14   Logger extension method for chaining

```
using Microsoft.Extensions.Logging;

namespace ACController
{                                                      Extensions go
  public static class RobustLoggerExtension     ◁──┘   in a static class.
  {
    public static LoggerFactory AddRobust(          "this" is what allows the
      this LoggerFactory factory)          ◁──┘     extension on LoggerFactory.
    {
      factory.AddProvider(new RobustLoggerProvider());   ◁──┐  All you need to do
      return factory;                                        │  is call AddProvider.
    }
  }
}
```

There are lots of custom logger implementations out there. Several are under the Microsoft.Extensions.Logging name and are easy to find in NuGet. Other custom implementations may be a bit harder to find. Before writing a custom logger, consider searching GitHub and NuGet first. If you end up creating a custom logger, consider putting it on GitHub and NuGet.

The only class you have left to implement is the `Telemetry` class. For that class, borrow your previous code that uses the `ResourceManager`, as shown in the next listing.

Listing 10.15   The air conditioner controller's `Telemetry` class

```
using System.Reflection;
using System.Resources;
using Microsoft.Extensions.Logging;

namespace ACController
{
  public class Telemetry
  {
    private readonly ILogger logger;
    private ResourceManager resMan;

    public Telemetry(ILogger logger)
    {
      this.logger = logger;
      this.resMan = new ResourceManager(
```

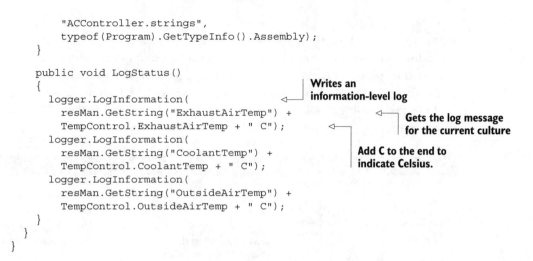

```
      "ACController.strings",
      typeof(Program).GetTypeInfo().Assembly);
  }

  public void LogStatus()
  {                                              Writes an
    logger.LogInformation(                       information-level log
      resMan.GetString("ExhaustAirTemp") +
      TempControl.ExhaustAirTemp + " C");        Gets the log message
    logger.LogInformation(                       for the current culture
      resMan.GetString("CoolantTemp") +
      TempControl.CoolantTemp + " C");           Add C to the end to
    logger.LogInformation(                       indicate Celsius.
      resMan.GetString("OutsideAirTemp") +
      TempControl.OutsideAirTemp + " C");
  }
 }
}
```

You'll need to add more entries to your restext files for the `CoolantTemp` and `OutsideAirTemp` resource strings, as shown in the following listing.

Listing 10.16   Updated strings.restext

```
ExhaustAirTemp=Exhaust Air Temp:
CoolantTemp=Coolant Temp:
OutsideAirTemp=Outside Air Temp:
```

Your ACController code is now functional and uses a logging library, but the application isn't world-ready. Before we get into the specifics of what's wrong with this application, let's take a look at the internationalization process.

10.2.2   Internationalization

Often abbreviated as i18n (*i* + 18 letters + *n*), *internationalization* means different things to different companies. In Microsoft and .NET terms, internationalization refers to the overall process, which consists of three steps:

- Globalization (g11n)
- Localizability review (l12y)
- Localization (l10n)

The definitions for these terms in Microsoft's documentation are vague and circular. A more helpful way to understand what they mean is to go through each step of the process.

10.2.3   Globalization

Globalization, aka world-readiness, involves designing and developing an application that can adapt to the region and culture of the user. Any data that can be exposed to the user, such as strings, dates, and numbers, needs to be adaptable to the region's and culture's language, sort order, and formats.

Note that although globalization means the software must be adaptable to the user's region and culture, it doesn't mean that each culture is supported. You shouldn't need to alter the code when you want to support an additional language or region, but you don't need to have that language built into your code when you ship. In the case of your ACController code, we've overlooked a whole class of languages.

Let's take another look at the code that writes the telemetry data. The code writes three values to the log. Each line looks like the following.

Listing 10.17   The air conditioner controller's `Telemetry` class

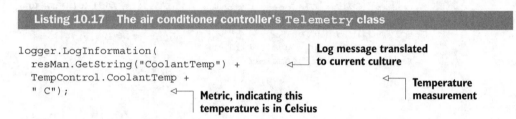

```
logger.LogInformation(
  resMan.GetString("CoolantTemp") +
  TempControl.CoolantTemp +
  " C");
```

Log message translated to current culture

Temperature measurement

Metric, indicating this temperature is in Celsius

The code in listing 10.17 writes the current temperatures to the log, but this code isn't world-ready. The problem is in the string concatenation. It makes an assumption about the order of elements in a sentence, which may not make sense in all languages. For instance, in languages that read right to left, the C should appear on the left.

To fix this, alter the strings in the strings.restext file to allow for substituting the temperature value wherever necessary. In the following example, the placeholders for string substitution are part of the resource file. Resource files in other languages can position the placeholders wherever appropriate.

Listing 10.18   strings.restext modified to use substitution for the temperature value

```
ExhaustAirTemp=Exhaust Air Temp: {0} C
CoolantTemp=Coolant Temp: {0} C
OutsideAirTemp=Outside Air Temp: {0} C
```

> **TEMPERATURES**   .NET doesn't provide facilities for converting temperatures based on region. If you want to show Fahrenheit for customers in the United States and its territories, you'll need to detect the region and do the conversion yourself. You'd also want to make the Celsius designation another substitutable parameter in the string.

It now seems like you've made your code world-ready. The next step is to go through a localizability review.

10.2.4   *Localizability review*

The localizability review is a chance to review your application and test that it's globalized (world-ready) and ready for localization (translating to different languages). Think of localizability as similar to a code review, but with a focus on globalization. Your team needs to check all the input and output to determine if it's user-facing or if it's persisting and could be affected by the culture it's run in.

In an earlier example, you set the culture as follows.

Listing 10.19   Setting the culture on the current thread

```
var culture = CultureInfo.CreateSpecificCulture("es-MX");
Thread.CurrentThread.CurrentCulture = culture;
Thread.CurrentThread.CurrentUICulture = culture;
```

There's no complete list of all cultures because that would be a constantly changing list. This means there's nothing that checks whether your culture code is a real one, so you can create a dummy culture for testing. Dummy cultures can be useful for finding areas of your code that break in build or test. For example, sometimes developers make assumptions about the length of strings. In some languages, translations may be much longer strings that could cause issues. This is easy enough to check with a dummy culture. Because translation of all the string resources (localization) usually happens very late in the product-development lifecycle, building a few dummy cultures early on can help you avoid some last minute fixes.

There's no prescribed way of doing a localizability review. Doing a code review and using dummy cultures are two helpful approaches. You can also enlist the help of a team or organization that specializes in internationalization.

Before we look at the localization step, there's still more you can do to make your code world-ready.

10.3   *Using the Microsoft localization extensions library*

The `ResourceManager` class, while useful, can be a bit cumbersome, because you have to create a key for each resource string and a file with the neutral culture resources. The ASP.NET Core team came up with a more intuitive solution called the `IStringLocalizer`. In ASP.NET Core, the localizer is already set up for you, but in libraries and console applications, you'll need to set this up yourself.

Start by adding a reference to this library in the project file, as follows.

Listing 10.20   Adding a reference to the localization extension in ACController.csproj

```
<Project Sdk="Microsoft.NET.Sdk">
  <PropertyGroup>
    <OutputType>Exe</OutputType>
    <TargetFramework>netcoreapp2.0</TargetFramework>
  </PropertyGroup>

  <ItemGroup>
    <PackageReference Include="Microsoft.Extensions.Logging"
                      Version="2.0.0" />
    <PackageReference Include="Microsoft.Extensions.Localization"
                      Version="2.0.0" />                          ←⎤ Add this
  </ItemGroup>                                                     ⎦ reference.
</Project>
```

Next, you'll want to initialize the localizer factory. Modify Controller.cs as follows.

Listing 10.21   Controller class modified to initialize the localizer factory

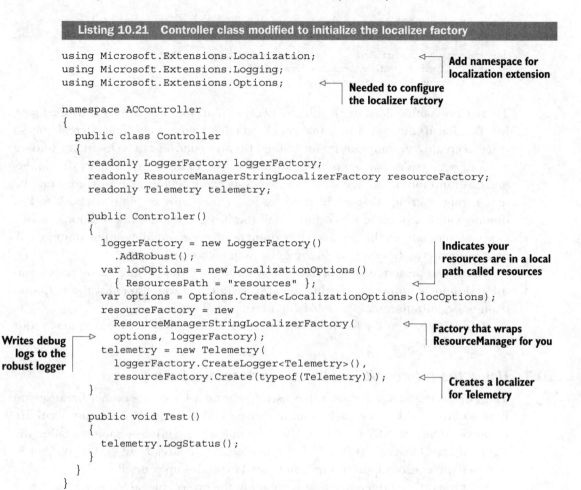

```
using Microsoft.Extensions.Localization;          ◁─┐ Add namespace for
using Microsoft.Extensions.Logging;                  │ localization extension
using Microsoft.Extensions.Options;        ◁─┐ Needed to configure
                                              │ the localizer factory
namespace ACController
{
  public class Controller
  {
    readonly LoggerFactory loggerFactory;
    readonly ResourceManagerStringLocalizerFactory resourceFactory;
    readonly Telemetry telemetry;

    public Controller()
    {
      loggerFactory = new LoggerFactory()
        .AddRobust();                                      Indicates your
      var locOptions = new LocalizationOptions()           resources are in a local
        { ResourcesPath = "resources" };          ◁        path called resources
      var options = Options.Create<LocalizationOptions>(locOptions);
      resourceFactory = new
        ResourceManagerStringLocalizerFactory(    ◁─┐ Factory that wraps
 Writes debug ┌─▷ options, loggerFactory);            │ ResourceManager for you
   logs to the    telemetry = new Telemetry(
 robust logger    loggerFactory.CreateLogger<Telemetry>(),
                  resourceFactory.Create(typeof(Telemetry)));  ◁─┐ Creates a localizer
    }                                                             │ for Telemetry

    public void Test()
    {
      telemetry.LogStatus();
    }
  }
}
```

Before, you kept the restext files in the same folder as the rest of the project. Going forward, you'll keep these files in a subfolder called resources. In large projects, this can help with organization.

The `ResourceManagerStringLocalizerFactory.Create` method creates an object that implements the `IStringLocalizer` interface. The following listing shows how to use this object in the `Telemetry` class.

Listing 10.22   `Telemetry` class modified to use the localizer

```
using Microsoft.Extensions.Localization;
using Microsoft.Extensions.Logging;

namespace ACController
{
```

```
public class Telemetry
{
  private readonly ILogger logger;
  private readonly IStringLocalizer localizer;

  public Telemetry(ILogger logger,
    IStringLocalizer localizer)               ◁──┐ Localizer passed
  {                                               │ in from Controller
    this.logger = logger;
    this.localizer = localizer;
  }

  public void LogStatus()
  {                                                  IStringLocalizer
    logger.LogInformation(localizer[           ◁──┘  defines an indexer.
      "Exhaust Air Temp: {0} C"],              ◁───── This string is the
      TempControl.ExhaustAirTemp);                    key you're looking
    logger.LogInformation(localizer["Coolant Temp: {0} C"],  for in the resources.
      TempControl.CoolantTemp);
    logger.LogInformation(localizer["Outside Air Temp: {0} C"],
      TempControl.OutsideAirTemp);
  }
 }
}
```

IStringLocalizer handles finding resources in a helpful way. With Resource-Manager, you need to provide a key, which is a token like ExhaustAirTemp. The problem with these keys is that the developer doesn't know what string will be written to the log without checking the resources file. And if ResourceManager can't find a value for a key, it throws an exception. By contrast, IStringLocalizer will write the key, which encourages you to use the full text as the key. This means that the full text of the log is used in the code, allowing developers to see the actual log message without referring to the resource file.

Because IStringLocalizer will write the key, the preceding code can be executed right away without creating any resources in the resources folder. Do a dotnet run, and you should see output similar to the following.

Listing 10.23 Telemetry output using robust logger and string localizer

```
6/23/2017 1:37:45 PM Information Exhaust Air Temp: 17 C
6/23/2017 1:37:45 PM Information Coolant Temp: 2 C
6/23/2017 1:37:45 PM Information Outside Air Temp: 26 C
```

10.3.1 *Testing right-to-left languages*

Imagine your company just signed a deal with a power company in Saudi Arabia (for some reason air conditioners are popular there). I mentioned before that some languages can have sentences in a different order. Arabic is written from right to left.

To allow your logs to be translated into Arabic, you'll need to create an Arabic resource file. First, create a new folder called resources as a subfolder of ACController.

Then create a new file called Telemetry.ar-SA.restext in the resources folder. This file will have contents like the following listing. You can get this file from the companion code on GitHub (http://mng.bz/F146) or by using Bing translate.

Listing 10.24   Resource file Telemetry.ar-SA.restext with Arabic version of telemetry logs

```
Exhaust Air Temp: {0} C=C{0} : درجة حرارة الهواء العادم
Coolant Temp: {0} C=C{0} :درجةحرارةالمبرد
Outside Air Temp: {0} C=C{0} :درجة حرارة الهواء الخارجي
```

Next you'll need to convert the restext files in the resources folder into embedded resources. Modify the project file item groups as follows.

Listing 10.25   ACController.csproj modified to get resources from resources subfolder

```
<ItemGroup>
  <Resx
    Include="resources\*.restext" />
  <EmbeddedResource
    Include="resources\*.resources" />
</ItemGroup>
```

Now all you need to do is set the culture so you can test.

Listing 10.26   Set the current culture to Arabic to test that the resources work

```
using System.Globalization;
using System.Threading;

namespace ACController
{
  class Program
  {
    static void Main()
    {
      var culture = CultureInfo
        .CreateSpecificCulture("ar-SA");        ← ar-SA is
                                                   Arabic-Saudi Arabia.
      Thread.CurrentThread.CurrentCulture = culture;    ← Affects date formats
      Thread.CurrentThread.CurrentUICulture = culture;  ← Affects output language
      var controller = new Controller();
      controller.Test();
    }
  }
}
```

DIAGNOSING RESOURCE ISSUES   If you're having trouble getting your resources to show up, you can modify the RobustLogger.IsEnabled method to return true for the debug level. Then you'll see what the ResourceManager tried before it settled on the text to use for your strings.

ARABIC CHARACTERS NOT SUPPORTED IN WINDOWS CONSOLE   If you're using Windows' command prompt, the Arabic strings will show up as "?????" in the console output. The fix for console output is complex. You'd need to install a font that supports Arabic, and then change the code page to see the results. Even then, the console doesn't support right-to-left languages. To check that your code works, redirect your output to a file: `dotnet run >> output.txt`. The strings should look correct in most text editors.

> ### Other ways to create resources
>
> We've only looked at one way to add localizable resources to a .NET application, and the restext approach is limited in that it can only handle string resources. You can probably imagine needing different images for different cultures. Also, there seems to be no good way to handle an equal sign (=) in the key. Because .NET Core and .NET Standard don't cover user-interface libraries, the restext format may be enough. Microsoft briefly experimented with a JSON file format, but that's not available in .NET Core.
>
> The more common way to specify resources in .NET is through the use of the .resx file format. .resx files are XML files that start with a large block of XML schema definition. Much like the .proj format before .NET Core, .resx files are meant to be created and edited with tools.
>
> You also have the option of creating a resources file programmatically. Just as you used a build tool to convert a restext file to a resources file, you can write your own code to generate a resources file. I won't cover that in this book.

10.3.2 *Invariant culture*

In the previous Saudi Arabia example, `Thread.CurrentCulture.CurrentThread` controlled how dates and times appear in the log, and the date shown used a lunar calendar. This may work for the customer, but the same log may not parse when consumed by the manufacturer's applications. Also Saudi Arabia may vote to use the Gregorian calendar as their primary calendar instead of the lunar calendar (most of Saudi Arabia uses the Gregorian calendar already, but the ar-SA culture code still officially uses the lunar calendar). That would change the definition of the ar-SA culture.

Your application shouldn't need to keep up with politics (well, at least not politics outside of the company). When sending data back to the services at the manufacturer, you need a culture that doesn't change and doesn't require separate installation—an invariant culture built into .NET. The following listing shows how to modify the `RobustLogger` to use the invariant culture.

Listing 10.27 Modifying `RobustLogger` class's `Log` method to use invariant culture

```
public void Log<TState>(LogLevel logLevel, EventId eventId,
  TState state, Exception exception,
  Func<TState, Exception, string> formatter)
{
  Console.WriteLine(string.Join(" ",
```

```
DateTime.Now.ToString(
CultureInfo.InvariantCulture.DateTimeFormat),
logLevel,
formatter(state, exception)));
}
```
DateTimeFormat implements IFormatProvider.

The dates in the log should now appear in "MM/dd/yyyy HH:mm:ss" format. Use the invariant culture for persisted data, such as what the controller sends back to the air conditioner manufacturer.

There are still two problems with the data sent to the manufacturer, though. The first is the time zone, which can be fixed by using `DateTime.UtcNow` instead of `DateTime.Now`. The second is the language used when writing the log message. You don't want to send the localized version of the log message back to the manufacturer. You could emit two logs—one localized for the user, and one using the default culture for the manufacturer—but the manufacturer only needs the temperature values and timestamp. Instead of writing the log directly, you could use a custom event.

10.3.3 *Using EventSource to emit events*

`EventSource`, part of the .NET Standard, is a powerful producer/consumer event system. On Windows, `EventSource` taps into the kernel-level Event Tracing for Windows (ETW). Users can create an event consumer that listens to multiple sources and combines the events together. The consumer can even be in a separate process. ETW isn't available in other operating systems, but `EventSource` still can be used on all platforms.

In your application, you want the telemetry data to go to two entities: the manufacturer and the customer. Each has a different requirement in terms of how the logs should be formatted. One approach you can take is to build an `EventSource` (publisher) to emit telemetry events and two `EventListeners` (consumers) to capture those events and send the data to both manufacturer and customer.

Start by creating a new `EventSource`, as shown in the following listing.

Listing 10.28   `ACControllerEventSource` is a custom event producer

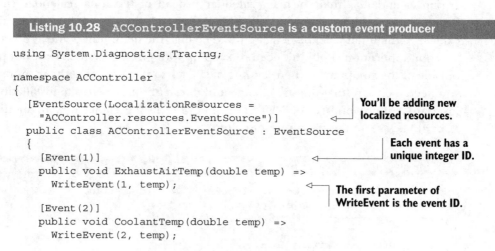

```
using System.Diagnostics.Tracing;

namespace ACController
{
  [EventSource(LocalizationResources =
    "ACController.resources.EventSource")]          You'll be adding new
                                                    localized resources.
  public class ACControllerEventSource : EventSource
  {
                                                    Each event has a
                                                    unique integer ID.
    [Event(1)]
    public void ExhaustAirTemp(double temp) =>
      WriteEvent(1, temp);                          The first parameter of
                                                    WriteEvent is the event ID.
    [Event(2)]
    public void CoolantTemp(double temp) =>
      WriteEvent(2, temp);
```

```
    [Event(3)]
    public void OutsideAirTemp(double temp) =>
      WriteEvent(3, temp);
  }
}
```

Create a singleton instance of this `EventSource` in the `Controller` class, as follows.

Listing 10.29 Add singleton instance of `ACControllerEventSource`

```
public class Controller
{
  internal static readonly ACControllerEventSource Events =
    new ACControllerEventSource();
}
```

In the `LogStatus` method in the `Telemetry` class, replace the logging calls with events, as follows.

Listing 10.30 Change the `LogStatus` method in `Telemetry` to emit events

```
public void LogStatus()
{
  Controller.Events.ExhaustAirTemp(TempControl.ExhaustAirTemp);
  Controller.Events.CoolantTemp(TempControl.CoolantTemp);
  Controller.Events.OutsideAirTemp(TempControl.OutsideAirTemp);
}
```

`EventSource` events have messages into which `WriteEvent` will substitute the parameters passed to it. You can localize these messages by indicating where to find the resources using the `LocalizationResources` property on the `EventSource` attribute.

The first step is to create a default resource file. Add a new file to the resources folder called EventSource.restext, with the following contents.

Listing 10.31 EventSource.restext default resource file

```
event_ExhaustAirTemp=Exhaust Air Temp: {0} C
event_CoolantTemp=Coolant Temp: {0} C
event_OutsideAirTemp=Outside Air Temp: {0} C
```

`EventSource` uses the convention that the key to find a resource string for an event is "event_EVENTNAME", where "EVENTNAME" is the name of the method used for the event.

You can also make a copy of the Arabic culture restext file and modify it to use the resource keys that `EventSource` understands. Add a file called EventSource.ar-SA.restext with the following contents.

Listing 10.32   EventSource.ar-SA.restext Arabic-localized resource file

```
event_ExhaustAirTemp=C{0} : درجة حرارة الهواء العادم
event_CoolantTemp=C{0} : درجة حرارة المبرد
event_OutsideAirTemp=C{0} : درجة حرارة الهواء الخارجي
```

Next, you'll need to add these to the project file. You can add the individual files to the `Resx` and `EmbeddedResource` item groups or use a wildcard as follows.

Listing 10.33   Adding files to `Resx` and `EmbeddedResource` item groups

```
<ItemGroup>
  <Resx Include="resources\*.restext" />
</ItemGroup>
<ItemGroup>
  <EmbeddedResource Include="resources\*.resources" />
</ItemGroup>
```

You're now able to emit the events, but there's one problem: nobody's listening.

10.3.4 *Using EventListener to listen for events*

There are many ways to listen to `EventSource` events, but the easiest is to create a subclass of `EventListener`. The following listing shows a simple version that writes to the console.

Listing 10.34   `EventListener` that writes to the console

```
using System;
using System.Diagnostics.Tracing;

namespace ACController
{
  public class ConsoleEventListener : EventListener
  {
    protected override void OnEventWritten(
      EventWrittenEventArgs eventData) =>
      Console.WriteLine(eventData.Message,          ◁── Localized event message
        eventData.Payload[0]);                      ◁── First event parameter, to be substituted into the message
  }
}
```

Modify the Program.cs file to use the `ConsoleEventListener`, as follows.

Listing 10.35   Using the `ConsoleEventListener` in the main program

```
using System.Diagnostics.Tracing;
using System.Globalization;
using System.Threading;
```

```
namespace ACController
{
  class Program
  {
    static void Main()
    {
      var culture = CultureInfo.CreateSpecificCulture("ar-SA");
      Thread.CurrentThread.CurrentCulture = culture;
      Thread.CurrentThread.CurrentUICulture = culture;
      using (var listener =                          EventListeners
        new ConsoleEventListener())                  are IDisposable.
      {
        listener.EnableEvents(Controller.Events,           Indicates which
          EventLevel.Verbose);                             EventSources to listen to
        var controller = new Controller();
        controller.Test();                         You can customize what
      }                                            types of events to listen to.
    }
  }
}
```

When running this code, you should see the localized events. If an error is reported about not being able to find the resources, try using the `--no-incremental` option when building and running.

Now build another listener that will use the Microsoft logging extensions library so you can use your `RobustLogger` code, as shown in the following listing.

Listing 10.36 Listen for `EventSource` events, and write them to the logging extension

```
using System.Diagnostics.Tracing;
using Microsoft.Extensions.Logging;

namespace ACController
{
  public class LoggerEventListener : EventListener
  {
    private readonly ILogger logger;
    public LoggerEventListener(ILogger logger) =>        Passes in the
      this.logger = logger;                              logger to use

    protected override void OnEventWritten(
      EventWrittenEventArgs eventData) =>
      logger.LogInformation(eventData.Message, eventData.Payload[0]);
  }
}
```

Note that with the `EventSource` and `EventListener` classes, you no longer need to have logging or localization classes in the `Telemetry` class. You can simplify that class as follows.

```
namespace ACController
{
  public class Telemetry
  {
    public void LogStatus()
    {
      Controller.Events.ExhaustAirTemp(TempControl.ExhaustAirTemp);
      Controller.Events.CoolantTemp(TempControl.CoolantTemp);
      Controller.Events.OutsideAirTemp(TempControl.OutsideAirTemp);
    }
  }
}
```

Because the `LoggerEventListener` needs an `ILogger` passed into the constructor, build it into the `Controller` class as shown in the next listing.

```
using System;
using System.Diagnostics.Tracing;
using Microsoft.Extensions.Localization;
using Microsoft.Extensions.Logging;
using Microsoft.Extensions.Options;

namespace ACController
{
  public class Controller : IDisposable          ⟵ Implements IDisposable since
  {                                                  the listener is disposable
    internal static readonly ACControllerEventSource Events =
      new ACControllerEventSource();
    readonly LoggerFactory loggerFactory;
    readonly ResourceManagerStringLocalizerFactory resourceFactory;
    readonly Telemetry telemetry;
    readonly LoggerEventListener listener;

    public Controller()
    {
      loggerFactory = new LoggerFactory()
        .AddRobust();
      var locOptions = new LocalizationOptions() {
        ResourcesPath = "resources" };
      var options = Options.Create<LocalizationOptions>(locOptions);
      resourceFactory = new ResourceManagerStringLocalizerFactory(
        options, loggerFactory);
      listener = new LoggerEventListener(                    ⟵ Creates the
        loggerFactory.CreateLogger<Telemetry>());              new listener
      listener.EnableEvents(Controller.Events, EventLevel.Verbose);
      telemetry = new Telemetry();
    }

    public void Test() =>
      telemetry.LogStatus();
```

```
    public void Dispose() =>
        listener.Dispose();
    }
}
```

⟵ **The listener is disposed of when the controller is disposed of.**

Running this application should print each temperature twice, since there are two listeners.

Although both the Microsoft logging extensions library and EventSource allow you to specify multiple places for your logs to go, EventSource has a more powerful filtering mechanism. You can set keywords on each event and have the listener filter by keyword. This can be handy if you want different events to go to different places.

10.4 *Other considerations for globalization*

The key to making world-ready applications is to not make assumptions about any communications with the user. When writing software, keep the following in mind:

- Sort order and string equality depend on culture.
- Numbers should be stored in the invariant culture, because number formats depend on culture.
- Although currency values don't depend on culture, they can depend on the denomination you're using. Store this data alongside the currency value.

Some things are not built into the .NET Framework but are culture-sensitive:

- Addresses
- Telephone numbers
- Paper sizes
- Units of measure
- Length
- Weight
- Area
- Volume
- Temperature

DOES THIS REGION USE THE METRIC SYSTEM? The RegionInfo.IsMetric property will tell you if the region uses the metric system.

10.5 *Localization*

In this chapter, you've already done some localization: you produced the Spanish and Arabic translations of the string resources used in the ACController application. Localization is the process of creating versions of your resources that apply to specific cultures.

Although Bing Translate may work for a sample application, the translations could be nonsensical, misleading, or perhaps offensive to a native speaker. Most companies will hire the services of a firm that specializes in translation.

AN EXAMPLE OF INCORRECT BING/GOOGLE TRANSLATION   If you were to use Bing Translate or Google Translate to convert the English word "turkey," meaning the animal, to Arabic, you'd get an appropriate translation referring to the animal. If you use these tools to translate "stuffed turkey," you'd get a translation of "stuffed Turkey" (the country).

You don't need all the localized resources while you're writing your code. The resource files are also independent enough that you can avoid giving the external translation company access to your source code by instead giving them only the resource files.

If you're developing with the Microsoft localization extension library, you'll be writing your default language resource strings as keys in the code. This means you don't have to create a resource file for the default language during development. This can be detrimental, because if you want to have an external company work on translations, you'll need to create a resource file for them by searching the code for every key string. I see this as another reason to create a dummy culture—doing so forces developers to create and update resource files during development.

Context is also important when it comes to translation—the resources file doesn't give the translator much context. You can help by adding comments to the restext file (use # at the beginning of the line), but sometimes it will take a bit more. You might decide to let the translator see the running application, but if it's a specialized application, such as an MRI machine, this might not be enough. You basically need a translator who understands your business, or you'll have to give them enough context to figure out the appropriate translations. Either way, don't take localization lightly.

Additional resources

To learn more about what we covered in this chapter, see the following resources:

- Microsoft's globalization documentation—http://mng.bz/1ID9
- The Microsoft.Extensions.Localization namespace—http://mng.bz/nu5v

Summary

In this chapter you learned about internationalization and how it affects your code. These key concepts were covered:

- Using the Microsoft localization extension library to avoid creating resource files until after you're done coding
- Logging with the Microsoft logging extension library
- Emitting events with localized messages through `EventSource`
- Understanding the globalization, localizability review, and localization steps in the internationalization process

These are some important techniques to remember from this chapter:

- String resources are easy to specify with restext files.
- Use the `GenerateResource` MSBuild task to generate resources files from restext files.

- Treat the resource key name as a default string when using the Microsoft localization extension library.
- You can use multiple `EventListeners` to write to different places.

Internationalization may seem daunting at first, but I hope that this chapter has helped you understand the process. Developers should keep globalization in mind when developing, because it will make the rest of the process go more smoothly. The most important concept of globalization is to not make assumptions about how the communication between your user and your application will be perceived.

11
Multiple frameworks and runtimes

This chapter covers

- The .NET Portability Analyzer
- Building projects that work on multiple frameworks
- Handling code that's operating-system specific

There are two features of .NET Core that we'll look at in this chapter. One is the ability to run .NET Core applications on many different operating systems. The other is the ability to write .NET code specific to each .NET framework if you need the code to operate differently.

You can take advantage of these capabilities in your own applications and libraries, which is particularly useful when you have to extend beyond the .NET Standard. It's also useful when you're trying to use OS-specific features or native components as the interfaces, because these will be different on each OS.

11.1 Why does the .NET Core SDK support multiple frameworks and runtimes?

The .NET Core SDK supports building for multiple frameworks. You can specify the desired framework with a command-line option.

Consider these examples:

```
dotnet build --framework netcoreapp2.0
dotnet run --framework netcoreapp2.0
dotnet test --framework netcoreapp2.0
```

So far in this book we've only targeted one framework at a time—either `netstandardxxx` or `netcoreappxxx`—so there was no occasion to exercise this capability.

If you're building a new library that adheres to the .NET Standard, it will work universally with other .NET frameworks. If you're porting a library from either Xamarin or the .NET Framework, it may be able to port directly to the .NET Standard Library without modifying the code. There are cases, though, where your code needs to be built for multiple frameworks.

For instance, suppose you have code that uses XAML that you want to make work on the .NET Framework, Xamarin Forms, and Universal Windows Applications. Or maybe your library is used by some existing applications that you can't change. The .NET Core SDK makes it possible to support multiple frameworks in the same NuGet package (generated by `dotnet pack`).

> **FRAMEWORKS VS. RUNTIMES** Runtimes and frameworks are not the same thing. A *framework* is a set of available APIs. A *runtime* is akin to an operating system (see section 3.1.3 for more details). Your code may have to work with some OS-specific APIs, which means that it will have different code for different runtimes.

One example of a library that works differently depending on the runtime is the Kestrel engine, which is used for hosting ASP.NET Core applications. Kestrel is built on a native code library called libuv. Because libuv works on multiple operating systems, it's a great foundation for the flagship ASP.NET Core web server. But even libuv has its limitations, so Kestrel doesn't work on all platforms.

Another example of needing to support multiple runtimes is the System.IO.Compression library. Instead of implementing Deflate/GZip compression in .NET managed code, System.IO.Compression relies on a native library called zlib. The zlib library isn't only the de facto standard for GZip compression and decompression, it's also implemented in native code, which gives it a slight performance advantage over any managed .NET implementation. Because zlib is a native library, the code in System.IO.Compression has to behave differently based on the runtime.

The .NET Standard Library gives you a great foundation on which to build libraries and applications for a broad array of platforms, but it's not comprehensive. Luckily, the .NET Core SDK is flexible enough to support different frameworks and runtimes, which can allow you to consolidate code into a single project and simplify packaging and distribution. This chapter introduces some techniques for supporting multiple frameworks and runtimes.

You'll start by trying to port code between .NET frameworks.

11.2   .NET Portability Analyzer

The .NET Portability Analyzer helps you migrate from one .NET framework to another. See figure 11.1, which shows that Xamarin, .NET Core, and the .NET Framework are all frameworks that implement the .NET Standard. The .NET Portability Analyzer has detailed information on where each framework deviates from the standard and how that translates into other frameworks.

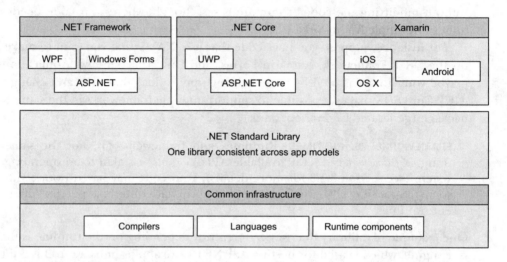

Figure 11.1   .NET Framework, .NET Core, and Xamarin are all different frameworks that support the .NET Standard Library.

If you want to port your Xamarin or .NET Framework library to .NET Core, the .NET Portability Analyzer can help. It identifies all the incompatibilities between the two frameworks and provides suggestions, where possible. The tool is available both as a command-line executable and a Visual Studio plugin. We'll explore the Visual Studio plugin version.

11.2.1   Installing and configuring the Visual Studio 2017 plugin

In Visual Studio, open the Tools menu and choose Extensions and Updates. In the Extensions and Updates dialog box, pick Online in the tree in the left pane. Type "portability" in the search box, and look for the .NET Portability Analyzer (shown in figure 11.2).

Download and install the plugin. After installing, you'll need to restart Visual Studio.

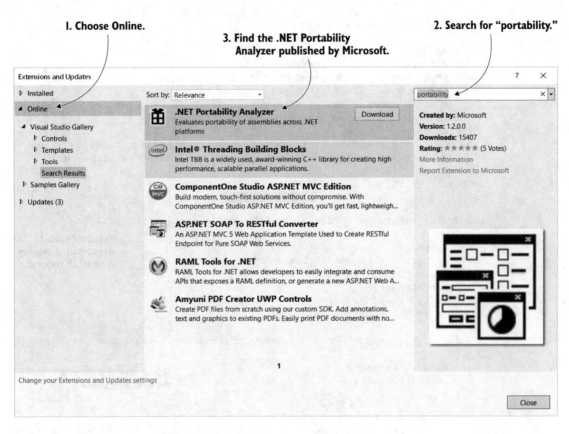

1. Choose Online.

3. Find the .NET Portability Analyzer published by Microsoft.

2. Search for "portability."

Figure 11.2 Search for the .NET Portability Analyzer.

11.2.2 Sample .NET Framework project

Now create a new project to test out the .NET Portability Analyzer. The sample project will execute a simple latency test by making HTTP requests to a given URI.

Create a new C# console application (listed as Console App (.NET Framework) in the New Project dialog box) in Visual Studio targeting .NET Framework version 4.5 or later. Alter the Program.cs file to contain the following code.

Listing 11.1 Program.cs for your test of the .NET Portability Analyzer

```
using System;
using System.Diagnostics;
using System.IO;
using System.Net;

namespace ConsoleApplication1
{
  class Program
  {
```

```
static void Main(string[] args)
{
  string uri = "http://www.bing.com";
  var firstRequest = MeasureRequest(uri);
  var secondRequest = MeasureRequest(uri);
  if (firstRequest.Item1 != HttpStatusCode.OK &&
      secondRequest.Item1 != HttpStatusCode.OK) {
    Console.WriteLine("Unexpected status code");
  } else {
    Console.WriteLine($"First request took {firstRequest.Item2}ms");
    Console.WriteLine($"Second request took {secondRequest.Item2}ms");
  }
  Console.ReadLine();
}

static Tuple<HttpStatusCode, long> MeasureRequest(string uri)
{
  var stopwatch = new Stopwatch();
  var request = WebRequest.Create(uri);
  request.Method = "GET";
  stopwatch.Start();
  using (var response = request.GetResponse()
         as HttpWebResponse)
  {
    using (var reader = new StreamReader(response.GetResponseStream()))
    {
      reader.ReadToEnd();
      stopwatch.Stop();
    }

    return new Tuple<HttpStatusCode, long>(
        response.StatusCode,
        stopwatch.ElapsedMilliseconds);
  }
}
```

> MeasureRequest measures the latency of an HTTP request.

> Makes sure you've read the whole response

The preceding code is a contrived example that measures the latency of web requests. It creates a `WebRequest` object pointing to the URI passed in. The response object exposes the `GetResponseStream` method, because the response may be large and take some time to download. Calling `ReadToEnd` makes sure you get the full content of the response.

The first request from the example project takes longer for many reasons, such as JIT compiling and setting up the HTTP connection. The latency for the second request is a more realistic measurement of the time it takes to get a response from the endpoint (http://www.bing.com in this case).

11.2.3   *Running the Portability Analyzer in Visual Studio*

Let's see how this code would port to .NET Core. First, change the settings for the Portability Analyzer. Open the settings as shown in figure 11.3. Choose all the options for .NET Core target platforms, as shown in figure 11.4.

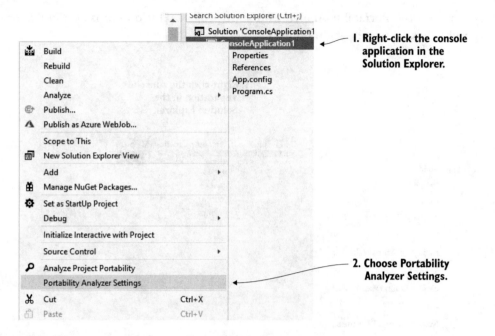

Figure 11.3   Open the settings for the Portability Analyzer.

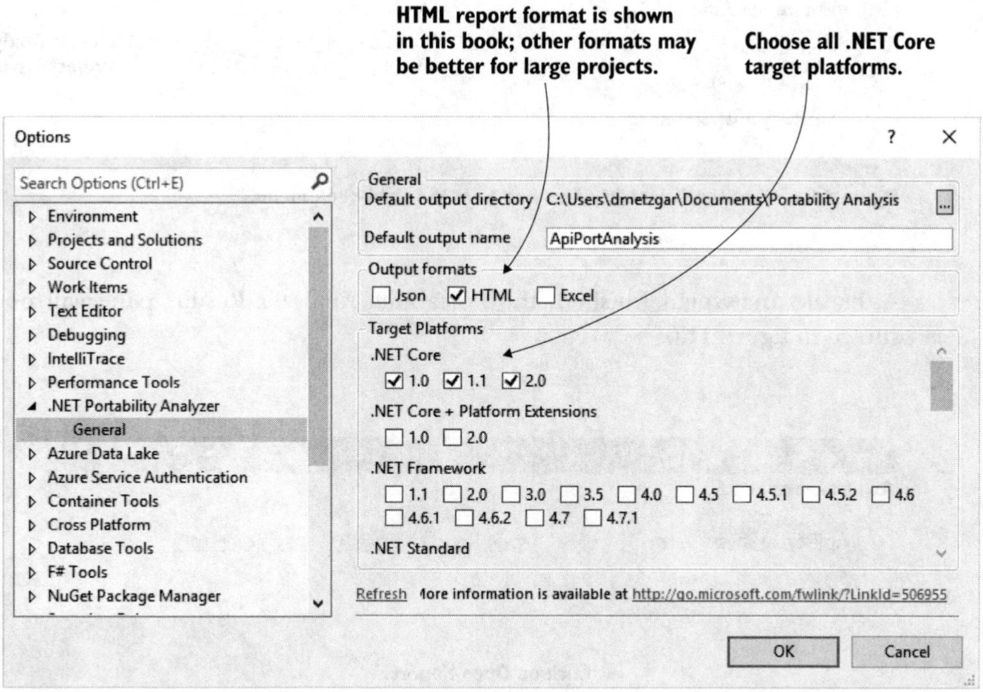

Figure 11.4   Choose all .NET Core Target Platforms in the Portability Analyzer settings.

Now run the Portability Analyzer on your project. This option is also in the project's right-click menu, shown in figure 11.5.

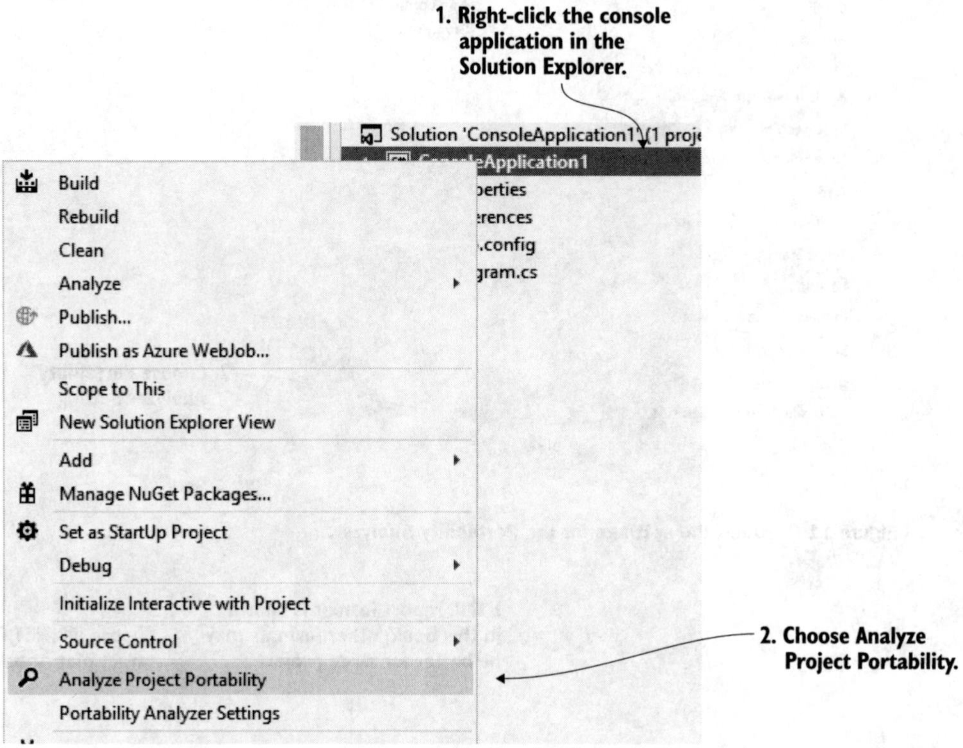

Figure 11.5 **Run the Portability Analyzer from the right-click menu.**

After the analyzer is finished, the Portability Analyzer Results pane will pop up, as shown in figure 11.6.

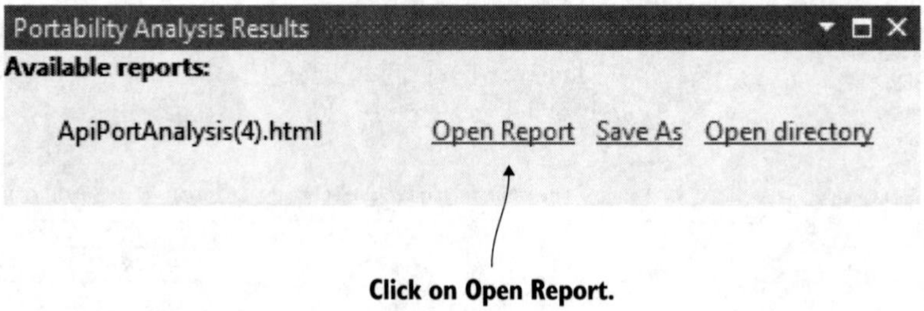

Figure 11.6 **Portability Analyzer Results pane**

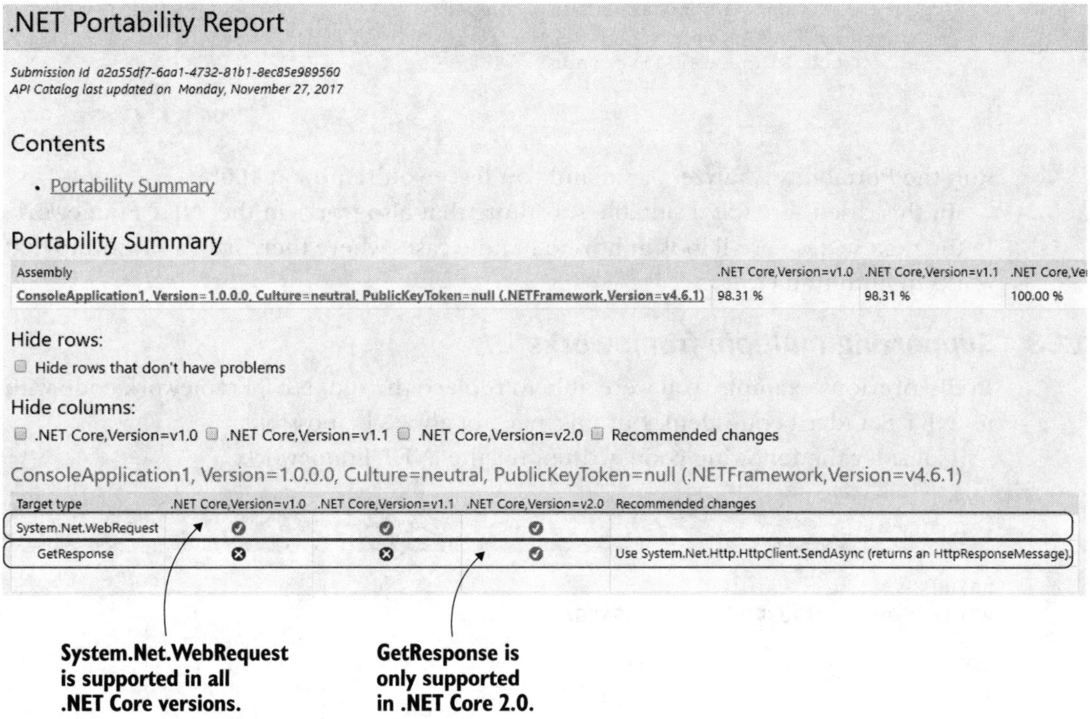

.NET Portability Report

Submission Id a2a55df7-6aa1-4732-81b1-8ec85e989560
API Catalog last updated on Monday, November 27, 2017

Contents

- Portability Summary

Portability Summary

Assembly	.NET Core,Version=v1.0	.NET Core,Version=v1.1	.NET Core,Ve
ConsoleApplication1, Version=1.0.0.0, Culture=neutral, PublicKeyToken=null (.NETFramework,Version=v4.6.1)	98.31 %	98.31 %	100.00 %

Hide rows:

☐ Hide rows that don't have problems

Hide columns:

☐ .NET Core,Version=v1.0 ☐ .NET Core,Version=v1.1 ☐ .NET Core,Version=v2.0 ☐ Recommended changes

ConsoleApplication1, Version=1.0.0.0, Culture=neutral, PublicKeyToken=null (.NETFramework,Version=v4.6.1)

Target type	.NET Core,Version=v1.0	.NET Core,Version=v1.1	.NET Core,Version=v2.0	Recommended changes
System.Net.WebRequest	✓	✓	✓	
GetResponse	✗	✗	✓	Use System.Net.Http.HttpClient.SendAsync (returns an HttpResponseMessage).

System.Net.WebRequest is supported in all .NET Core versions.

GetResponse is only supported in .NET Core 2.0.

Figure 11.7 Portability analysis of the sample code

Figure 11.7 shows an HTML version of the report.

If you're targeting .NET Core 1.0 or 1.1, the suggested method for fixing the code is to use a different means of making HTTP requests entirely, via HttpClient. You learned about HttpClient back in chapter 7. Change Program.cs to use Http-Client as shown in the following listing.

Listing 11.2 New method that implements the suggestion from the Portability Analyzer

```
using System.Net.Http;                          ◁─┐ Add this using
                                                   │ statement.
class Program
{
  static HttpClient client = new HttpClient();

  static Tuple<HttpStatusCode, long> MeasureRequest(string uri)
  {
    var stopwatch = new Stopwatch();
    stopwatch.Start();
    var response = client.GetAsync(uri).Result;            ◁─ Result waits for the Task to
    response.Content.ReadAsStringAsync().Wait();           ◁─ finish and gets the result.
    stopwatch.Stop();                                         You don't need the result
                                                              here, so you just Wait().
```

```
        return new Tuple<HttpStatusCode, long>(
          response.StatusCode,
          stopwatch.ElapsedMilliseconds);
    }
}
```

Run the Portability Analyzer again and you'll see you're now at 100%.

In this case there was a suitable substitute that also works in the .NET Framework. In the next section, we'll look at how to handle cases where there isn't a substitute that works in both frameworks.

11.3   Supporting multiple frameworks

In the previous example, you were able to replace the old .NET Framework code with its .NET Standard equivalent. But this may not always be possible.

Consider the following code, written for the .NET Framework.

Listing 11.3   `EventProvider` **.NET Framework sample**

```
using System;
using System.Diagnostics.Eventing;

namespace ConsoleApplication3
{
  class Program
  {
    private static readonly Guid Provider =          ◁─┐ The actual Guid
      Guid.Parse("B695E411-F53B-4C72-9F81-2926B2EA233A");  is not important.

    static void Main(string[] args)
    {
      var eventProvider = new EventProvider(Provider);  ◁─┐ Writes events
      eventProvider.WriteMessageEvent("Program started");   to Windows

      // Do some work

      eventProvider.WriteMessageEvent("Program completed");
      eventProvider.Dispose();
    }
  }
}
```

You may have legacy code that uses some Windows-specific features like the preceding code. This code produces an event in Windows under a given provider Guid. There may be logging tools that listen for these events, and slight changes in how the events are emitted might break those tools.

11.3.1   Using EventSource to replace EventProvider

Try running the .NET Portability Analyzer on the preceding code to see the suggested .NET Core alternative. Figure 11.8 shows an example analysis.

Portability Summary

Assembly	.NET Core,Version=v1.0	.NET Core,Version=v1.1	.NET
ConsoleApplication3, Version=1.0.0.0, Culture=neutral, PublicKeyToken=null (.NETFramework,Version=v4.6.1)	89.19 %	89.19 %	89.1!

Hide rows:

☐ Hide rows that don't have problems

Hide columns:

☐ .NET Core,Version=v1.0 ☐ .NET Core,Version=v1.1 ☐ .NET Core,Version=v2.0 ☐ Recommended changes

ConsoleApplication3, Version=1.0.0.0, Culture=neutral, PublicKeyToken=null (.NETFramework,Version=v4.6.1)

Target type	.NET Core,Version=v1.0	.NET Core,Version=v1.1	.NET Core,Version=v2.0	Recommended changes
System.Diagnostics.Eventing.EventProvider	✖	✖	✖	Use System.Diagnostics.Tracing.EventSource instead.
#ctor(System.Guid)	✖	✖	✖	Use System.Diagnostics.Tracing.EventSource instead.
Dispose	✖	✖	✖	Use System.Diagnostics.Tracing.EventSource instead.
WriteMessageEvent(System.String)	✖	✖	✖	Use System.Diagnostics.Tracing.EventSource instead.

**EventProvider isn't supported
in any .NET Core version.**

Figure 11.8   Portability analysis of the sample code using `EventProvider`

The recommended change in this case is to use an `EventSource`. An `EventSource` is definitely the way to go when writing events without relying on platform-specific features. You learned about `EventSource` back in chapter 10. Unfortunately, if you're replacing an existing Windows event provider, the `EventSource` implementation may not produce the exact same events.

Let's look at a similar version written for .NET Core using `EventSource`, shown in the following listing.

Listing 11.4   Writes events using `EventSource`

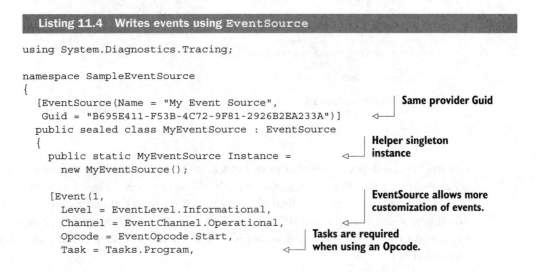

```
using System.Diagnostics.Tracing;

namespace SampleEventSource
{
  [EventSource(Name = "My Event Source",                    Same provider Guid
  Guid = "B695E411-F53B-4C72-9F81-2926B2EA233A")]
  public sealed class MyEventSource : EventSource
  {
    public static MyEventSource Instance =                   Helper singleton
      new MyEventSource();                                   instance

    [Event(1,                                                EventSource allows more
      Level = EventLevel.Informational,                      customization of events.
      Channel = EventChannel.Operational,
      Opcode = EventOpcode.Start,                            Tasks are required
      Task = Tasks.Program,                                  when using an Opcode.
```

```
        Message = "Program started")]
    public void ProgramStart()
    {
        WriteEvent(1);
    }

    [Event(2,
      Level = EventLevel.Informational,
      Channel = EventChannel.Operational,
      Opcode = EventOpcode.Stop,         ◁─┐  Start and Stop are
      Task = Tasks.Program,                 │  standard Opcodes.
      Message = "Program completed")]
    public void ProgramStop()
    {
        WriteEvent(2);
    }

    public class Tasks
    {
      public const EventTask Program = (EventTask)1;
    }
  }
}
```

In the preceding code, you took advantage of some of the capabilities that Event-Source has to offer. It also makes the Program code much cleaner, as you can see in the following listing.

Listing 11.5   Program.cs refactored to use the new EventSource

```
using System;

namespace SampleEventSource
{
  public class Program
  {
    public static void Main(string[] args)
    {
      MyEventSource.Instance.ProgramStart();

      // Do some work

      MyEventSource.Instance.ProgramStop();
    }
  }
}
```

The events are slightly different than before, so there's a risk that the new code will break existing tools. But because those tools will have to be changed to work with the .NET Core version of the application anyways, don't worry about making the events exactly the same. Instead, you'll focus on allowing the .NET Framework version of the application to continue to work as before. That means you have to support multiple frameworks.

Start by creating the .NET Core project. Create a folder called SampleEvent-Source, and open a command prompt in that folder. Run `dotnet new console` to create a new .NET Core console application. Modify the Program.cs file to match listing 11.5. Also create a new file called MyEventSource.cs with the code in listing 11.4.

Feel free to build and run the application. You won't see any output from it. To view the logs that are emitted from the EventSource, you'll need to create a consumer, which was covered in chapter 10. For this chapter, we'll just assume it works.

11.3.2 Adding another framework to the project

Indicating support for another framework is straightforward. Modify the SampleEventSource.csproj file as follows.

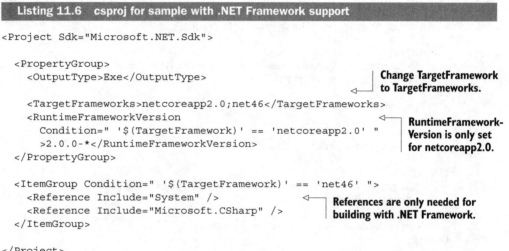

Listing 11.6   csproj for sample with .NET Framework support

```
<Project Sdk="Microsoft.NET.Sdk">

  <PropertyGroup>
    <OutputType>Exe</OutputType>                        Change TargetFramework
                                                         to TargetFrameworks.

    <TargetFrameworks>netcoreapp2.0;net46</TargetFrameworks>
    <RuntimeFrameworkVersion                             RuntimeFramework-
      Condition=" '$(TargetFramework)' == 'netcoreapp2.0' "  Version is only set
      >2.0.0-*</RuntimeFrameworkVersion>                 for netcoreapp2.0.
  </PropertyGroup>

  <ItemGroup Condition=" '$(TargetFramework)' == 'net46' ">
    <Reference Include="System" />                      References are only needed for
    <Reference Include="Microsoft.CSharp" />            building with .NET Framework.
  </ItemGroup>

</Project>
```

Notice that you specifically need net46. net45 won't work in this case because the EventChannel class wasn't defined in that version. If you remove the Channel specification from the MyEventSource class, however, you should be able to usenet45.

You can now build this code for the .NET Framework using the following command:

```
dotnet build --framework net46
```

This will use the EventSource on the .NET Framework and .NET Core, but you want it to revert to the old code when using the .NET Framework. Because the framework is something you know at build time, you can use preprocessor directives. Listing 11.7 shows how this works.

WHAT IS A PREPROCESSOR DIRECTIVE?   A preprocessor directive is a statement that's executed before compilation starts. If you're familiar with C or C++, you may be familiar with creating macros using preprocessor directives. Although macros aren't available in C#, you can still have conditionally compiled code.

Listing 11.7   Program.cs rewritten to use preprocessor directives

```
using System;

#if NET46
using System.Diagnostics.Eventing;        ⟵——  NET46 is automatically
#endif                                           defined.

namespace SampleEventSource
{
  public class Program
  {
#if NET46
    private static readonly Guid Provider =
      Guid.Parse("B695E411-F53B-4C72-9F81-2926B2EA233A");
#endif

    public static void Main(string[] args)
    {
#if NET46
      var eventProvider = new EventProvider(Provider);
      eventProvider.WriteMessageEvent("Program started");
#else
      MyEventSource.Instance.ProgramStart();
#endif

      // Do some work

#if NET46
      eventProvider.WriteMessageEvent("Program completed");
      eventProvider.Dispose();
#else
      MyEventSource.Instance.ProgramStop();
#endif
    }
  }
}
```

The #if and #endif are preprocessor directives that will include the code contained between them only if NET46 is defined. NET46 is created automatically from the name of the framework. The special characters are usually replaced with underscores, and everything is in uppercase. For instance, the framework moniker netcoreapp2.0 would be defined as NETCOREAPP2_0.

ALTERNATIVES TO PUTTING #IF/#ENDIF IN THE MIDDLE OF YOUR CODE Putting #if directives all over your code can make it hard to read. There are a couple of ways that I avoid this. The first is to have two copies of the file (for example, one for NET46 and one for NETCOREAPP2_0) with #if/#endif surrounding the entire contents of each file. Another way is to also have these two different versions of the file, but to exclude or include one based on conditions in the project file. This has the obvious drawback of maintaining two files, so it's helpful to isolate the framework-specific code in one class to reduce duplication.

You should now be able to build the application by specifying the target moniker at the command line, as follows:

```
dotnet build --framework net46
dotnet build --framework netcoreapp2.0
```

You can also build all frameworks by running `dotnet build` with no `--framework` specification.

11.3.3 *Creating a NuGet package and checking the contents*

When you build the NuGet package, it should contain both frameworks. To test this out, run `dotnet pack`. Browse to the folder that has the SampleEventSource.1.0.0.nupkg file, and change the extension to .zip. NuGet packages are essentially zip files organized in a particular way. Use your normal zip tool to see the contents.

The contents of SampleEventSource.1.0.0.nupkg should look like this:

- _rels
- .rels
- lib
- net46
  - SampleEventSource.exe
  - SampleEventSource.runtimeconfig.json
- netcoreapp2.0
  - SampleEventSource.dll
  - SampleEventSource.runtimeconfig.json
- [Content_Types].xml
- SampleEventSource.nuspec

In the NuGet package, the .nuspec file defines the contents, dependencies, metadata, and so on. The two frameworks supported by the application get their own folder and copy of the binary. In the case of the .NET Framework, the binary is in .exe form because this is an executable application. The .NET Core version of the binary is a .dll because it's not a self-contained application (see chapter 3).

11.3.4 *Per-framework build options*

One thing we've overlooked in the previous scenario is the MyEventSource.cs file. By default, all the .cs files in the project folder are included in the build. This means that MyEventSource.cs is being built even when you target the `net46` framework.

The build doesn't fail because .NET 4.6 has all of the `EventSource` features used by your code, but suppose the requirement for this application is that it has to work on an older version of the .NET Framework, like 4.5. Change the framework moniker to net45 as follows.

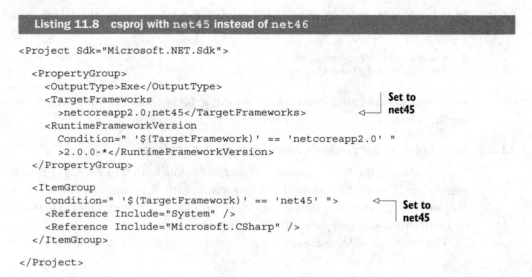

Listing 11.8   csproj with net45 instead of net46

```
<Project Sdk="Microsoft.NET.Sdk">

  <PropertyGroup>
    <OutputType>Exe</OutputType>
    <TargetFrameworks
      >netcoreapp2.0;net45</TargetFrameworks>        ⟵— Set to net45
    <RuntimeFrameworkVersion
      Condition=" '$(TargetFramework)' == 'netcoreapp2.0' "
      >2.0.0-*</RuntimeFrameworkVersion>
  </PropertyGroup>

  <ItemGroup
    Condition=" '$(TargetFramework)' == 'net45' ">      ⟵— Set to net45
    <Reference Include="System" />
    <Reference Include="Microsoft.CSharp" />
  </ItemGroup>

</Project>
```

Also, be sure to fix the preprocessor directives in the Program.cs file, as follows.

Listing 11.9   Program.cs using NET45 instead of NET46

```
using System;

#if NET45
using System.Diagnostics.Eventing;
#endif

namespace SampleEventSource
{
  public class Program
  {
#if NET45
    private static readonly Guid Provider =
      Guid.Parse("B695E411-F53B-4C72-9F81-2926B2EA233A");
#endif

    public static void Main(string[] args)
    {
#if NET45
      var eventProvider = new EventProvider(Provider);
      eventProvider.WriteMessageEvent("Program started");
#else
      MyEventSource.Instance.ProgramStart();
#endif

      // Do some work

#if NET45
      eventProvider.WriteMessageEvent("Program completed");
      eventProvider.Dispose();
```

```
#else
      MyEventSource.Instance.ProgramStop();
#endif
    }
  }
}
```

Try to build it, and you'll see the following errors.

Listing 11.10 Errors when building for .NET Framework 4.5

```
C:\dev\SampleEventSource\MyEventSource.cs(14,7): error CS0246: The type or
 namespace name 'Channel' could not be found (are you missing a using
 directive or an assembly reference?)
C:\dev\SampleEventSource\MyEventSource.cs(14,17): error CS0103: The name
 'EventChannel' does not exist in the current context
C:\dev\SampleEventSource\MyEventSource.cs(25,7): error CS0246: The type or
 namespace name 'Channel' could not be found (are you missing a using
 directive or an assembly reference?)
C:\dev\SampleEventSource\MyEventSource.cs(25,17): error CS0103: The name
 'EventChannel' does not exist in the current context

Compilation failed.
    0 Warning(s)
    4 Error(s)
```

You need to remove the MyEventSource.cs file from compilation when building for the net45 framework. Change the csproj to exclude the MyEventSource.cs file from compilation under net45. You learned how to do this in chapter 3. The following listing shows how this would be done in your project.

Listing 11.11 csproj with framework-specific `buildOptions`

```
<Project Sdk="Microsoft.NET.Sdk">

  <PropertyGroup>
    <OutputType>Exe</OutputType>
    <TargetFrameworks>netcoreapp2.0;net45</TargetFrameworks>
    <RuntimeFrameworkVersion
      Condition=" '$(TargetFramework)' == 'netcoreapp2.0' "
      >2.0.0-*</RuntimeFrameworkVersion>
  </PropertyGroup>

  <ItemGroup Condition=" '$(TargetFramework)' == 'net45' ">
    <Reference Include="System" />
    <Reference Include="Microsoft.CSharp" />
    <Compile Remove="MyEventSource.cs" />        Add this
  </ItemGroup>                                   line.

</Project>
```

You should now be able to successfully build and run this application in either framework.

11.4   *Runtime-specific code*

In section 11.1 we looked at examples of .NET Core libraries taking a dependency on a native library, like libuv or zlib, to do some low-level operations with the operating system. You may need to do this in your library or application.

To do so, you'll need to define the runtimes you support in the `Runtime-Identifiers` in the csproj, as follows.

Listing 11.12   Enumerating multiple runtimes in csproj

```xml
<PropertyGroup>
  <TargetFrameworks>netcoreapp2.0;net46</TargetFrameworks>
  <OutputType>Exe</OutputType>
  <RuntimeIdentifiers>osx.10.11-x64;ubuntu-x64</RuntimeIdentifiers>
</PropertyGroup>
```

To illustrate code that's OS-dependent, you'll attempt to get the process ID of the process your code is running in, without the help of .NET Core. If you peek into how .NET Core does it, you'll find the code that I'm using in this section (see https://github.com/dotnet/corefx).

To get the process ID on Windows, you can use the code in the following listing.

Listing 11.13   Interop.WindowsPid.cs—code to get the process ID on Windows

```csharp
using System.Runtime.InteropServices;

internal partial class Interop
{
  internal partial class WindowsPid
  {
    [DllImport("api-ms-win-core-processthreads-11-1-0.dll")]
    internal extern static uint GetCurrentProcessId();
  }
}
```

Note that this code doesn't have an implementation. It uses `DllImport` to make an interop call to a native assembly. The native assembly has a method called `Get-CurrentProcessId` that does the real work.

Similarly, the following listing shows the code .NET Core uses to get the process ID on Linux systems.

Listing 11.14   Interop.LinuxPid.cs—code to get the process ID on Linux

```csharp
using System.Runtime.InteropServices;

internal static partial class Interop
{
  internal static partial class LinuxPid
  {
    [DllImport("System.Native",
```

```
      EntryPoint="SystemNative_GetPid")]
    internal static extern int GetPid();
  }
}
```

The question is how you can use the Linux code on Linux runtimes and the Windows code on Windows runtimes. Given our discussion in the previous section on supporting multiple frameworks, you might think the answer is to use preprocessor directives and a per-runtime setting in the project file. Unfortunately, there are no extra build settings you can provide for specific runtimes. NuGet packages don't distinguish the runtime in the same way that they do frameworks.

That leaves detecting the operating system up to the code. Try this out by using the previous process ID code. First, create a new folder called Xplat, and open a command prompt in that folder. Run `dotnet new console`. Then create the Interop.WindowsPid.cs and Interop.LinuxPid.cs files, as listed earlier.

Now create a file called PidUtility.cs with the following code.

> **Listing 11.15 Contents of PidUtility.cs**

```
using System;
using System.Runtime.InteropServices;

namespace Xplat
{
  public static class PidUtility
  {
    public static int GetProcessId()
    {
      var isWindows = RuntimeInformation.IsOSPlatform(OSPlatform.Windows);
      var isLinux = RuntimeInformation.IsOSPlatform(OSPlatform.Linux);

      if (isWindows)
        return (int)Interop.WindowsPid.GetCurrentProcessId();
      else if (isLinux)
        return Interop.LinuxPid.GetPid();
      else
        throw new PlatformNotSupportedException("Unsupported platform");
    }
  }
}
```

This utility class detects the OS at runtime and uses the appropriate implementation of the process ID interop class. To test it out, write a simple `Console.WriteLine` in the Program.cs file, as follows.

> **Listing 11.16 Contents of Program.cs**

```
using System;

namespace Xplat
{
```

```
public class Program
{
  public static void Main(string[] args)
  {
    Console.WriteLine($"My PID is {PidUtility.GetProcessId()}");
  }
 }
}
```

Do a `dotnet run`. If you're running on a Windows or Linux machine or a Docker container, you should see the process ID.

If you're writing a library, you should indicate in the csproj that you only support the two runtimes. This lets any projects that depend on yours know what runtimes they will function on. The following listing shows how to do this.

Listing 11.17   Xplat.csproj modified to indicate support for only two runtimes

```
<Project Sdk="Microsoft.NET.Sdk">

  <PropertyGroup>
    <OutputType>Exe</OutputType>
    <TargetFramework>netcoreapp2.0</TargetFramework>
    <RuntimeIdentifiers>win;linux</RuntimeIdentifiers>
  </PropertyGroup>

</Project>
```

Note that the `win` and `linux` runtimes are pretty broad categories. I picked them for demonstration purposes, but it may be necessary to be more specific about which operating systems the native code will work on.

Additional resources

To learn more about what we covered in this chapter, see the following resources:

- .NET Core GitHub repo—https://github.com/dotnet/corefx
- .NET Portability Analyzer—http://mng.bz/P5qN

Summary

In this chapter we looked at how to build applications that work differently depending on the framework or runtime in which they're used. We covered these key concepts:

- Using the .NET Portability Analyzer to assist in porting code between frameworks
- Using precompiler directives to build different code for different frameworks
- Creating code that uses OS-specific features

These are some important techniques to remember from this chapter:

- Precompiler directives can be used to optionally build code based on build properties.

- The .NET SDK `pack` command will generate NuGet packages that have all the frameworks you target.

Many of the early .NET Core projects undertaken by .NET Framework developers will involve porting existing code to .NET Core or .NET Standard. The .NET Portability Analyzer provides useful suggestions for these kinds of migrations. With the multiple framework support in .NET SDK, you can use newer features in .NET Core while still preserving functionality from existing applications.

You also learned about the flexibility in the .NET Core SDK for supporting multiple operating systems. This is useful when writing code that works with OS-specific libraries or features.

These two features in .NET Core—support for multiple frameworks and runtimes—are useful when porting existing projects. Whether you're moving from .NET Framework to .NET Core, Windows to Linux, or both, these features should give you the ability to tackle some of the more difficult issues encountered when converting a project to a new development platform.

Preparing for release

Once your library is coded, tested, and localized, you're ready to release it to your organization or the world. This chapter covers a few of the considerations for release. You want credit for your hard work, and there are ways to prevent someone else from copying it and taking credit themselves. You also want to ensure that developers using your library have a way to verify that they're getting the real version.

Let's first explore how to build a package.

12.1 Preparing a NuGet package

Back in chapter 2 you learned about the `dotnet pack` command. This is the simplest way to build a NuGet package. You can easily share the resulting NuGet package with others in your organization through a custom NuGet store. You can also publish to the official nuget.org site and allow developers from all over the world to use it.

Before publishing to nuget.org, take a moment to consider some of the properties of your package that will be displayed on nuget.org. Figure 12.1 shows an example package and highlights the properties under your control.

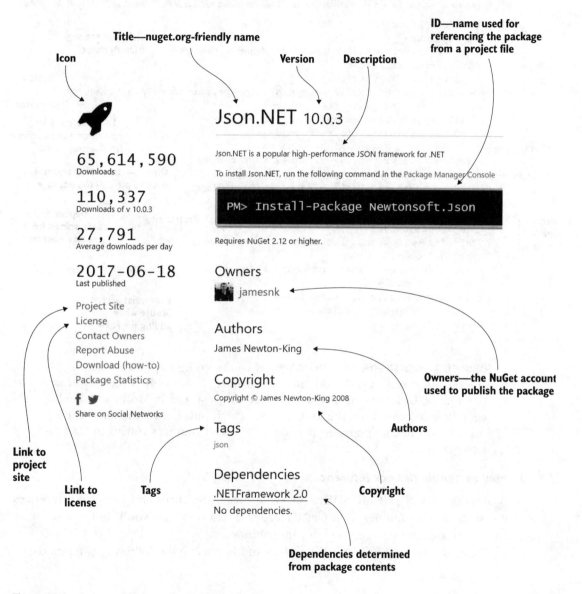

Figure 12.1   An example of a NuGet package on nuget.org

Let's assume you're the author of the package in figure 12.1. Your code could be in a folder called Newtonsoft.Json with a project file named Newtonsoft.Json.csproj, which would look something like the following.

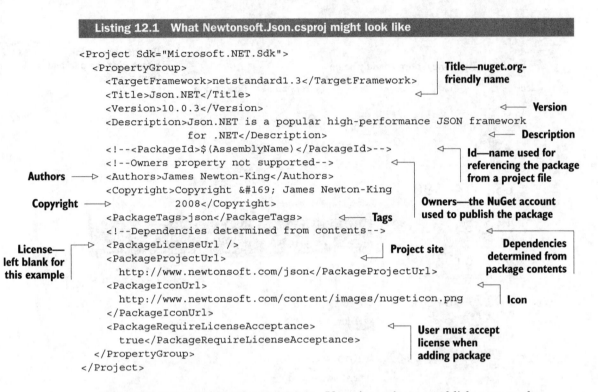

Listing 12.1   What Newtonsoft.Json.csproj might look like

```
<Project Sdk="Microsoft.NET.Sdk">
  <PropertyGroup>
    <TargetFramework>netstandard1.3</TargetFramework>
    <Title>Json.NET</Title>
    <Version>10.0.3</Version>
    <Description>Json.NET is a popular high-performance JSON framework
                for .NET</Description>
    <!--<PackageId>$(AssemblyName)</PackageId>-->
    <!--Owners property not supported-->
    <Authors>James Newton-King</Authors>
    <Copyright>Copyright &#169; James Newton-King
               2008</Copyright>
    <PackageTags>json</PackageTags>
    <!--Dependencies determined from contents-->
    <PackageLicenseUrl />
    <PackageProjectUrl>
      http://www.newtonsoft.com/json</PackageProjectUrl>
    <PackageIconUrl>
      http://www.newtonsoft.com/content/images/nugeticon.png
    </PackageIconUrl>
    <PackageRequireLicenseAcceptance>
      true</PackageRequireLicenseAcceptance>
  </PropertyGroup>
</Project>
```

Annotations on listing:
- Title—nuget.org-friendly name
- Version
- Description
- Id—name used for referencing the package from a project file
- Authors
- Copyright
- Tags
- Owners—the NuGet account used to publish the package
- License—left blank for this example
- Project site
- Dependencies determined from package contents
- Icon
- User must accept license when adding package

CHOOSE A LICENSE FOR YOUR PACKAGE   If you're going to publish your package on nuget.org, you should choose a license. It not only protects you as the author, but it lets others know where they can use it. Most .NET packages from Microsoft use the MIT license, which puts few restrictions on the user. If you need to change the license, NuGet requires you to upload a new version.

12.1.1   How to handle project references

By default, the .NET Core SDK will treat project references and package references the same when building a NuGet package. It assumes that you'll build a separate NuGet package for each project in your solution.

For example, create two packages, Foo and Bar, using the following commands:

```
md PackTest
cd PackTest
dotnet new classlib -o Foo
dotnet new classlib -o Bar
```

Modify Bar.csproj to reference Foo, as follows.

Listing 12.2 Project Bar references project Foo

```
<Project Sdk="Microsoft.NET.Sdk">

  <PropertyGroup>
    <TargetFramework>netstandard2.0</TargetFramework>
  </PropertyGroup>

  <ItemGroup>
    <ProjectReference Include="../Foo/Foo.csproj" />
  </ItemGroup>
</Project>
```

Run `dotnet pack` in the Bar folder to build the NuGet package. Then look in the bin/Debug folder under Bar for the Bar.1.0.0.nupkg file. You can rename this file to have the .zip extension and examine the contents.

Within the package is a lib folder that only contains Bar.dll, not Foo.dll. At the root folder is a Bar.nuspec file that will have contents similar to the following.

Listing 12.3 Contents of the Bar.nuspec file

```
<?xml version="1.0" encoding="utf-8"?>
<package xmlns="http://schemas.microsoft.com/packaging/2013/05/nuspec.xsd">
  <metadata>
    <id>Bar</id>
    <version>1.0.0</version>
    <authors>Bar</authors>
    <owners>Bar</owners>
    <requireLicenseAcceptance>false</requireLicenseAcceptance>
    <description>Package Description</description>
    <dependencies>
      <group targetFramework=".NETStandard2.0">
        <dependency id="Foo" version="1.0.0"          ◁── This is a package
          exclude="Build,Analyzers" />                     dependency.
      </group>
    </dependencies>
  </metadata>
</package>
```

PACKAGE ID The `id` property used in the package dependency is the `PackageId` field for the Foo project.

.NET developers may argue that publishing both the Foo and Bar packages to the NuGet store is the right way to do it. But this was not a restriction for NuGet in the past, and some developers may want to keep the original structure of their packages. To do this, you can use a workaround or use the `nuget` command directly.

USING A WORKAROUND TO PACKAGE PROJECT REFERENCES

This workaround was provided by Rohit Agrawal (http://mng.bz/11yT). It modifies the MSBuild item group controlling what build output goes into a package to include the project references. The following listing shows how you could do this with the Bar project file.

Listing 12.4   Project Bar packaging its project references

```
<Project Sdk="Microsoft.NET.Sdk">

  <PropertyGroup>
    <TargetFramework>netstandard2.0</TargetFramework>
    <TargetsForTfmSpecificBuildOutput>$(TargetsForTfmSpecificBuildOutput);
      CopyProjectReferencesToPackage
      </TargetsForTfmSpecificBuildOutput>
  </PropertyGroup>


  <ItemGroup>
    <ProjectReference Include="../Foo/Foo.csproj" />
  </ItemGroup>

  <Target Name="CopyProjectReferencesToPackage"
    DependsOnTargets="ResolveProjectReferences">
    <ItemGroup>
      <BuildOutputInPackage
        Include="@(_ResolvedProjectReferencePaths)"/>
    </ItemGroup>
  </Target>
</Project>
```

Executes this custom target during build

Custom build target (see section 3.3.2)

BuildOutputInPackage item group controls what goes into NuGet package

Includes your referenced projects

USING THE NUGET COMMAND TO PACKAGE PROJECT REFERENCES

The nuget command comes with the .NET SDK, but the version installed on your machine may not be the latest version. To update your NuGet client, use this command:

```
nuget update -self
```

This should verify that you're running NuGet version 4.0 or higher.

Now, from the Bar folder, run the following command:

```
nuget pack Bar.csproj -IncludeReferencedProjects
```

The IncludeReferencedProjects option tells the .NET SDK to treat project references differently than package references. This will cause Foo.dll to be included in the Bar package.

NOT YET SUPPORTED   As of the writing of this book, there's a bug that causes the preceding command to fail. The bug is tracked at http://mng.bz/11yT.

12.1.2 NuGet feeds

If you'd like to have a version of nuget.org for your organization, there are many options:

- Create a local feed using a file share.
- Build a website and add the NuGet.Server package for hosting a feed on IIS.
- Copy the source code from NuGet Gallery (https://github.com/NuGet/NuGet-Gallery) to get a site similar to nuget.org using ASP.NET.
- Purchase private feeds, such as
  - MyGet
  - ProGet
  - Artifactory

The simplest way to create a feed is with a file share. There's no setup involved. For example, if you have a folder on a file share called \\myfileshare\nuget, you can publish the Bar package directly to it by going to the bin/Debug folder and executing this command:

```
nuget add Bar.1.0.0.nupkg -source \\myfileshare\nuget
```

You can then add this feed to your global NuGet configuration by running the following command:

```
nuget sources add -Name myfeed -Source \\myfileshare\nuget
nuget sources list
```
◁─┐ **List the sources
     in the config.**

Another option is to add a NuGet.config file to your project or in a folder above the project. Create a new file called nuget.config with the following contents.

Listing 12.5 Empty nuget.config file

```
<?xml version="1.0" encoding="utf-8"?>
<configuration>
</configuration>
```

Now you can add your local feed, or any other feed, to this file with the `nuget` command. Here's an example:

```
nuget sources add -Name myfeed -Source \\myfileshare\nuget
  -configfile nuget.config
```

This should alter the nuget.config file to look like the following.

Listing 12.6 nuget.config file with local feed

```
<?xml version="1.0" encoding="utf-8"?>
<configuration>
  <packageSources>
```

```
        <add key="myfeed" value="\\myfileshare\nuget" />
      </packageSources>
</configuration>
```

HOW DOES NUGET LOCATE CONFIG FILES?   If the nuget.config file is in the folder
you're running .NET SDK commands from, or in a folder above that (all the
way up to the root), that file will be used as the first configuration file. There
are other global configuration files that will be used afterwards, when a package reference can't be found in the earlier configuration files. The .NET SDK
commands will list the NuGet configuration files used if a restore was
performed.

PACKING WITH SYMBOLS OR CODE   You may wish to include the debug symbols
with your NuGet package, especially if the package is intended for internal
consumption. Simply add the `--include-symbols` option to the `dotnet
pack` command. This will generate an additional NuGet package with a dif-
ferent name—MyLibrary.1.0.0.symbols.nupkg—so you're not confused about
which one has symbols. Another option, `--include-source`, also creates
the symbols package and it includes a src folder with the source code.

Advanced NuGet features

When building for the .NET Framework, you can assume that most users will install
your NuGet package through Visual Studio. This means that the user has a .NET project they're adding the package to. NuGet has a few advanced features to improve the
user experience in this scenario.

One option is to allow scripts to run when the package is installed or uninstalled.
These scripts are written in Windows PowerShell and can do all sorts of things. For
example, Newtonsoft's Json.NET has an install script that tells Visual Studio to open
the URL for the Json.NET splash screen. The .NET SDK tools don't give you the ability
to add scripts, which makes sense because scripting for every operating system
could get tricky.

Another option is to use XML Document Transforms (XDT). A common use of XDT is
to modify the config file of a project. For example, the Microsoft Azure Service Bus
NuGet package will add WCF client configuration to the app.config or web.config file.
But unlike in the .NET Framework, .config files are no longer the one true way to spec-
ify configuration. With so many configuration options available (see chapter 6), this
NuGet feature doesn't make sense for .NET Core and is therefore not available.

12.1.3 *Packaging resource assemblies*

In chapter 10 you learned how to add localized resources to a library. The build system will create satellite assemblies for each locale. Unfortunately, the `dotnet pack`
command won't automatically recognize these satellite resources assemblies and add
them to your NuGet package. Packaging with localized resources is more of a manual
process—at least at this point in time.

There are generally two options for packaging resource assemblies. The first option is to include all the localized resource assemblies in a single package, along with the default locale. The other is to create a NuGet package for each locale. Both options have their pros and cons. For simplicity, we'll look at the first option.

As you may recall from the examples in chapter 10, the project you created was called ACController (you can get the code for this project from GitHub at http://mng.bz/F146). When you execute `dotnet pack` on this project, you get a nupkg file, which is a zip file. You can go into this file, extract the ACController.nuspec file, and place it in the root of the project.

You're going to take the ACController package and add the satellite resource assemblies to it. Create a new folder for the contents of the new package. The name of the folder doesn't matter—it just shouldn't contain anything that you don't want in the package. Mine is called pack and has the following contents:

- pack/
- lib/netcoreapp2.0/
- ACController.dll
- ACController.runtimeconfig.json
- ar-SA/
- ACController.resources.dll

Now use the following command from the project folder:

```
dotnet pack /p:NuspecFile=ACController.nuspec /p:NuspecBasePath=./pack
```

These steps are a bit cumbersome, but they'll generate a nupkg with the resource satellite assemblies inside. In the case of the ACController example, the Arabic resources are necessary for the application to run.

12.2 Signing assemblies

Earlier in this chapter you created a mock of the Newtonsoft.Json.csproj file. Let's say that I'm malicious and want to put some tracking code or a virus into the NuGet package for Json.NET. It's easy enough to mock the package, but how would anybody know if they were getting the real version of Json.NET or my hacked version?

On nuget.org, you can see the owner of the package. This is one way to verify authenticity.

But how can you be assured of the package's contents? The assemblies in the package can be signed with strong names, giving you another level of authenticity checking. A strong name proves that an assembly was signed with the developer's private key. Unsigned assemblies can't be verified for authenticity and pose a risk to the user.

Microsoft signs all of the .NET Framework assemblies with a well-known set of keys (see listing 12.7 for an example). Very few people in Microsoft have access to the actual keys. Instead, all signing is handled by a strictly controlled internal system. Keeping the assembly-signing keys safe is important for any individual or organization distributing a library.

Listing 12.7   Full name of the System.Core assembly in the .NET Framework

```
System.Core, Version=4.0.0.0, Culture=neutral,
    PublicKeyToken=b77a5c561934e089
```
◁── **The signing key creates
the public key token.**

12.2.1   *Generating a signing key*

As of the writing of this book, there's no cross-platform tool for creating signing keys. The tool used to generate signing keys only works on Windows and is distributed with the Windows Software Development Kit (SDK). If you're using Visual Studio, open a developer command prompt and use the following command to create a new key and extract the public key:

```
sn.exe -k mykey.snk
sn.exe -p mykey.snk mykey.public.snk
```

In order to understand what the public key is for, you'll have to explore the concept of delay-signing.

12.2.2   *Delay-signing*

When a project references a signed assembly, it uses the full name of the assembly (as shown in listing 12.7). Let's say you're a developer working on this assembly— you shouldn't need to have a copy of the signing key on your workstation to make changes to the assembly for internal testing. Changing how projects reference the assembly every time you switch from internal build to official build isn't a good strategy either.

To handle this situation, .NET Framework developers use a technique called *delay-signing*. Each signing key is a public/private pair. A step in the build process signs the assembly with the private key. Projects using the signed assembly can then verify the signature using the public key. The public key gets stored in the assembly's manifest.

> **DELAY SIGNING NOT SUPPORTED BY .NET CORE**   Delay-signing currently isn't supported by .NET Core. This is a very useful feature, so I hope this is fixed soon.

> **VIEWING AN ASSEMBLY MANIFEST**   You can view the assembly's manifest using another Windows SDK tool called ildasm.exe.

A delay-signed assembly marks the public key in the assembly manifest. This allows projects referencing the assembly to keep the same full assembly name. But in order to prevent .NET from rejecting the assembly because the public key doesn't match the assembly signature, you need to use the sn.exe tool again to turn off signature verification. The following command skips signature verification for an assembly:

```
sn.exe -Vr myassembly.dll
```

The unfortunate result of the sn.exe tool only working on Windows is that verification skipping also only works on Windows, and only with the .NET Framework. The skip-verification command adds an entry to the Windows registry that the .NET Framework reads before loading assemblies. This same functionality isn't currently available in .NET Core.

12.2.3 Signing an assembly in .NET Core

With the signing key generated, all you need to do to sign an assembly is modify the project file, as follows.

> **Listing 12.8 Project file with signing options turned on**

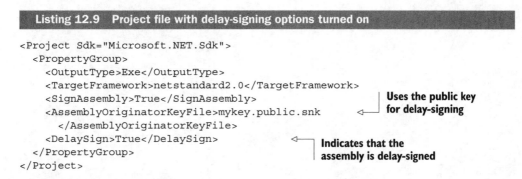

```
<Project Sdk="Microsoft.NET.Sdk">
  <PropertyGroup>
    <TargetFramework>netstandard2.0</TargetFramework>
    <SignAssembly>True</SignAssembly>
    <AssemblyOriginatorKeyFile>mykey.snk              ◁──┐  Use the private key
      </AssemblyOriginatorKeyFile>                          for proper signing.
  </PropertyGroup>
</Project>
```

If you're building for the .NET Framework and can use delay-signing, you'd add the properties shown in the following listing.

> **Listing 12.9 Project file with delay-signing options turned on**

```
<Project Sdk="Microsoft.NET.Sdk">
  <PropertyGroup>
    <OutputType>Exe</OutputType>
    <TargetFramework>netstandard2.0</TargetFramework>
    <SignAssembly>True</SignAssembly>                       Uses the public key
    <AssemblyOriginatorKeyFile>mykey.public.snk   ◁──┘      for delay-signing
      </AssemblyOriginatorKeyFile>
    <DelaySign>True</DelaySign>                ◁──┐  Indicates that the
  </PropertyGroup>                                    assembly is delay-signed
</Project>
```

Additional resources

To delve deeper into some of the subjects introduced in this book, check out Manning's other .NET Core books:

- *ASP.NET Core in Action* by Andrew Lock (Manning, 2018)—http://mng.bz/DI1O
- *Entity Framework Core in Action* by Jon P Smith (Manning, 2018)—http://mng.bz/cOH4
- *Xamarin in Action* by Jim Bennett (Manning, 2018)—http://mng.bz/bgT5

Summary

In this chapter you learned about NuGet packages and feeds, as well as assembly signing. These are the key concepts from this chapter:

- Assembly signing is used to verify the authenticity of the assembly.
- There are many kinds of NuGet feeds that can work in your organization.
- Most of the properties shown in nuget.org can be manipulated in the project file.

You also used a few techniques that you should keep in mind when preparing for release:

- Delay-signing is helpful during development, but it only works on Windows when targeting the .NET Framework.
- You can use the SN Windows SDK tool to generate signing keys for your assemblies.
- A local file share can make a quick and easy NuGet feed.
- NuGet configuration files are simple to construct and to include in source repositories.

Congratulations on finishing this book! I hope that you've acquired enough knowledge of .NET Core to build first-rate libraries and applications. In this last chapter we covered some of the aspects of releasing your code into the wild. It's important to package, distribute, and protect your intellectual property. As you can see from this chapter, with a few simple steps you can be ready to release your code properly.

appendix A
Frameworks and runtimes

This appendix contains two tables that will be handy if you need to look up a target framework moniker or runtime identifier for use in your .NET Core applications.

CONSTRUCTING THE RUNTIME IDENTIFIER STRING The runtime identifier string obeys a hierarchy: `linuxmint.17.1-x64` is a child of `linuxmint.17.1`, which is a child of `linuxmint.17`, then `linuxmint`, and finally `linux`. If a runtime doesn't work, try a more specific version.

Table A.1 Runtimes

OS	Flavors	Version examples
linux	rhel	7.0, 7.1, 7.2
	ol	7.0, 7.1, 7.2
	centos	7
	debian	8
	ubuntu	14.04, 14.10, 15.04, 15.10, 16.04
	linuxmint	17, 17.1, 17.2, 17.3
	fedora	23
	openuse	13.2
	musl (Alpine)	
osx		10.10, 10.11
win	win7	
	win8	
	win81	
	win10	

Table A.2 Target frameworks available in .NET CLI

Name	Abbreviation	Moniker
.NET Framework	net	net11
		net20
		net35
		net40
		net403
		net45
		net451
		net452
		net46
		net461
		net462
		net47
		net471
		net472
		net48
.NET Standard	netstandard	netstandard1.0
		netstandard1.1
		netstandard1.2
		netstandard1.3
		netstandard1.4
		netstandard1.5
		netstandard1.6
		netstandard2.0
.NET Core app	netcoreapp	netcoreapp1.0
		netcoreapp1.1
		netcoreapp2.0
		netcoreapp2.1

appendix B
xUnit command-line options

Because of the way the .NET CLI works, it isn't obvious that it's possible to specify command-line options when running tests. If you execute dotnet test -?, you'll only see the help for the dotnet test command. The -? is picked up first by .NET CLI instead of being passed to the xUnit entry point.

To see the command-line options for xUnit, you have to look at the code. I've included it here for reference.

Listing B.1 Command-line options for xUnit

```
Copyright (C) 2015 Outercurve Foundation.

usage: {executableName} <assemblyFile> [configFile] [assemblyFile
    ➥ [configFile]...] [options] [reporter]
    ➥ [resultFormat filename [...]]

Note: Configuration files must end in .json (for JSON) or .config
    (for XML)

Valid options:
  -nologo              : do not show the copyright message
  -nocolor             : do not output results with colors
  -noappdomain         : do not use app domains to run test code
  -failskips           : convert skipped tests into failures
  -parallel option     : set parallelization based on option
                       :   none        - turn off all
                       :                   parallelization
                       :   collections - only parallelize
                       :                   collections
                       :   assemblies  - only parallelize
                       :                   assemblies
                       :   all         - parallelize assemblies &
                       :                   collections
```

```
    -maxthreads count        : maximum thread count for collection
                             : parallelization
                             :    default   - run with default (1 thread
                             :                   per CPU thread)
                             :    unlimited - run with unbounded thread
                             :                   count
                             :    (number)  - limit task thread pool size
                             :                   to 'count'
    -noshadow                : do not shadow copy assemblies
    -wait                    : wait for input after completion
    -diagnostics             : enable diagnostics messages for all test
                             : assemblies
    -debug                   : launch the debugger to debug the tests
    -serialize               : serialize all test cases (for diagnostic
                             : purposes only)
    -trait "name=value"      : only run tests with matching name/value
                             : traits if specified more than once, acts
                             : as an OR operation
    -notrait "name=value"    : do not run tests with matching name/value
                             : traits if specified more than once, acts
                             : as an AND operation
    -method "name"           : run a given test method (should be fully
                             : specified;
                             : i.e., 'MyNamespace.MyClass.MyTestMethod')
                             : if specified more than once, acts as an OR
                             : operation
    -class "name"            : run all methods in a given test class
                             : (should be fully specified; i.e.,
                             : 'MyNamespace.MyClass') if specified more
                             : than once, acts as an OR operation
    -namespace "name"        : run all methods in a given namespace
                             : (i.e., 'MyNamespace.MySubNamespace')
                             : if specified more than once, acts as an OR
                             : operation

Reporters: (optional, choose only one)
   -appveyor                 : forces AppVeyor CI mode (normally
                             : auto-detected)
   -json                     : show progress messages in JSON format
   -quiet                    : do not show progress messages
   -teamcity                 : forces TeamCity mode (normally
                             : auto-detected)
   -verbose                  : show verbose progress messages

Result formats: (optional, choose one or more)
   -xml                      : output results to xUnit.net v2 XML file
```

Note that the `method`, `class`, and `namespace` options give you the ability to execute specific test cases.

appendix C
What's in the
.NET Standard Library?

.NET Framework developers who are looking to port to .NET Core may wonder what's supported in each version of the .NET Standard Library. This section gives a general description of what's supported by each version. If you're not familiar with the .NET Framework, this section will still be useful as an indication of what's available in the Standard Library.

netstandard 1.0

- Collections
- Globalization
- Generic I/O (streams)
- Linq
- Networking primitives
- Reflection
- Regular expressions
- Threads
- Tasks
- XML reader/writer
- XML document

netstandard 1.1

Includes everything in 1.0 plus

- Concurrent collections
- ETW support
- Zip/Deflate compression (not zip files)

- HTTP
- Numerics (`BigInteger` and `Complex`)
- Parallel Linq

netstandard 1.2

Includes everything in 1.1 plus thread timers

netstandard 1.3

Includes everything in 1.2 plus

- AppContext (used to opt out of functionality)
- Console output
- Globalization calendars
- Zip file compression
- File I/O
- Sockets
- Cryptography

netstandard 1.4

Includes everything in 1.3 plus isolated storage

netstandard 1.5

Includes everything in 1.4 plus `AssemblyLoadContext`

netstandard 1.6

Includes everything in 1.5 plus OpenSSL cryptography

netstandard 2.0

Includes everything in 1.6 plus

- XML
  - XLinq
  - XmlDocument
  - XPath
  - Schema
  - XSL
- Serialization
- BinaryFormatter
- DataContract
- XML
- Data
- Abstractions
- Provider Model

- DataSet
- Networking
- Sockets
- HTTP
- Mail
- WebSockets
- Memory-mapped files
- Thread pools

appendix D
NuGet cache locations

There are two caches used by NuGet. The first cache holds the nupkg files down-loaded from the feed. You'll find those nupkg files here:

- Mac and Linux: ~/.local/share/NuGet/Cache
- Windows: %LocalAppData%\NuGet\Cache

The second cache holds the files extracted from the .nupkg files. This is the cache NuGet will use during build time. These are the folders:

- Mac and Linux: ~/.nuget/packages
- Windows: %UserProfile%\.nuget\packages

index